INFOTRENDS

INFOTRENDS

The Competitive Use
of Information

Jessica Keyes

McGraw-Hill, Inc.

New York   St. Louis   San Francisco   Auckland   Bogotá
Caracas   Lisbon   London   Madrid   Mexico   Milan
Montreal   New Delhi   Paris   San Juan   São Paulo
Singapore   Sydney   Tokyo   Toronto

Library of Congress Cataloging-in-Publication Data

Keyes, Jessica, date.
   Infotrends: the competitive use of information / Jessica Keyes.
     p. cm.
   Includes bibliographical references and index.
   ISBN 0-07-034464-7
   1. Management—United States—Communication systems—Technological
innovations—Case studies. 2. Corporations—United States—
Communications systems—Technological innovations—Case studies.
3. Information resources management—Case studies. 4. Information
technology—United States—Case studies. I. Title.
HD30.3.K49   1992
658.4'038—dc20   92-29939
                                        CIP

 This book is printed on recycled, acid-free paper containing a minimum of 50% recycled de-inked fiber.

1 2 3 4 5 6 7 8 9 0 DOC/DOC 9 8 7 6 5 4 3 2

ISBN 0-07-034464-7

The sponsoring editor for this book was Betsy N. Brown, and the production supervisor was Pamela A. Pelton. This book was set in Baskerville by Caliber/Phoenix Color Corp.

Printed and bound by R.R. Donnelley & Sons Company.

*This book is most appreciatively dedicated
to my clients and friends, old and new,
my family, and editors.*

Contents

Preface

After fifteen years of haunting the corridors of American industry, I can say, with a certain amount of confidence and justification, that I've just about seen it all—that is, the Good, the Bad, and the Ugly.

What I'm talking about here is not personages but strategies. In particular, the strategy of using technology as a competitive hedge. Often talked about in corporate boardrooms, and certainly not lacking for its fair share of media attention given today's economic doldrums, competitive technology certainly seems that pot of gold at the end of the rainbow. And corporations, large and small, East and West, are rushing, dollars in hand, to fund a plethora of seemingly promising technology projects. But what are these companies really funding?

Technology does not necessarily beget competitive advantage any more than painting a canvas begets a Van Gogh. There is more, much more, to the art of using technology to gain a competitive toehold than just a mere application of technology. The real art lies in wrapping technology around a company, much like a glove, so that the company can more flexibly extend its reach and take advantage of the new market opportunities it finds there.

The motivation for this book is quite simple really. It is to make the reader aware of the technology paradox—massive funding does not necessarily translate into higher productivity or higher profits. Rather, companies that understand the *strategic placement* of technology seem to move ahead at a more rapid clip than those that don't. Included in this category are such companies as American Express, Federal Express, and Banker's Trust. These, and others, have joined me in showing readers how to prosper from a competitive use of technology.

This book wouldn't have been possible without the help and encouragement of many people. First of all, I'd like to thank my husband and parents without whose unwavering support this book would never have been finished.

If there is one other person who was involved in the publication of this book as I, it was my editor at McGraw-Hill. Betsy Brown has been an inspiration as well as a great source of organization, style, and content advice from the very first outline of this book. Her help shaped this book in more ways than one.

But many other people were involved in this book as well—people like Carmine Vona at Banker's Trust and Ron Ponder at Federal Express. These people gave willingly of their time and information to help me understand better the nature of competitive use of technology, and I offer them my grateful thanks.

Jessica Keyes

INFOTRENDS

1

Techno-Strategizing the Corporation

Although Information Technology (IT) started its life in the early 1950s far from the strategic ups and downs of the corporate mainstream, corporate visionaries over the last four decades have discovered how diverse seeds of data could be harvested into a bounty of knowledge for their companies. But this advance was only made possible by harvesting data with the right tools and techniques. This book is an examination of these visionary companies, their tools, and their IT strategies. Although we'll talk about some intriguing IT systems, this is *not* a book about systems themselves, but of the *strategy behind the systems.*

In the world of botany, the strategy of "cross-hybridization" is common to fuse the strengths of two very different genera of plants to produce a plant that is superior. Companies which have fused their technology strategy with their business strategy find superior strength as well.

Read on then to find out how the visionaries of Federal Express, American Express, Bankers Trust, Time Warner, and many, many others cross-hybridized their strategies to grow a competitive advantage. Read on to find out how you can do it, too.

Visionary use of technology is multidimensional. Not all companies achieve a competitive advantage in the same way. This is why this book divides its discussion into identifiable technology trends that are becoming, and quite possibly already are, the "hot tickets" of the 1990s.

Each of these chapters, or trends, is discussed by providing *insight,* through the liberal use of case studies of firms who have successfully maneuvered that particular trend, and *intelligence,* through the discussion of procedures and techniques that can be used by the reader to get on the fast track to success. Just one paragraph into Chapter One, the reader begins to understand what a "techno-strategy" is and how one can create a technology team that will be able to successfully implement this strategy.

Beginning with Infotrend #1: Using Technology to Prosper in a Down Market in Chapter Two, the reader will find advice on how to stay on an even keel, and maybe ever prosper during lean economic times through the use of technology. In Chapter Three, Infotrend #2: Downsizing, we will discuss the growing trend toward moving off Big Iron, that is, large and expensive mainframes, and down to more reasonably priced, and more functional, personal work stations.

Infotrend #3: From Flying Solo to Partnering, in Chapter Four, explores the push to strengthen a company externally—rather than internally, known as partnering. Some surprising insights are offered into the pros and cons of this process by those firms who have taken this road. Chapter Five, Infotrend #4: Integration, should be read carefully by those firms which have a proliferation of nonconnected systems. In order to survive in the 1990s, these systems must be integrated.

For the first time, in Chapter Six, Infotrend #5: Outsourcing (The Inside Story), we get a full, unbiased picture of outsourcing. Should you or shouldn't you? This chapter will give you the info you need to make that crucial decision. If the instructions in Chapter Seven, Infotrend #6: Info-Marketing, are carried out, readers, for the first time, will be able to successfully implement a "business intelligence" program in their companies. Having a product is only the first step on a company's path to success. Understanding the market, competitors, and customers are the next important steps. The information that serves as a basis for these types of decisions is unavailable internally, but it can be bought. There are then tools that can help you sift through this mass of raw data to turn it into competitive gold.

Chapter Eight, Infotrend #7: Turning Data into Knowledge, explores the growing movement to "intelligent" systems. These are the systems that must be put into place if the company of the 1990s is to become productive enough to compete. Infotrend #8: The Distinctive Edge, in Chapter Nine, reveals the discovery of companies that have gone beyond the normal use of technology—using technology to set themselves apart from the rest of the pack. It's in this chapter that we find out how the NASD made its move on the New York Stock Exchange.

Finally, in Chapter Ten, Infotrend #9: Ushering in the Age of Techno-Business, we reach the pinnacle of the technology mountain. Here we read about firms the very existence of which depends upon the use of technology. In this chapter, we'll read about Federal Express—a success story that has become legend. Chapter Eleven offers a summary that pulls together the threads of techno-strategy so that you, too, can profit.

The Basics of Techno-Strategy Development

The big question: With global competition intensifying and closing in rapidly will U.S. companies wind up, as *USA Today* once so succinctly put it, as "an easy target in the slow lane"? This particular phrase comments on the results of a 1989 M.I.T report[1] that concludes that the nation is slipping, and industry, not government, is primarily responsible. Although the report targeted many culprits, perhaps the most interesting was what they labeled outdated corporate strategies. One such strategy might well be the omission of technology from the corporate weave.

A company's technology strategy is often subordinate to its business strategy. Here a management committee, or some other planning body, meticulously develops the company's long-range plan. The technology chiefs are called from their basement perches only to plan for one or another automated system as it meets a comparatively short-term goal from one or more of the business units. In some companies, this planning process is akin to weaving cloth. In weaving, thread after thread is woven so tightly that, when complete, the cloth's individual threads are nearly impossible to distinguish from one another. The strength and resiliency of the completed cloth is the result of this careful weaving.

A company, too, is made up of many threads, each with its own strategy. Only when all of these unmatched threads, or strategies, are woven evenly together can a successful general competitive business strategy be formulated. If the technology thread is not as tightly woven as the others, the final strategy will be as a cloth missing threads—full of holes and weak.

If this chapter conveys any one principle, it is that senior executives must take an active interest in the merger between technology and business in their organizations. The one common denominator among the firms described in this book is the availability of a senior executive who understands and appreciates the value of technology—coupled with a strong advocate, who understands business, in the technology department. This dynamic duo possesses the understanding, and ultimately the know-how, of how the information technology resource can be used strategically.

Although many systems are described by their respective organizations as strategic, in reality there are but a few legitimate examples of truly competitive systems. This small number stems from a lack of strategic information systems vision. Information technology managers and executive level managers view strategic use of the information technology resource quite differently. Although strategic issues are important to both levels of management, technology managers are much more complete and accurate in

---

[1] "Made in America," M.I.T. Sloan School Study, 1989.

identifying potential strategic technology strengths and weaknesses than are executives.

The root of the problem is a difference in perspective within organizations about the strategic use of information technology. It is worthwhile, then, to spend a few minutes in discussing the components of corporate strategy so we can relate this important process to information technology.

Components of Strategy

There are three factors that define strategy and strategic processes: the scope of strategic decision making, the factors or forces to be considered in formulating a strategy, and the approach to strategic planning.

The scope of strategic decision making defines the decision's impact on the organization. For it to be strategic, it must deal with the organization's relationship with the external environment and must have some impact on the success of the organization as a whole.

In his excellent book on competitive strategy, Michael Porter[2] identifies several competing forces that need to be considered in business strategy formulation:

Bargaining power of customers

Bargaining power of suppliers

Current competitors

Threat of new entrants into the market

Threat of substitute products or services

These forces are affected by barriers to entering or exiting markets. Porter advises that a company should flexibly employ its assets to ease its entry, mobility, and exit in a market area. Alternatively, the company can attempt to put up barriers to other companies entering the marketplace. Advantages for this strategy include "cornering the market," but this may be more than offset by the expense involved in doing so.

The process of strategy formulation consists of many activities, according to other business theorists.[3] In the best-case companies :

■ Create a strategic profile which includes how the company defines itself as well as the steps it has taken to be competitive.

---

[2] Michael Porter, *Competitive Strategy.* (New York Macmillan, 1980).

[3] H. Uyterhoeven, R. Ackerman, and J. Rosenblum, *Strategy and Organization*, (Homewood, Illinois, Richard D. Irwin, Inc.,1977).

- Develop a strategic forecast of the environment. This should encompass political, economic, market, product, competitive, and technological issues.

- Perform an audit of the strengths and weaknesses of the organization.

- Compare the audit results with the environmental scan; from this comparison, create a set of strategic alternatives.

- Test the consistency of the alternatives to make sure that they fit the capabilities of the organization as well as the external opportunities defined by the organization. These alternatives must also be consistent with the profile that the organization has created for itself. This step permits the alignment of what it is possible for the company to do in its particular environment versus what the company has the capability to do.

- Review the alternatives and make a choice.

Strategic Use of Information Technology

Most corporations are besieged by demands from their internal divisions and departments for funding to automate. Even in the best of economic times, it is indeed foolhardy for an organization to invest in all comers. The savvy organization should attempt to separate the wheat from the chafe and fund only those projects that offer a positive contribution to the organization's bottom line—economics or productivity.

Because of this necessity, it is important to be able to determine the strategic level of an existing, or potential, system. One useful tool is the framework developed by the Harvard professors F. Warren McFarlan and James Cash, which assesses the strategic significance of a system to an organization.[4]

A matrix function is to assist in determining a company's classification and to determine the appropriate way to manage the technology resource based on whether it serves a support or strategic role in the organization. As shown in Figure 1-1, the McFarlan/Cash grid is two-dimensional showing four different types of management environments:

1. Strategic firms have a very tight relationship of a firm to technology. These firms have an "excruciating" dependence on technology. Systems that these companies develop are critical to its competitive success.

2. Turnaround firms, while considering technology to be very important, don't quite have the dependence on technology as do strategic firms. These

[4] James I. Cash, and F. Warren McFarlan, "Competing Through Information Technology" (Harvard Business School Video Series, 1989).

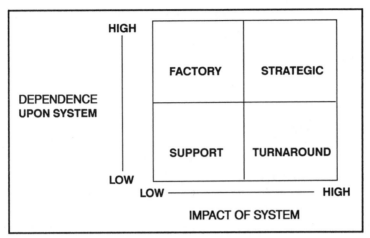

Figure 1-1. Framework for assessment of strategic importance of an
IT system. (*Source: F. Warren McFarlan and James Cash*).

firms are making the transition to the strategic level. Their current systems
are not considered strategic, but the development of new ones are making
them crucial to the competitiveness of the organization.

3. In factory type firms, while technology is heavily depended upon for
smooth running of their operations, it is not seen as a major differentiator.

4. In support type firms technology is considered important, and useful
but not on the short list of things this company needs to do.

The many forms of technology in relation to busines strategy require different sets of techniques. In using technology to support the mission and
strategy of the organization a well-known technique, and one that should be
employed by all organizations, is "strategy set transformation"[5]:

- Identify the "strategy set" of the organization. This consists of a firm's
  mission statement, its organizational objectives, the organizational strategy, and strategic organizational attributes.

- Identify stakeholder groups within the organization.

- Identify the operating objectives of the stakeholder groups and the constraints related to the development of systems.

- Develop information strategies using these results.

[5] G. Parsons, "Information Technology: A New Competitive Weapon," *Sloan Management
Review* 25:1 (Fall 1983), pp. 3–14.

This set of questions is quite elegant in its simplicity. Its employment assures the organization that the proper fit between technology and business is, indeed, being achieved.

The Role of the CIO in Managing Strategy— Time Warner's Model

This fit between business and technology has an ally. It is the CIO, or Chief Information Officer. Ideally, this man, or woman, must be a hybrid technologist-businessperson, making the fusion between technology and business a more natural process.

On this, our first stop on our quest for competitive technology, we'll meet such a person. When Don Winski was CIO of Time Warner, he had already completed his quest. His doing so forced Time Warner to realize that it is the componentization of technology into strategy that services the organization best.

Winski had long recognized that technology must be woven into the very fiber of the company as the key to Time Warner's vast information and entertainment empire. But could this goal be accomplished in a $11 billion company that is so widely dispersed?

Time Warner figures big in everyone's mind, but the first thing that most think of when this conglomerate's name is mentioned is magazine publishing. During the fast eighties, the number of Time Warner magazines tripled from 8 to 25 through a series of acquisitions, joint ventures and start-ups. Few realize that *Time, Life, Fortune, Sports Illustrated, People, Money,* and *Entertainment Weekly* are all cut from the same Time Warner cloth. But Time-Warner is more than magazines, everyone recognizes the name Warner Brothers, makers of big hits such as *Batman, Gremlins,* and *GoodFellas,* but few realize that these are the same folks that bring you your favorite TV shows like "Murphy Brown" and "Night Court." Madonna and Michael Jackson figure in, too, under Time Warner Music, as does Home Box Office and Cinemax—under the aegis of Time Warner Cable. Also memorable are the Time-Life Books series, *Mysteries of the Unknown,* and the Book-of-the-Month Club. All these thriving businesses are expected to continue thriving since, as Time Warner so succinctly states in their annual report, "feeding the appetite for information and entertainment doesn't satisfy the hunger . . . it increases it."

In a technological sense, Don Winksi was at the center of this $11 billion empire. In his position as senior information executive, he was responsible for the corporate oversight and coordination of worldwide information systems and telecommunications activities. Winski exemplifies the type of individual that makes for a successful CIO. Prior to joining Time Warner in 1987, Winski *was* part of the management team responsible for the buildup and integration of new business enterprises at Bell Atlantic following the AT&T divestiture. Under Winski's tutelage, these businesses grew to revenues of $1 billion annually within two years. Holding graduate degrees in chemical engineering and operations research from Polytechnical Institute of New York has given Winski a good technical background that he applies to good advantage in productively cultivating his passion for business.

It was this passion that executives took note of when Winksi was hired to help plan strategy for the premerger Warner. At the time the business was growing extremely rapidly, and part of Winksi's job was to figure out just where it was going. Warner wanted part-technologist and part-businessperson. Winksi describes his function, at that time, as 10 percent making sure the telephones work and ninety percent coordinator/facilitator/catalyst. Premerger, Warner was almost a family business, built up and run by Steve Ross, still in charge today. Therefore, those in the corporate office, including Winksi, had a much stronger oversight responsibility for keeping track of what's going on out there in the business units. Since Warner's individual business units were very small, Winksi could become very intimately involved.

Time, on the other hand, was a holding company with a very hands-on policy because of its origins as a magazine publisher. After the merger, Winski was confronted with two very diverse corporate policies: Time, on one hand, could be considered quite decentralized; Warner, on the other hand, could be considered centralized—the complete opposite of Time. According to Winski, there really is no right or wrong, so he worked hard on understanding the disparate cultures of the two very different organizations. He predicted that there will most likely be a swinging back and forth of the centralization-decentralization pendulum.

Winksi spent a great deal of time developing his role of Time Warner CIO. But what is the role of the CIO, in general? In those companies where information is a critical part of the business, as in financial services, the CIO has much more direct line management over the Information Technology (IT) group(s). This may be the result of the nature of financial services, which although marketing diverse financial products, is still primarily a single product company. The tenure of DeWayne Petersen at Merrill Lynch exemplifies this role. Before his retirement, Petersen was intimately involved in the day-to-day affairs of IT—right down to attending meetings on specific data-export requirements.

In businesses that promote autonomy, one will usually find a management view that the business is really composed of several businesses—each having their own market focus. In these types of organizations, the CIO tends to be much more of a coordinator/facilitator. Don Winski at Time

Warner, Leo Haile at ITT, and Larry Ford at IBM are good examples of this genre. Each of these CIOs is more strategic thinker, ombudsman, and visionary than technology managers concerned with taking care of business around the company on a daily basis.

In the Time Warner scheme of things, each business unit (BU) has its own mission, its own goals, and its own technology group. It's the vice-president of the BU's technology group whose responsibility it is for the day-to-day tasks. Don Winski, as CIO coordinator/facilitator, must diplomatically assert the strategic plan into the BU's tactical plan. According to Winski, the easiest way to effect expertise among the BUs is to bring someone in from the outside. In the tactician's eyes, this makes it much more palatable and preferable to the perceived heavy hand of the CIO.

In a decentralized environment, the CIO and his or her staff (referred to as Corporate at Time Warner) often worked effectively with the autonomous BUs as a technology utility. In this environment, the autonomous BUs can join together with Corporate to achieve economies of scale in utilization of computer horsepower. But it's more than acting just as the company store. By virtue of its position in the company hierarchy, Corporate has the ability, some say luxury, of walking around to see what's going on in the individual BUs. In this way, Corporate can keep track of the "islands of excellence," as Winski refers to them, that are being quietly created in the BUs and ultimately act as a sort of marriage broker. For example, at Time Warner an impressive array of desktop publishing skills can be found deep within Home Box Office (HBO). Winski discovered and, ultimately, brokered these skills to other Time Warner groups.

How CIOs Can Build Effective Technology Teams

If a CIO had the ability to build a technology team from scratch, how could it be done to achieve the causal effect of better technology leading to a competitive edge? The best place to start our creative exercise is at the top. What type of person should the vice-president of Information Technology be? Although this is a discussion about how to select the head of technology for a particular business unit, much of the selection criteria described is equally applicable to selecting a CIO.

Recently, there's been much debate about whether or not the person chosen needs in-depth experience in technology. Some say that it's more important to have good business acumen about the particular business unit as well as savvy political skills. Others suggest that it is of paramount importance that the day-to-day chief of technology demonstrate practical experience in the applications of technology. Still others take a middle-of-the-road approach when they advocate that a person's set of skills depends upon the type of business he/she is in. If a business is high-tech oriented, then the technology chief should be more tech-oriented and less business-oriented. If technology plays primarily a support role, then the split should be somewhere around 70 percent business savvy and 30 percent technology savvy.

Interestingly, in those companies surveyed for this book, apparently what ultimately determines the decision as to the appropriate techno-intelligence ratio possessed by the head of technology for any individual business unit, is the comfort level of this person's superior. If this person is highly uncomfortable with the notion of technology, then the subordinate is likely to be more business-oriented and less technically oriented. On the other hand, if the superior officer is comfortable with the notion of technology, and its demands, then the position of chief of technology for the business unit is likely to be filled by a strong technologist.

What is really needed in this position is a *golem*. In Jewish legend, the sixteenth-century Prague Rabbi Low brought to life a robot of clay given life by means of a charm. Molded out of clay, the golem could be made to take on any of the characteristics desired by the one who molded him. If we could "build" the perfect head of technical services, what would we sculpt into its final form? First and foremost, this person **must** have an extensive background in technology—preferably, hands-on. Time Warner's Winski advises, "You can't manage technical people if you don't have their respect. And you won't get their respect until you can demonstrate that you once were, and still are, one of them."

Now comes for the hard part. There's been much criticism about the managerial prowess of most technical people. Most die-hard, techno-gurus just can't manage. Most have an inability, or perhaps lack of desire, to understand the business unit's mission and subsequent goals. What's more, most techno-gurus lack the political savvy, or finesse, to deal on a daily basis with people who are less technically inclined.

In general, managements across the board operate on the premise that in-depth technical expertise precludes managerial expertise. Although this is true for technical-types, it's also true for accountants, for marketers, etc. In fact, this is a corporate-wide truism. What most senior managements fail to remember is that the "all does not represent the one." Senior management needs not promote, or hire, all technical staff to the position of head of technology. Just one. The right one. There will always be that one unique individual who possesses both technical smarts and business savvy that makes for the right choice.

At a minimum, then, senior management should look for a good grounding in technology coupled with a deep understanding of the business. This goes beneath the surface of the business, and into its culture and personalities.

If such a golem can be found, or nurtured from within, then two tasks must be tackled simultaneously. The first is to understand the business and its goals, the second is to be able to recommend applicable technological solutions.

We've all heard horror stories about projects that failed due to an insistence on the part of technical leadership for "technology for technology's sake." Unfortunately, this problem is a double-edged sword. On the one hand, senior management has a right to be wary of the request to once again dip into the budget for what they perceive to be the next hottest techno-toy. On the other hand, these managers, ever-wary of the boy who cried wolf once too often, may mistakenly discount a technology with positive competitive advantages. This confusion over the question of whether to apply budget dollars to any particular project has contributed to what some call the "productivity paradox."

Technology's Productivity Paradox

A corporation's foundation rests on the skills and productivity of its workers, and if that foundation is weak, the corporation will falter. In spite of American industry's investment—to the tune of about $25 billion a year—in

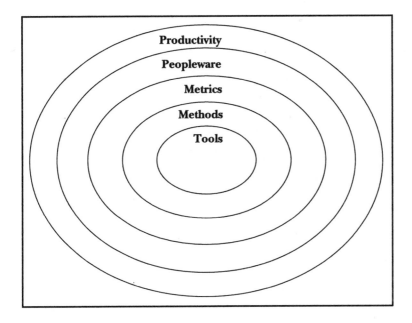

teaching their employees the basic skills that should have been learned in school, the outlook is still bleak.

An antidote to this corporate woe just may be technology. Savvy organizations have long realized that technology could be used, not only to *replace* assembly line clerical workers in doing repetitive and mechanical tasks, but also to *assist* white-collar workers in performing their functions more productively and more accurately. No where is this more evident than in the productivity boon that followed the introduction of the personal computer.

On the other hand, businesses that expected a big productivity payoff from investing in information technology are, in many cases, still waiting to collect. According to research by Paul Attewell, then professor at the State University of New York at Stony Brook, "There is an absence or paucity of productivity payoffs from information technology (IT), despite massive investment in IT over the last 25 years."

In 1988 alone, U.S. companies invested some $51 billion in hardware, $20 billion in purchased software and over $44 billion in computer services, representing up to 25 percent of a firm's capital stock. This huge commitment was made at the expense of other kinds of investments while the United States placed its bet that IT investment would raise economic productivity.

Instead of increasing productivity, though, computers often generate more work for the end user. Attewell points to a study done by the Internal Revenue Service in which IRS auditors supplied with laptops found no productivity gain. In fact, the same work took longer to do.

Perhaps the real problem here is not that technology has proven ineffective in America's push for productivity, but that American corporations have chosen the wrong systems to automate. As Chris Kemerer, Assistant Professor at M.I.T.'s Sloan School, so succinctly puts it, "we will not only have to build systems right, but will also have to build the right systems."

To ensure technological productivity, technologists must go beyond the traditional approaches of system development to be able to make a correct match between technology and process, and between problem and solution. One way this can be done is by evaluating the critical success factors (CSF) of a business or business line. Managers are intimately aware of their missions and goals, but they don't necessarily consciously define the processes required to achieve these goals—in other words, "How are you going to get there?" In these instances, technologists must depart from their traditional venue of top-down methodologies and employ a bottom-up approach. They must work with the business unit to discover the goal and work their way up through the policies, procedures, and technologies that will be necessary to arrive at that particular goal. For example, the goal of a fictitious business line is to be able to cut down the production/distribution cycle by a factor of 10, providing a customized product at no greater cost than that of the generic product in the past. To achieve this goal, the technology group needs to get the business managers to walk through the critical processes that need to be invented or changed. It is only at this point that any technology solutions are introduced.

IBM's Approach to Determining Critical Success Factors

A technique, called Process Quality Management or PQM, makes use of this concept of critical success factors. We will focus on IBM's approach to solving a persistent problem that plagues most companies: How do you get a group to agree on goals and ultimately deliver a complex project efficiently and productively? PQM is a really a combination of methodologies that many companies use independently, but IBM culled these diverse techniques together to create a method that is used today by a broad array of companies including Time Warner.[6]

PQM is initiated by gathering, preferably off site, a team of essential staff. The team's components should represent all facets of the project. Obviously, all teams have leaders and PQM teams are no different. The team leader chosen must have a skill mix closely attuned to the projected outcome of the project. For example, in a PQM team where the assigned goal is to improve plant productivity, the best team leader just might be an expert in process control, albeit the eventual solution might be in the form of enhanced automation.

Assembled at an off-site location, the first task of the team is to develop, in written form, specifically what the team's mission is. With such open-ended goals as, "Determine the best method of employing technology for competitive advantage," the determination of the actual mission statement is an arduous task—best tackled by segmenting this rather vague goal into more concrete subgoals.

In a quick brainstorming session the team lists all the factors that might inhibit the mission from being accomplished. This serves to develop a series of one-word descriptions. Given the 10-minute time frame, the goal is to get as many of these inhibitors as possible without discussion and without criticism.

It's at this point that the team turns to identifying the critical success factors (CSFs), which are the specific tasks that the team must perform to accomplish its mission. It is vitally important that the entire team reach a consensus on the CSFs.

---

[6] This overview is based on an article by Maurice Hardaker and Bryan K. Ward published in the November-December 1987 issue of the *Harvard Business Review* that encapsulates rather neatly IBM's approach to helping a team develop a specific plan of action for a particular approach.

The next step in the IBM PQM process is to make a list of all tasks necessary in accomplishing the CSF. The description of each of these tasks, called business processes, should be declarative. Start each with an action word such as: study, measure, reduce, negotiate, eliminate.

Figures 1-2 and 1-3 show examples of the Project Chart and Priority Graph, respectively, that diagram this PQM technique. The team's mission, in these examples, is to introduce just in time (JIT) inventory control, a manufacturing technique that fosters greater efficiency by promoting stocking inventory only to the level of need. The team, in this example, identified six CSFs and 11 business processes labeled P1 through P11.

The Project Chart is filled out by first ranking the business process by importance to the project's success. This is done by comparing each business process to the set of CSFs. A check is made under each CSF that relates significantly to the business process. This procedure is followed until each of the business processes have been analyzed in the same way.

The final column of the Project Chart permits the team to rank each business process relative to current performance, using a scale of A—excellent, to D—bad, and E—not currently performed.

The Priority Graph, when completed, will steer the mission to a successful, and prioritized, conclusion. The two axes to this graph are Quality, using the A through E grading scale as shown above, and Priority, represented by the number of checks noting each business process received. These can be lifted easily from the Project Chart from the Quality and Count columns respectively.

The final task as a team is to decide how to divide the Priority Graph into different zones representing first priority, second priority and so on. In this example, the team has chosen as a first priority all business processes, such as in our example negotiate with suppliers and reduce number of parts, that are ranked from a quality of fair degrading to a quality of not currently performed and having a ranking of three or greater. Most groups employing this technique will assign priorities in a similar manner.

Determining the right project to pursue is one factor in the push for competitive technology. It is equally as important to be able to "do the project right." Which is of paramount importance in a company that aims to run a productive and quality-oriented software factory.

A Case for Productivity

Many CIOs live by the 10-percent rule. That is the greatest productivity you can get comes from hiring within the Top Ten percentile. One of technology's leading gurus, Ed Yourdon, agrees when he says the easiest approach to developing an efficient technology department is to bring in the better

# Business Process	CRITICAL SUCCESS FACTORS 1 2 3 4 5 6	COUNT	QUALITY
P1 Measure delivery performance by suppliers	x x	2	B
P2 Recognize/reward workers	xx	2	D
P3 Negotiate with suppliers	x x x	3	B
P4 Reduce number of parts	x x x x	4	D
P5 Train supervisors	xx	2	C
P6 Redesign productionj line	x x x	3	A
P7 Move parts inventoryp	X		E
P8 Eliminate excessive inventory buildups	X X	2	C
P9 Select suppliers	X X	2	B
P10 Measure	X X X	3	E
P11 Eliminate defective parts	X X X	3	D

CSF 1 = Rapid access to parts
CSF 2 = Supplier cooperation
CSF3 = Products engineered for JIT assembly
CSF4 = Supportive workforce
CSF5 = Worker knowledge of JIT procedures
CSF6 = Supervisor knowledve of JIT procedures

Figure 1-2. Project chart. (*Source: Maurice Hardaker and Bryan K. Ward*)

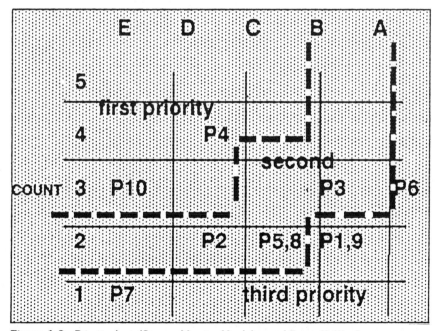

Figure 1-3. Priority chart. (*Source: Maurice Hardaker and Bryan K. Ward*)

people. Since, according to Yourdon, there is a 25 to 1 differential between the best people and the worst people, and a 4 to 1 differential between the best teams and the worst teams, maybe the best way to improve productivity and quality is just to improve hiring practices.

But who are the people that improved hiring practices would find? According to Yourdon, these are the people who are just innately better programmers. "If you take a random group of 100 people and put them in a room with a complex programming exercise, one of them will finish 25 times faster than the others."

The Challenge of Peopleware

In addition to hiring, other "peopleware" techniques could go a long way towards increasing productivity. Recent studies have shown that the productivity of people with adequate office space is substantially higher than people with traditionally allocated smaller amounts of space. Training also makes a difference, particularly if workers can accrue their training days the way they accrue their vacation days.[7]

Productivity can also be improved in many other ways: by training managers to develop more skill in handling employee performance reviews, or even by focusing on the psychological makeup of the development team. Much work has been done, in recent years, on team dynamics. In order for a team to work together successfully, team members must complement each other. Each team needs a distribution of leaders, followers, idea people, testers, problem solvers, and so on. Even in an industry where personality profiles are skewed towards introversion, it is still possible to build an effective working team. All it needs is some good management.

Metrics—the Yardstick for Measuring IT

When Ed Yourdon was asked to pick one single technology-based approach to make people more productive, and produce a product of higher quality, he recommended metrics. "If you don't know where you are now and you don't know where your productivity problems are, any solution you seek may turn out to be the wrong one."

However, measurement is more than just taking a count. In fact, Professor Howard Rubin, chairman of the computer science department at Hunter College in New York, emphasizes that often a company's concept of measure-

---

[7] Tom DeMarco, *Structured Analysis and Systems Specification* (New York: Prentice-Hall, 1979).

ment is itself flawed. Most organizations start a measurement program without understanding the requirements for measuring. Thus, companies should know what the destination target is and to achieve it they need to develop navigational measures.

In tracking the field of measurement for over 15 years, Rubin has found that measures have evolved from measurement of lines of code to productivity analysis relying on more business directed measures. Today, the lingo of IT measurement is rooted squarely in the lingo of user and management concerns where these users are often referred to as "measurement stakeholders."

It is these stakeholders that have driven some advanced companies to adopt a dashboard-oriented framework for program implementation. As developed by Rubin, these dashboards consist of the appropriate gauges to show current performance, baselines, directional trends, and performance targets. The most useful gauges represent core management concerns: quality, productivity, delivery, demand, overall work distribution, work profile within projects, tool penetration, process maturity, and technology readiness. But for this type of measurement program to work, it is critical the IT organization must fully understand how the company itself measures its business success and how IT performance links to company performance.

Achieving Efficiency from Methodology

Companies that will win the competitive battles of the '90s are those firms that will leverage their technology investments to create new possibilities. What are necessary for IT to make a productive contribution are good management, good technical staff—including good estimators and testers, good measurements, good tools, and a good methodology.

IT management can choose from many well-known and well-documented methodologies, the most popular being Martin, Gane/Sarson and Yourdon. A methodology represents the processes, or steps, that a technology unit goes through in order to successfully specify, develop and then implement a computer system. Pursuing technology development without a methodology is akin to finding your way through the Yukon without a map. It's surprising, therefore, to find that many companies develop a majority of their systems without a map. Perhaps this is one of the root causes of the productivity paradox that Professor Attewell decries.

The Software Engineering Institute, located in Pittsburgh, Pennsylvania, is the author of a well-known chart depicting the software process maturity framework. As shown in Figure 1-4, the framework consists of five levels of maturity that an IT department goes through on its way to becoming completely optimized and productive. An oft-quoted statistic is that a full 80 per-

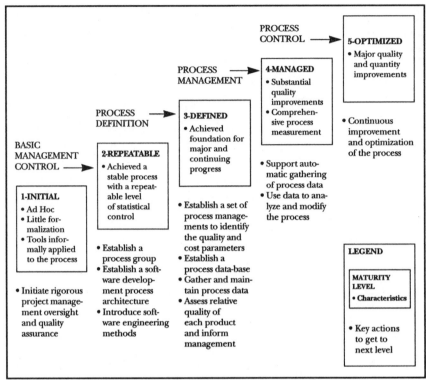

Figure 1-4. Five steps to IT maturity. According to the Software Engineering Institute, an Information Technology department goes through five levels of maturity on its way to becoming optimized and productive. Few IT departments have reached Level 5. (*Source: Software Engineering Institute*)

cent of us are sitting squarely on top of level one. This may be because the general computing public has not exactly found what it wants or what it needs from any one of these methodologies. Instead, technologists are all back in their shops trying to put a little bit of what sounded good in one with what sounded good in another. They're asking, "Is there a way for me to create my own version of these methodologies? And then have some tool that would enforce them for me?"

In choosing a methodology IT would do well to understand the dynamics of the relationships between methodology, CASE, and measurements. Many interviewed for this book agreed that the proper sequence of implementation to foster the improvement in systems development productivity and quality, as shown in Figure 1-5, is to develop a measurement program first, a methodology second, and pick a CASE product last of all. Surrounding this trio are the prickly issues of "peopleware," as Ed Yourdon so succinctly labeled perhaps the most important factor of all.

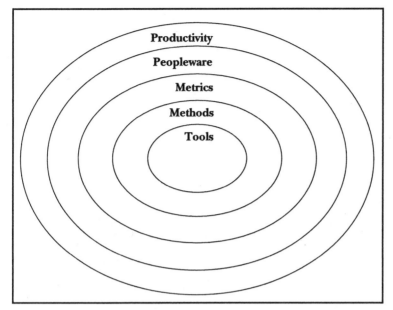

Figure 1-5. Multilayer approach to quality/production.

The Quality Issue

The quality issue is necessarily inseparable from the productivity issue if a company is going to "do systems right." As a rule of thumb, quality in the short term translates to productivity in the long term.

Quality is frequently overlooked in the race to implement on or before deadline. However, no matter what the time pressure, certain measures undertaken seriously can enhance the quality of output of any software investment. Figure 1-6a lists some of the possible measurement programs from which a company can choose to assist it on the road to quality computer systems; Figure 1-6b can be used as a quick measure of system quality. By answering the questionnaire, it is possible to score a system's overall quality.

The Hewlett-Packard Way

Perhaps one of the best examples of a company tracking the quality and productivity of its software team from an engineering perspective comes from Hewlett Packard. Quality and productivity have been part of Cupertino-based Hewlett Packard (HP)'s corporate objectives for years. But it's only within the last few that this concept has filtered into the world of software development. To help develop and utilize metrics company-wide, HP created the Software Metrics Council. Today, 80 productivity and quality

1)	Lines of code
2)	Pages of documentation
3)	Number and size of tests
4)	Function count
5)	Variable count
6)	Decision count
7)	Number of modules
8)	Depth of nesting
9)	Count of changes required
10)	Count of discovered defects
11)	Count of changed lines of code
12)	Time to design, code, test
13)	Defect discovery rate by phase of systems development
14)	Cost to develop
15)	Number of external interfaces
16)	Number of tools used
17)	Reusability percentage
18)	Variance of schedule
19)	Staff years experience with team
20)	Staff years experience with language
21)	Staff years experience with software language
22)	MIPS per person
23)	Support personnel to development personnel
24)	Nonproject time to project time ratio

Figure 1–6a. Productivity/Quality metrics.

managers within HP perform a variety of functions, from training to communicating the best software engineering practices to establishing productivity and quality metrics.

HP has adopted a methodology called Total Quality Control (TQC). A fundamental principle of TQC is that all company activities can be scrutinized in terms of the processes involved; metrics can be assigned to each process to evaluate effectiveness. HP has developed numerous measurements (Figure 1-7).

The TQC approach places software quality/assessment high on the list of software development tasks. When projects are first defined, along with understanding and evaluating the process to be automated, the team defines the metrics that are to be used to measure the process.

When HP decided to revolve the future of the company around a new type of computer architecture, software reliability was deemed critical. The development of the systems software for this enterprise was the largest devel-

		1 = low to 5 = high				
1)	How easy is it to use?	1	2	3	4	5
2)	How secure is it?	1	2	3	4	5
3)	Level of confidence it it?	1	2	3	4	5
4)	How easy is it to upgrade?	1	2	3	4	5
5)	How well does it conform to requirements?	1	2	3	4	5
6)	How easy it it to change?	1	2	3	4	5
7)	How portable is it?	1	2	3	4	5
8)	How easy is it to locate a problem and fix?	1	2	3	4	5
9)	Is the response time fast enough?	1	2	3	4	5
10)	How easy is it to train staff?	1	2	3	4	5
11)	Ease of testing?	1	2	3	4	5
12)	Is the software efficient in terms of computing resources?	1	2	3	4	5
13)	Ease of coupling this system to another?	1	2	3	4	5
14)	Does this system utilize the minimum storage possible?	1	2	3	4	5
15)	Is the system self-descriptive?	1	2	3	4	5
16)	Does the system exhibit modularity?	1	2	3	4	5
17)	Is there a program for on-going quality awareness for all employees?	1	2	3	4	5
18)	Do you check supplier quality?	1	2	3	4	5
19)	Is there a quality department?	1	2	3	4	5
20)	Is this the "right" system to be developed?	1	2	3	4	5

Circle the applicable number next to each measure. Add for total score.

Figure 1-6b. Quality factors. Rating these quality factors and then totaling the score is a way to measure overall quality of a software project. Taking the time to enhance quality (improve the score) can also enhance a company's software development investment.

opment effort in HP's history, and the first that required multiple divisions to produce software systems.

Charles A. Krueger, a professor at the University of Wisconsin in Madison, points out the productivity paradox of budget versus getting to market: Is it more important to stay within the targeted confines of money allocated, or to get the product out on time? He quotes a McKinsey & Company study which indicates that going over budget by 50 percent and

Metric	Goal
Break-even time	Measures return on investment. Time until development costs are offset by profits.
Time to market	Measures responsiveness and competitiveness. Time from project go ahead until release to market.
Progress rate	Measures accuracy of schedule. Ratio of planned to actual development time.
Post-release defect density	Measures effectiveness of test processes. Total number of defects reported during first 12 months after product implementation.
Turnover rate	Measures morale. Percentage of staff leaving.
Training	Measures investment in career development. Number of hours per staff per year.

Figure 1-7. Hewlett-Packard Productivity/Quality measurements. (*Source: Hewlett-Packard*)

getting a product out on time reduces profits by only 4 percent. But staying on budget and getting to market five months late reduces profits by two-thirds. Obviously, productivity is really a measure of how successful you are in achieving your results.

Hewlett Packard came to the same conclusion as Krueger, and the company insisted on reliable software and delivery on time. HP established the Systems Software Certification program to ensure measurable, consistent, high-quality software through defining metrics, setting goals, collecting and analyzing data, and certifying products for release. This program developed four metrics for their new architecture program:

1. *Breadth*—measures the testing coverage of user-accessible and internal functionality of the project

2. *Depth*—measures the proportion of instructions or blocks of instructions executed during testing

3. *Reliability*—measures the stability and robustness of a product and its ability to recover gracefully from error conditions

4. *Defect density*—measures the quantity and severity of reported defects and a product's readiness

HP's results were impressive. Defects were caught and corrected early, when costs to find and fix are lower. Less time was spent in the costly system test and integration phases, and on maintenance. This resulted in lower overall support costs and higher productivity. It also increased quality for HP's customers. HP's success demonstrates what a corporation-wide commitment to productivity and quality measures can achieve.

2

Infotrend #1: Using Technology to Prosper in a Down Market

The gold rush of the 1980s is over. Back in those halcyon days, it was quite possible to have a bad idea, bad execution of that idea, and still make a profit. In the rush for these profits, good management practices and principles often fell by the wayside—replaced by huge infusions of capital to correct any possible problematic situation.

The era of the 1980s gave rise to such notables as Ivan Boesky and Mike Milken. The 1980s also saw an entire industry fall prey to what it thought would be easy money. Of course, when the boom ended in the late 1980s, Boesky, Milken, and the entire Savings and Loan industry were only notable for the amount of red ink spilled as an entire economic boom period went bust.

Today's economic weather is clearly much darker and more stormy. There are no spare dollars to throw around. Today, in this down market, the watchword is caution.

The recession of the early 1990s saw many managements make a 180-degree reversal. Once freewheeling spenders, they turned into scrooges, spending nary a cent and slicing through their ranks cutting staff and key projects seemingly indiscriminately.

In the financial services sector, based in the hard-hit northeast, the cuts were heavy and unforgiving. In some companies, entire departments were let go. Of course, this cyclical pattern of hiring during flush times and lay-ing off during lean times is nothing new. But by analyzing just what functions are let go, it is quite possible to perceive some of the business strategy of a particular firm. In the case of technology, a definite pattern emerges.

The Equitable Life Assurance Company and American Express represent both ends of the technology spectrum as it pertains to a down market. American Express believes that even during troubling times, technological investment must be maintained. On the flip side, the Equitable, faced with mounting losses, made major cuts irrevocably slicing through its technology departments. Nowhere is the difference between the two companies more apparent then in their Research and Development (R&D) departments, for it is this department that represents the "future" of the company.

To demonstrate that firms that link their technology strategy with their business strategy are at a definite competitive advantage to firms that do not—especially in times of economic downturn—we will detail several case histories of companies whose stature is heavily dependent on their understanding of this technology—strategy relationship and invest in technologies that support this view.

Having a technology R&D department is always advantageous to a firm, and this book strongly advocates investment in research and development to enable companies to take advantage of newer technologies. Knowing about leading-edge technologies positions companies to take advantage of the technology to enjoy greater efficiencies and even leadership positions.

Michael Porter, a leading management consultant well-known for his books on competitive strategy, talks about a concept called *first mover.* A company which is in a position to be "first" in that company's industry is in the position of deriving great benefits. This company is, therefore, called a first mover. Slanting this to a technology perspective, we can find many examples of this in practice. McKesson Drug Company developed an information system which it provided its customers. The system, Economost, was a state of the art order-entry system. Not only did it provide efficiencies both for McKesson and McKesson's customers, but—since none of McKesson's competitors had a system quite like it—Economost provided McKesson with first-mover status.

In times of lean markets, as mentioned, there are two general reactions typified by American Express and the Equitable. Indiscriminate cutting of technology staff—especially R&D—effectively slices segments out of that company's future. American Express, also faced with a down market, had to make cuts as well, but it understood the principle that by cutting R&D during a lean year, AMEX would effectively impede progress toward technological innovation for several years to come.

In down markets, the most effective strategy is somewhere in between the excessive spending of the 1980s and the excessive cuts of the 1990s. If a company truly understands the value of technology, then surviving in hard-pressed economic times means combining innovative technology, good management, good service, and a good product to produce success.

Perhaps the best example of this guiding principle in action can be found in Columbus, Ohio. Surprisingly, this example comes from an industry in the midst of great, and often bloody, upheaval. Banc One has combined conservative lending, innovative technology, and superior customer service to make itself into a superregional bank which threatens to compete head on with the big money-center banks such as Citicorp and Chase Manhattan.

Banc One's corporate culture—a culture taught in two-week, 18 hour-a-day "boot camps" for officers of newly acquired banks—synergizes technology with a sort of supermarket approach to banking. This, coupled with a conservative lending policy (no third-world or Donald Trump-like loans need apply), makes Banc One the bank of the present, and most surely, the bank of the future. Banc One's management skill in all of these areas is what makes it a contender for the title of best-run bank in America. The age is over when a bank's significance and importance directly relates to its size. Today, analysts indicate that it is management skill in being able to handle growth, people, product innovation, and technology which are more important.

Banc One has quietly gone about its business of technology. It was one of the first banks to install automated teller machines. The first was in 1970, while a more recent one was in a McDonald's restaurant in Mansfield, Ohio. But if banking officials had to choose one technological innovation as representative of Banc One's understanding of the value of technology to their position, it would be in the area of management reporting.

Management reporting may seem too innocuous a choice to be called innovative. However, given Banc One's far-flung empire and the industry's seeming inability to track the strengths and weaknesses of its portfolio, their particular version of a management reporting system clearly stands out.

Monthly reports are produced in a standardized fashion for all of Banc One branches and the bank's 21 affiliates, tracking hundreds of categories of revenue and expenses, and measuring performance against monthly forecasts made by the managements of each bank. The reports measure each bank's performance against comparable institutions in the Banc One system.

This complete confluence of technology and business strategy has proven quite profitable. From 1984 through 1990, Banc One had quadrupled in size to $30.3 billion in assets.

R&D as a Starting Point to New Markets— The American Express and Texas Instruments Model

Nearly every technical innovation on which a company might rest its laurels stems from corporate R&D. One can draw the conclusion, therefore, that setting up a R&D group should be a priority for any company wishing to gain a competitive position in the best of times and remain competitive in the worst of times.

An R&D lab can be simply or extensively built. The simple side is represented by hiring, or grooming, a staffer whose specific function is to keep abreast of all the latest in information technology, and then disseminate this information to the project directors in the business units. American Express represents the type of firm which heavily invests in R&D and has, out of necessity, built an extensive R&D superstructure.

American Express's R&D team is large, and staffed with holders of advanced degrees. The Advanced Technology Group at American Express is divided into separate departments that handle the different advanced and emerging technologies. Not only do they keep fully informed on the latest breaking news about a particular technology, but they fund prototypes which permit them to experiment with the technology and thereby gain hands-on experience. Thus American Express is fully prepared to be a "first-mover" in using technology when the need arises or a future need is perceived.

Of course, not all research becomes fruitful. There exists an erroneous assumption, specifically among senior managers, that any technological innovation coming out of the lab will be fully marketable and therefore lead to competitive advantage. This is, unfortunately, not so.

Eliminating Misconceptions about IT Development

Business analyst and academician Lowell Steele itemized seven misconceptions about technological innovation that often compromise R&D projects and make them difficult to manage[1]. By using Steele's checklist to assist in making a decision about whether to fund a particular R&D project or not will greatly assist in boosting the success rate of the R&D lab in general. The following assumptions, although seemingly right on target, are wrong according to Steele:

---

[1] Lowell Steele, Managers' Misconceptions About Technology, *Harvard Business Review* (November/December 1983), pp. 133–40.

Misconception #1: Best-fit possible technology should be implemented. The company would be better off in looking for "best fit" rather than the "best," i.e., most technically advanced. Always striving for the best is overkill leading to excessive costs and an inevitable hindrance of adoption. There is always a trade-off among performance, cost, and product life. It is better to optimize this trade-off by developing a technology that is just good enough to do so.

This particular misconception is easily visible in practice in nearly every company. Many technology people like to experiment. When a new technique or tool is first announced, these staffers strive to force fit the new technology to any number of projects—whether or not the project warrants it. A case in point occurred at a large financial services company. In the late 1970s, when database technology was first making its entrance into corporate America, this company purchased a database tool set. At the time, an important new project was in its planning stages. Since the database tool was new, the development team decided to apply the new technology to this highly visible project. As it turned out, the project did not need database technology. Since the team little understood how to apply this new technology, what was ultimately developed was excessively costly and prone to failure. The system was replaced within two years.

Misconception #2: A system solution is deemed "good enough" if the solution was determined rationally. Just because it appears that a technical solution to a business problem is "good enough" to solve the problem, and was rationally and carefully considered, doesn't mean that that *particular solution* provides technological innovation. Understanding this forces the issue of looking outside of the organization to determine what market forces must be used to shape the technology project. User expectations must be considered when determining what is good enough. Sometimes, the market will demand a "glitzy" application of technology that is more involved and more costly than really needed to solve the problem. Sometimes a market will not accept a technology at all—even though it is better. According to Steele, R&D groups must consider "widely shared beliefs" or face failure.

Misconception #3: Innovations are generally successful. Failure rates for innovative products are extraordinarily high. In fact, there are many more failures than successes. It may appear that there are many successes, but that's because successes are often publicized while failures seldom are.

Misconception #4: Once discovered, technical innovation goes smoothly. Even though a first pass at using a new technology sometimes goes extremely well, it can be expected that future uses of the technology may not go as well. This is particularly true for situations where a prototype has been used as a proof of concept. If the prototype is not truly representative of the problem the technology is attempting to solve, then it is likely that difficulties will occur as the project progresses.

Misconception #5: Success is directly related to the novelty of the idea. There is risk in the unknown. Most successes, interestingly, are advances based on existing technology. This misconception has lead to the development of R&D groups which look only to the future, or emerging, technologies while ignoring R&D into possible uses of existing technologies into new corporate areas. Possibly, this is due to the charter of most R&D groups where the stated goal is to look to the future. Existing corporate information services groups, therefore, are charged with applying these found technologies across the board. Wherever it is done, whether R&D or corporate information services, it is equally as important to disseminate existing technologies as it is to research new technologies. Both lead to competitive advantage.

Misconception #6: The most important factors leading to success are the technical factors. Unfortunately, many information systems are built in just this vacuum. Only technological factors are considered when judging success. Ultimately, when the product reaches the market or the end user, it may be found lacking since the team failed to consider market forces or user concerns. One should ask the question, "Assuming that the system works, what can stand in the way of its success?" Possible answers are marketing and consumer behavior.

Misconception #7: Measurements and standards stand in the way of true technical innovation. Managements should strive to force R&D teams from the "creative" mind set of research and towards the engineering side. A structured development environment, one in which true measures and standards apply, will lead to developments more likely to be successful and suitable for production.

Planning R&D

In times of downward spiraling markets, it is necessary to apply Steele's principles to make sure that the R&D group is working effectively according to the realities of the marketplace. Of course, Steele's checklist of misconceptions about technology serve only as a springboard to monitoring the R&D group's efforts.

If R&D within a company is to be truly effective, then the R&D group must not operate in a vacuum. R&D must be the responsibility of the entire company. Managers at all levels, tactical, strategic, and operational must provide input and become responsible for efforts that affect their respective domains.

When Texas Instruments (TI) began to grow larger, it developed a planning system for R&D that permits it to maintain the innovative spirit so indicative of its early years[2]. Its methodology for planning has proven extremely successful in helping management identify the most promising of innovations. Since the method is meant to be employed by all levels of management, it is a worthy tool for encouraging managers to innovate as well.

TI's method includes assigning operational managers the responsibility for reviewing and prioritizing R&D project proposals on three levels. Committees —composed of managers—are formed on the operational, tactical, and strategic levels. Thus, not only do operational managers have the responsibility for ensuring smooth running of day-to-day operations, they must also constantly search out and consider innovation.

Managers need to be recognized and rewarded for their contributions and their willingness to champion new ideas. Criteria should be developed by the company employing this strategy so that innovation is as objectively rewarded as operational management success. Some companies start out by publicizing employee participation in such programs. Promotional opportunities and financial incentives should also be explored as reward alternatives.

Three levels of R&D budget are required for operational, tactical, and strategic initiatives. Proposals, therefore, have a chance to receive funding from three different sources. In order to receive funding, each proposal is subjected to competitive review and prioritized at each level. What may not be appealing at one level is often appealing at another level. This is especially true for long-term or risky proposals which often have a second chance for life when turned down by the tactical level, but are approved at the strategic level. Budget considerations come into play after prioritization, as projects are funded based on their ranking. Those proposals that go unfunded are put back into a pool for consideration when additional funding becomes available.

The benefits of this three-tier hierarchy are great. First, multiple levels of management are involved in the project—providing better communications within the company. Another benefit is that projects that get "killed" at the lower rungs of the hierarchy are often resurrected by senior management, seeing potential in spite of the risk associated with the project. A third benefit is that, perhaps for the first time, redundancy of projects can be eliminated. Too many companies spend too many budget dollars in developing information systems with similar functionality to those already in existence. The three-tier competitive review process permits senior managers to determine if the there are relationships between proposals or between proposals and existing systems for which there might be a synergy.

Occasionally, there will be a project that is too underdeveloped to be considered by the process used by Texas Instruments. TI created an informal

[2]"Texas Instruments Shows US Business How to Survive in the 1980s," *Business Week* (September 18, 1978), pp. 66–92.

source of secondary funding or "seed" money available through venture managers. This fund provides small amounts of funding enabling feasibility demonstration or proof-of-concept systems. These proposals are reviewed outside of the main review process by an experienced manager whose sole criteria is simply that the idea be a good one.

Bankers Trust Goes Global and Wins

Remaining competitive in lean times requires a dedication to innovation coupled with no small dose of managerial acumen. It also requires being able to foster a spirit of cooperation between often noncooperating, diverse business units and the information services department, as well as being able to separate the technological wheat from the chaff.

Bankers Trust has turned technology into profit, an especially notable achievement, as much of it has occurred during the doldrums starting after the 1987 market crash. First, we'll discuss the man behind their technological innovation. If you look carefully at a company that appears to be aggressively pursuing technological innovation, you'll often find one person acting as the technology champion.

Carmine Vona is a unique man. Perhaps it is his background as a nuclear physicist and a teacher that make him the perfect catalyst for technological revolution. Or it may be his uncanny knack for picking the right projects and getting them to work right on target. As a result of Vona's technological strategies, Bankers Trust has sailed through banking's toughest days and on into uncharted waters to rack up an astonishing array of successes. But Vona, the man, is probably proudest of a testament to him that appeared in a 1977 issue of *Computerworld*.

In a letter to the editor, someone who had worked with Vona was decrying the popularization of a test which would measure the value of a programmer. The writer was scandalized that the test seemed to imply that the field was being overrun by lazy, careless less-than-professionals.

Carmine Vona's name was brought up as an example of superior technical leadership—as someone who never had, and never would, warrant such a test. The writer went on to say that Vona's systems all worked, his managers got promoted and his users loved him. He ended the letter by saying, "I just want to be like Carmine Vona when I grow up."

Thus, by virtue of his technical prowess, his managerial skill, his personality, and his academic background, Vona was well suited for the job of turning Bankers Trust from "a second-rate, ill-focused, near-insolvent commercial bank into a dynamic, well-capitalized, and highly profitable merchant bank."[3]

Computerworld, an computer industry newspaper, selects 100 companies each year which are then known as the Computerworld Premier 100. These premier 100 are deemed leaders in the use of technology in several industry categories. In the banking category, Bankers placed first two years running. In 1989, Bankers won for its then unusual restructuring of a centralized technology group into decentralized business units. In 1990, Bankers won for its global information systems support plan, which feeds off the decentralization of the technology groups.

Of course, when viewed across time, Bankers Trust's two awards may seem to be two discrete events. When viewed from within, however, they are synergistic—very much part and parcel of Vona's vision to "make technology an integral part of the fabric." The net result is that Bankers is a more powerful and secure bank which, in times of down markets, can move ahead forcefully.

Innovations of an IT Champion

There is no doubt that Bankers' technical infrastructure has permitted them to enjoy profits not available to other big money-center banks. Their decision to expand this infrastructure to move into the global arena was a decisive strategic move, and one that pushed the bank's profitability to new highs.

The details of Bankers' technical architecture are worthy of consideration for those who might glean some new direction for their own firms. But before we launch into a specific discussion of this plan, it is necessary to reiterate that the successful implementation of this plan was due to the efforts and the talents of one man: Carmine Vona.

Vona has been with the bank for 20 years, which is itself unusual, the average lifespan for somebody in his position is about two years.

Life at the bank wasn't always so smooth for Vona. In fact, he often had to fight to persuade others of his point of view. According to Vona, the secret in fighting is in believing in what you are fighting for and in fighting in a way not to get you thrown out.

Vona rose to a level of prominence in Bankers when a study was performed to select the bank's best system-development efforts. It turned out that all of the systems that worked well, were well-received by the users, and made the bank more profitable were developed by Carmine Vona. This recognition enabled Vona to progress rapidly through several levels of promotions to achieve his current status.

Perhaps part of Vona's success comes from his background. As part of his school curriculum, in pursuing a degree in nuclear physics, he studied Latin for nine years and Greek for five. His academic background gave him

---

[3] Peter Lee, "BT Looks to Sanford's Sorcery," *Euromoney* (Jan. 1991), pp. 24–32.

the background for scientific thinking as well as the ability to communicate. As Vona puts it, "if you have an idea and you can't express it, it's like not having an idea at all."

Prior to Vona, the bank had twice tried to implement some sort of technical infrastructure—and twice failed. A combination of factors led to these failures; the projects were too huge, too complex a maze of transactions flowing in all directions.

When Vona was assigned the project, he spent several months trying to unravel what he calls "spaghetti." Finally he realized that there were two incestuous functions that needed to be separated. Understanding this, he was able to create a scheme whereby everything became clear.

The two functions interfering with each other were Foreign Exchange and Money Transfer, at the time under one umbrella called Foreign Exchange Operations.

When he realized that the integration of these two functions under one roof was causing the problem, he went to the business manager of the unit and asked him to create two divisions out of the one. "I had a suspicion that if we split the division in two, we'd need fewer than the 600 people they currently had to run it." Vona felt that if you make things more linear, efficiency will follow. For all his efforts, Vona got chased out of that manager's office after a somewhat tense meeting.

When Vona came back from that meeting, he had only two choices open to him. He could resign or go over the manager's head. He choose the later. He presented his case to a senior manager, "I have the following problem here. If we were to carry on automation of this area, I will be no more successful than the last several managers who attempted to automate this area." The senior manager understood the wisdom of Vona's words; ever since, there are two divisions rather than the original one.

Vona's deintegration of the Foreign Exchange Operations group into two discrete business units became the basis for his plan to decentralize the entire company and provide it with the technological tools necessary to compete. His goals are to create new products and services while minimizing costs.

Thus, in 1985, Bankers Trust was the first of the big banks to restructure its information systems to support self-managed profit centers. According to Raphael Soifer, a banking analyst at Brown Brothers Harriman and Company, this change has radically transformed the bank from a traditional commercial bank into a powerful trading and merchant institution.

The key to the success of this radical department from the norm was a comprehensive technology architecture that provides a backbone of information systems support to the profit centers.

The move to decentralization was coincident with a total restructuring of the bank. In the early 1980s, senior managers of the bank decided that in order to become more competitive, it was necessary to weed out the unprofitable and reorganize the bank from the typical hierarchical structure to a more innovative, and less bureaucratic, horizontal structure. With this more horizontal structure, the senior managers hoped that the new company-wide policy of integration and cooperation would be fostered.

At the same time, the information services group had grown to 1,400 employees. Vona, then a division manager, clearly saw the signs of malaise responsible for long lead times in application development, the delivery of flawed applications, and alienation from the user community. Since the bank was undergoing a restructuring at the time, Vona recommended the same medicine for the information services group.

The architecture recommended then, now commonplace, was revolutionary in the beginning of the 1980s. Vona reorganized the information services group into decentralized profit centers. This dramatically altered the job of the information services staff. Not only did they have to excel at technology, they also had to learn, and master, the business indicative of the unit to which they were assigned. Ultimately, the centralized group was organized into more than 20 decentralized, self-managed business units, each with its own information services support center. It was only in this way, Vona reasoned, that Bankers could assure the creation and implementation of competitive systems. In fact, this was the route that Vona himself had taken when he first started at the bank. The first thing he did when he got the job at Bankers was to "get my hands on every business document I could find."

To ensure that there would be no proliferation of technologies leading to an inability to integrate, Vona specified that ultimate control over the technologies and methodologies used would stay in the domain of a small central staff of technology managers, Every expenditure over $10,000 would have to be approved by this small central group. Bankers seems to have successfully found the elusive middle ground between a decentralized and centralized approach to technology. In many organizations, decentralization has lead to redundancy and lack of integration, while many totally centralized firms experience difficulty in merging technology with business.

In January 1991, Salomon Brothers published a stock-research report that shows that Bankers Trust reported net earnings of $665 million dollars for 1990 with an impressive 27.9 percent return on equity. In fact, these glowing earnings have been consistent since 1984. Bankers, in fact, is the only New York-based bank the shares of which Salomon recommends for purchase, citing the bank's technical systems as largely responsible for its profitability. Of the three areas that Salomon specifically mentions as being contributing factors to Bankers's balance sheet, global trading accounts for the largest share (40%) of profits—a department that relies heavily on technology.

The innovation of decentralization has permitted Vona—and Bankers—to be able to compete effectively in the global arena. Vona's architecture is flexible enough to be able to support the bank's long-term global requirements. Bankers Trust's global plan calls for regenerating the architecture itself as the market changes and the technology progresses. In this way, Vona has been able to build a worldwide systems infrastructure which permits real-time operation from Bankers Trust branches as far away as the Far East.

If there is one system that helps Bankers Trust keep under the profitability umbrella, whatever the weather outside, it is the RAROC system. "Rate of return on capital" measures the level of risk associated with financial products and lines of business that the bank is in, and then allocates capital appropriate to that risk. The system's genesis dates back to the 1970s, when the bank's current chairman, Charles Sanford, ran the global markets area and needed a way to reduce risk. By the mid-1980s, the RAROC system—greatly enhanced—was in use as a benchmark by which all business lines are assessed for profit potential.

Since capital is a scarce resource during down markets, it is very important to make the strategically correct tactical decisions. In the global arena, RAROC is indispensable. It's woven right into the trading information systems used by top management. For example, managers use it to determine the risk characteristics of the foreign-exchange business.

RAROC is only one of a number of tools used by the bank in the global arena. The global operations and information services group (GOIS) has invested rather heavily in technology. Services include BT-World, an on-line account management system as well as the Remos trading software. Remos currently supports foreign exchange, money market, futures and options, and Eurobond government securities.

A Bank-wide Technical Architecture as Key

Vona's Bankwide Technical Architecture is the culmination of Vona's goals and his history at the bank. The term technical architecture, as used here, refers to a set of concepts, technical facilities, policies, standards, guidelines, procedures, and organizational responsibilities which work together to create an integrated, flexible, and effective technology environment for Bankers.

The increased integration and flexibility resulting from this architecture are essential ingredients to Bankers Trust's global merchant banking strategy, providing significant advantages to their more traditional lines of business as well. The architecture provides a framework within which individual business units are given the broadest possible autonomy while functioning cooperatively to achieve corporate objectives. The development of the architecture was based on their perception of five specific corporate and technical objectives.

1. *Customer Service.* Technology must be applied directly in the delivery of transaction processing and information services to customers. These services must be accurate, timely, flexible, innovative, and available worldwide.

2. *Internal Service.* The same criteria apply to services provided internally to product and marketing staff. These services include information delivery and the automation of information-intensive internal functions.

3. *New Product Creation.* The architecture must support rapid implementation of new services and create modular and reusable product components.

4. *End-User Development.* Nontechnical staff must develop the capability to manipulate information for local presentation and analysis.

5. *Data Processing Effectiveness.* The data-processing effort itself must be business focused and increasingly productive. The architecture addresses this issue through the application of advanced tools, shared facilities, and uniformity.

Conceptual Architecture   Vona developed four basic, but interrelated, technological concepts that provide Bankers Trust with the flexibility, and power, to support its global market within the confines of the bank's stated objectives:

Clusters   The architecture groups related products and services onto clusters of data-processing equipment. This localizes decision making along independent business lines. Each cluster may support a single business unit, or may be shared by multiple business units.

Networks   The architecture provides local and global communication facilities. These shared utilities reduce duplication among business units and provide more capability than a single unit could justify independently

Security   Specific policies and facilities within the architecture provide a basic security environment for each business application. By building upon this base, each application can implement the degree and form of security best suited to its business function without concern for the impact on other neighboring systems.

Integration   The standards provided by the architecture ensure the rational evolution of application components which, while developed independently, will function smoothly together. When combined with the architecture's communication facilities, they permit a free flow of processing and information services among these independently developed applications.

These features of the architecture support varying levels of functional distribution, while avoiding duplication of expenses and ensuring the ability of independent units to function cooperatively.

Lessons Learned

Vona's global architecture was created as a direct result of understanding the business of banking. He had often heard the terms "distribution network" and "placement power." If you are in the business of originating loans and placing securities, you must have this distribution network which enables you to turn over your assets by selling them to investors wherever they might be located. This gives the bank a great power of placement of these assets. Vona translated this requirement into the technical architecture described in detail above. It was built to encompass three key attributes that were the key to success:

1. *The network must be global.* Given the fluidity and shifting pattern of worldwide political and economic situations, the bank could not afford to build a distribution network that would permanently leave out any continent or even a specific country.

2. *The distribution network must be able to reach every corner of the world.* Vona compares this to the circulatory system bringing oxygenated blood to every cell in the body. In the same way, the bank's network must be able to reach every potential investor, in his bedroom if needed, and deliver the financial service that he desires.

3. *The network must have instantaneous response time.* Vona well understood the paranoia of financial market operators around the world. They react instinctively when a rumor spreads. If you are an investor or a market operator, it is possible that a slow reaction time will lead to major losses. Thus, instantaneous response time of the technical environment is a necessity.

Thus, Vona's ability to integrate communication and computer resources into a solid technical foundation enables Bankers Trust to excel as a worldwide merchant bank. Even to this day, this strategy is evolving. As experimentation proceeds, the new insights it brings are used to adjust and refine their formula for success. According to Vona, the key to the future is the creativity to refine their business and technical strategies and keep the two working closely together, "that's the entrepreneurial spirit" in worldwide merchant banking.

Getting the Biggest
Technology Return—
Advice from the Big Six

In a study of CEOs appearing in *Fortune* magazine[4], a question was asked concerning how improvements resulting from information technology compared to expectations. Fully 26 percent of those surveyed responded that, in their view, information technology just hadn't lived up to expectations.

Companies have billions invested in technology people, technology software, and technology hardware—and with every passing year, technology budgets increase. In lean times, senior managers—especially those that fit into the 26 percent category of the Fortune survey—often look for ways to ease expenses by cutting information technology budgets. These cuts are often made across the board and indiscriminately.

Some senior managers attempt to strategize wholesale cuts by prioritizing projects and cutting only those in the lower range. However the cut, it is most often in relation to budget dollars only and takes little business strategy into account.

If a company is to get the highest possible utilization of its information technology resource, it must readjust its perspective on the role of information technology in the company and what the relationship between information technology and the organization as a whole must become.

Perhaps the best insight into developing an information technology infrastructure along these lines comes from the Big Six. The Big Six accounting firms are actually in the forefront of working with business and technology units of a firm to coalesce these separate entities into a more uniform, and profitable, structure.

Stephen Simmerman is the Managing Partner of the KPMG Peat Marwick Technology practice based in Philadelphia, Pennsylvania. According to Simmerman, many of his clients exhibit disorganized infrastructures— grown over many years when systems were built independently and often at cross-purposes. It has become very hard for them to operate efficiently and effectively because of the patchwork quilt of different systems based on different management theories that were in place at different points in time.

What we find, even in the more progressive companies, is that companies are very willing to spend money on research and development, product development, and production, but are unwilling to spend an equal sum of money on administrative systems (i.e., infrastructure). Thus, over a number of years, that infrastructure, just like the roads in the United States, have started to deteriorate. Couple that now with the need for getting informa-

---

[4] "CEOs Don't Share White Collar Blues," Fortune (Feb. 25, 1991), p. 87.

tion to people in a useful form faster, and a problem begins to materialize. In addition, the watchword for most companies — especially in a recession — is organizational simplicity. Companies are very aggressively moving to create leaner organizational structures. In doing so, they are letting people go, oftentimes not reorganizing the work flow, so some work is simply not getting done.

The net result is a labyrinth of unrelated systems, referred to by Simmerman as stovepipes (i.e., payables are not related to receivables are not related to the ledgers are not related to the manufacturing systems), which are totally obsolete. As a result, many companies are facing a massive bill to correct past systems development sins that are just catching up to them now. It will be a very expensive capital expenditure to go back and rearchitect their businesses and the way they do things and wrap the current technologies around that.

Even among the Fortune 10, the thought processes are along the path of the functional hierarchies. This may, indeed, be the route of the problem. These companies are going through alot of process redesign and work simplification but are doing this without regard to the technology infrastructure. In essence, they are trying to redesign business processes, the tentacles into their customers and suppliers, using technology almost as an afterthought. This makes it difficult to make a change and be nimble because most don't understand the reality that a company's infrastructure can't be changed without massive expenditures in technology modification.

An Effort at Simplification

Simplification is the first task that must be undertaken in the many companies that have automated their clerical processes to the hilt. Now that all of these functions have been automated, and some lower-priced head count have been eliminated, senior managers have taken the long view and asked, "What am I really getting from all of this automation?" Some have come to the conclusion that not enough head count have been eliminated to justify the huge expenditures, and these large technology expenditures haven't enabled their workers to make any better, and more profitable, decisions. Therefore, in order to successfully simplify, it is absolutely imperative for the company to really take a real long, hard look at the running of the business.

There is probably no area within a company that cannot be simplified. Complexity has eroded the organization's flexibility, responsiveness, and morale. A start in simplification comes by assigning a senior executive mandated working team(s) composed of representatives of the business unit and the technology group. Their task is to review the processes of the organization unit and make recommendations for clarification. More than likely they will, according to Simmerman, find many things that "are dumb" and can be done better.

The culmination of this simplification effort will be a series of projects geared to develop new applications and reengineer old ones. However, in order for this to be effectively accomplished, newer approaches to systems development must be utilized. The Peat solution is to move into RAD (rapid development) techniques, prototyping, and interactive systems development with the users.

These newer techniques, when combined with newer hardware and software, will permit technology to be wrapped around the business in such a way as to foster immense productivity benefits. Client-server architectures will play a major role in granting the ability to download important information, on a timely basis, to the desktop. In times of simplification, and resultant downsizing, the middle managers and senior managers who are left will need access to more information then they ever needed before. This information will be needed at the desk pushing the desktop computer into the forefront of the information technology architecture. Of all the technologies that will have a positive effect on the simplification of the workplace, Simmerman forecasts that it will be telecommunications that will drive the process home. It is telecommunications—the telephone wires, and the cabling that connect the desktop computers to each other, to mainframes, and to minicomputers—that will be ultimately put the desktop revolution on the desks of newly simplified staff, perhaps renamed "information agents."

Technology as Enabler

In order to achieve this new order, the organization must actually forget about the technology and concentrate solely on the business. Senior managers should begin to think of information technology as an enabler, not as an end unto to itself. The business should be looked at like an onion: each layer must be peeled away uncovering the mission, the goals, and the objectives. Next, the organization must decide how they need to be organized to fulfill the mission, goals, and objectives.

Next, the engine of the process must be considered. This is the component that actually drives the organization that we created here to be able to accomplish those business goals and objectives. Peat's approach is to spend alot of time in working through the business side of their client prior to considering technology. This often frustrates systems staffers who have an immediate need to take a pencil and start coding. This must be prevented since premature system development—that is, developing a system before the full extent of the businesses strategy is well-understood—leads to those disconnected and noncompetitive systems alluded to in the beginning of this section.

It is preferable to spend more time up front making sure that the business problem, as well as constraints surrounding the business problem, is well understood. Only after the problem is well understood should technology be considered, and since technology is really a composite of discrete technologies, more than one technological solution can apply. The goal, then, is to pick the best solution.

Since it is likely that this process will be accompanied by fitting the company with a new set of technological methodologies and tools, it is important to assess how well the company can absorb such change. Even if it is determined that change can be absorbed, it is useful to calculate the rate at which change can be absorbed to better forecast time and budget dollars to effect the overall change to the company's organizational infrastructure.

All of this will lead to monumental change. According to Simmerman, most of his larger clients who are engaged in this process are involved in difficult make/buy decisions when it comes to staff. He finds that more and more managements are becoming focused on a return to shareholders. With this focus, the emphasis is increasingly turning to outsourcing many of the functions that 20-year information technology employees have long regarded as their private domain.

The Difficulty of Technology Transfer

The great difficulty seems to be in technology transfer of the new techniques to staff used to the old ways. This is a thorny, double-sided issue. On one side, technology staff complains they don't have the opportunity to learn newer techniques. On the flip side, organizations who do invest in the educations of their technology staff often see this investment jump ship and move over to the competition. As a result, organizations are finding themselves saddled with technology staff with obsolete skills and no way to quickly move into the newer technologies that show some competitive promise. Outsourcing, as you will see in Chapter Six, is one solution. However, there is a caveat here. The balance between outsourced services and insourced services should be carefully measured. A firm cannot maintain a competitive position if it cannot get to its information on a timely and analytical basis.

The Promise of Re-engineering

Once the business strategies are well understood and the technology requirements are folded in, it is necessary to step back and make a comparison between what exists today and what the firm has devised as its plan for tomorrow. Usually, the two have no similarity. This leads to the question of "should the firm throw out what they have and start from scratch or should they attempt to salvage some of their existing technology by a process called re-engineering.

Re-engineering is a set of technologies and processes whereby a firm can "update" old and archaic codes. It is a laborious and, often, costly process. Simmerman relates the case of a subsidiary of a large manufacturing firm with a billion dollars in sales. Its systems were antiquated and nonintegrated. They had literally not put money into systems for about 15 years. The staff did little new development and was primarily responsible for "band-aiding" the systems that were already there. Peat was requested to re-engineer existing systems since the company was not displeased with the functionality of these systems. Once Peat did a careful analysis they found that the re-engineering price tag was five times what it would take if they were to get rid of everything and start from scratch—which is essentially what they ended up doing.

The firm opted to get rid of their mainframe and move into distributed processing. This example is excellent in that it demonstrates the sometimes courageous actions of senior management to bite the bullet to gain a long-time benefit. This firm's management well understood that the information technology resource that they currently had was actually detracting from the profitability of the firm. This, then, might well be a trend. When a company's entire technology infrastructure needs to be overhauled, possibly the best solution might be to throw out the old and bring in the new.

Of course, there will be detractors to this statement. After all, billions of dollars have been invested. But those arguing against this solution should understand that this is just that—one solution. But it is a viable solution. For, if the technology resource as it stands today does not add a measurable profit to the bottom line, then it is most assuredly detracting from the bottom line. The net result will be a loss of competitive position, which can be deadly during economic downturns. Haven't many mature firms within an industry watched meekly as a new entrant comes in with all new technology? Hasn't that same mature firm envied the upstart's "start-from-scratch-status"?

Biting the Bullet

Given the complexity of today's technology infrastructures, it is often better bite the bullet and start from scratch. If you were to lay out the application information system structure in most of Peat's clients, you will find that it closely aligns with the organization's functional hierarchy, which is where the stovepipes come in. If you look at where business problems are being created, it is generally not vertically.

If you try to process an invoice through a payable system, it does that pretty well because all of those clerical functions have already been automated. But what if you have to pass information from payables to some other system? Now the process is no longer vertical, but horizontal: from system to system to system. The problem with this path through the systems is that the systems usually have no commonality. Some of these disparate systems may have been developed in-house, some may have been purchased and all exhibit different file structures. In this situation, it is all but guaranteed that the company will have horizontal interface problems.

The latter half of the 1980s saw the proliferation of new techniques such as Just In Time (JIT) and Total Quality Management (TQM). Moving towards these disciplines pushed the organization to somewhat reorganize themselves along the lines recommended by these methods. This reorganization, in effect, changed the functional hierarchy and saw the formation of business teams forcing the company into a more horizontal organizational structure. These teams were often composed of an R&D person, working with an engineering person, working with a technology person as a team trying to solve a problem. In essence, what has been created is an organizational structure that is totally unsupportable by the vertical architecture that the firm spent the last 20 or 30 years creating. According to Simmerman, this is the crux of the problem for which there is no simple solution.

Again, the real solution is to simply bite the bullet and invest in realigning the organization into a structure that is most effective for that organization. This should be followed by wrapping a technology architecture around the process, similarly to Bankers Trust, that can grow and evolve as the company grows and evolves. Bankers is one of the few fortunate firms who developed this strategy and made the migration before becoming enmeshed in Simmerman's stovepipes. But even at this late date, and after a capital investment in the millions if not billions, many large companies are traveling this same road.

Perhaps one of the most forward thinking of Peat's clients along these lines is General Electric. Like Bankers, they too believe in continuous change and are especially reactive to times of economic stress. GE senior management clearly understands that change is an integral part of its business. What this means is that the infrastructure at General Electric needs to be able to accept that change. GE senior management is proactive rather than reactive in this regard. Senior management at GE aggressively searches out problems to solve in an attempt to evolve in such a way to make itself better, more responsive to its customers, more responsive to its shareholders, more responsive to the people who work for them, and thus more competitive. Its focus is on change and continuous improvement.

3
Infotrend #2: Downsizing (or Running Lean, Mean, and Fast)

The term "downsizing" has come to have various meanings to various people. From a human resource perspective, downsizing means flattening the corporate hierarchy—a phenomena that began in earnest after the stock-market crash of 1987, and deepened during the recession that followed. Even during the recovery beginning in late 1992, the trend toward downsizing continued as senior managements increasingly realized the benefits and efficiencies of running lean and mean. In this chapter, we'll examine the many issues surrounding successful downsizing, discuss a host of cases, such as Salomon Brothers and Pillsbury Brands, where downsizing was successfully implemented, and ultimately develop a plan for the process that can be tailored to any organization.

A Case for Downsizing

As companies began to search for a way to bring a better use of computing power to these flattened organizational structures, it became apparent that a company's large investment in personal computers could be strategically leveraged. Thus, to IT departments, downsizing represents the trend to downsize computing power from mainframes to work stations and personal computers.

Merrill Lynch Trades Down

Right around the time of the stock-market crash in 1987, Joseph Freitas, director of investment banking systems for Merrill Lynch & Company, decided that the $1 million price tag for maintenance and leasing fees on his mainframe was too high, and the functionality that the machine itself afforded him was much too low.

In addition, Freitas realized that the use of the mainframe would never let him achieve his goal of building a 13-city computer network that would be able to immediately provide information to bankers all over the world. Freitas made the dramatic decision to dispense with his mainframe altogether and downsize to a series of networked personal computers.

Connecting up the 1,100 personal computers was only one part of Freitas's downsizing equation. He still needed a larger computer to serve as a database server. The database server would provide generally available information accessible to each of the 1,100 users on the network. Compared to the $1 million dollar a year mainframe price tag, the $500,000 purchase price of a new Sequent Computer was minimal. The multiple Intel microprocessors that made up the Sequent Computer virtually made this smaller box as powerful as the expensive mainframe.

The tricky part of Freitas' puzzle was in being able to track what information is stored in the network—no matter where it is stored. For example, if a banker in London needs a prospectus stored on a PC in New York, then there had to be some way of instantaneously grabbing the information from New York and depositing it on the PC in London. The real key behind the downsizing issue for Freitas, then, was not actually the hardware but the software. For this challenge, he needed to have some software specially developed. A small start-up company in Bellevue, Washington was assigned this challenge. Saros Corporation designed a system called Mezzanine for Merrill and several other big computer buyers with the same problem. Mezzanine works similarly to a library's card catalog, keeping track of what information is kept in each computer on the network. Once it locates requested information, Mezzanine also has the knowledge of how to retrieve all that data and deliver it to the requestor.

However, Mezzanine wasn't the only trick up Freitas's sleeve. Using another specially written program, this one from Gupta Technologies, client reports—tracked by individual bankers on their private PCs—are made instantly available to all other PCs on the network. When a client report is entered on a remote PC, the Gupta software automatically routes the information back to a central database in New York which can then be tapped by other users on the network.

Freitas's own Merrill-written Cicero program provides a similar cross-networking feat by allowing a banker to ask for current and projected price-earning ratios for up to five companies, and then going out across the network to various computers and databases to retrieve and calculate the answer. Merrill believes that its decision to downsize gives it an edge over its competitors. According to Freitas, "our survival depends on fast information and knowing how to analyze it."

If you were to ask Freitas what downsizing means, he would be sure to answer hardware, network, and software—for this was the solution to his thorny problem. A similar approach was taken by a Deloitte & Touche customer in trying to solve an even more global problem.

The United Nations Gets Smaller

When one thinks of the United Nations, one thinks of the dozens of flags waving in the breeze at the U.N.'s New York headquarters. Each of these flags represents a member nation—and each of them needs to be hooked up to the U.N.'s administrative system. Charles Popper, currently CIO at Merck Pharmaceuticals, was formerly a technology partner at Deloitte & Touche's New York office and worked on the U.N. project. Popper emphasizes the pioneering work that was done in developing the requirements for this effort. The U.N. administrative system is expansive. All financial systems, budgeting systems, payroll systems, procurement systems, inventory systems, as well as travel management systems form the infrastructure. This administrative hub had to be made efficiently available to the different member nations. But each member nation had different requirements for the functionality of the system and the size of the system.

Popper's team realized that it made no sense to have a large, traditional mainframe at the core of all this, and opted to recommend a Unix-based distributed work-station approach that could be tailored to the specific requirements of each member nation. Indeed, Popper would be hard-pressed to find an example of an instance where he would put a new application on a mainframe at all.

So what is the real issue behind downsizing? Is it moving from more expensive hardware to less expensive hardware? Popper contends that the price of MIPS, or the power of the computer, is coming down dramatically so that in the future it is likely that expense will be a moot issue. Is the functionality of a work station or PC much greater than that of a mainframe? There are two sides to this particular issue. On the one hand, mainframes are vast powerhouses that are able to support large numbers of users and even larger amounts of data. On the other hand, work stations have the capability of providing workstation-to-work station networking that is unparalleled by the large central processors. Perhaps the real power behind the growing favor of workstations is the ability to tailor the technological workplace to the human workplace as the U.N. did. Australia will get one size box to suit their needs, and the United States will get a larger sized box to suit their larger needs.

The issues then come down to, according to Popper, "How are you going to do software development? Downsizing is more of a software issue than a hardware issue."

Costs and functionality are largely software dependent. So, unless a company is making the right software decisions, moving to a smaller box or remaining on a larger box will not make much of a difference. Perhaps, then, what is really driving the move to downsizing is the availability of some novel software tools on workstation and PC devices which are unavailable, or inflexible, on the mainframe.

Salomon Downsizes for the Twenty-First Century

In 1988, Salomon Brothers began a five-year project that they dubbed TP–21, or Technology Platform for the twenty-first century. Downsizing from its bulky mainframe to a more flexible workstation environment was its objective, thus permitting its business units to have more authority over technology. In doing so, Salomon becomes truly representative of firms looking at downsizing from the dual perspective of both hardware and software.

Salomon's current environment is familiar to most: a patchwork of incompatible systems that makes it hard to give traders timely information about their systems. As are most securities firms that began automating in the late seventies, Salomon is mainframe-based. Currently, it is said that the firm leases somewhere around 30 Prime mainframes costing the firm somewhere between $1 million and $2 million a month to lease.

The reasons behind downsizing were twofold. First, and foremost was the cost consideration. Obviously, leasing 30 Primes at a cost of between $1 and $2 million a month nets out to a whopping $30 million to $60 million a year. Since the power of a mainframe leased five years ago can be readily found in the less-expensive work stations of today, Salomon decided to downsize to a Sun workstation environment.

Cost, however, was not the only consideration. Since the mainframe systems were largely incompatible and traders were not getting timely enough information, the migration to new software was necessary as well. The Sun Microsystems workstations are equipped with Unix software applications which will permit Salomon to fully integrate market data services, trade execution, and analytical applications with clearance and settlement.

At this same time, Salomon decided to restructure the relationship between the trading function and the systems that they use. Under the new structure, the technology division must justify its costs on a desk-by-desk basis. This will ensure that the technology and associated costs will stay competitive with the evolving marketplace. The way this will be accomplished is by assigning an account manager to each trading desk who will be responsible for meeting its specific technology needs.

The move to downsizing was accompanied by a move to a new facility in the World Trade Center. This enabled Salomon to implement a radically altered advanced technological trading environment. The new site consists of two complete computer rooms, one above and one below the trading floors. The trading floors themselves have somewhere around 700 Sun workstation positions surrounded by Pyramid computers, which are used to perform extremely complex and computer-intensive calculations such as collateralized mortgage obligations (CMOs).

Salomon offers a good example of a firm undergoing radical technology change. Not only have they radically altered their hardware and software platform, but they have made the decision to alter the way in which they do business.

Salomon also offers a good example of a firm that has and continues to have problems in bringing this new technology to bear. The first problem was a result of the technology group being moved to new headquarters in East Rutherford, New Jersey. Many of the technology staff, experts in the securities industry, chose to remain behind. This, and some trading personnel's hesitation to agree with all the principles of TP–21, prompted many of them to "go it alone."

Results of going it alone are rarely positive. In Salomon's case, one trading desk decided to automate an application called the Yield Book. It was named after a book entitled *Inside the Yield Curve* written by Marty Liebowitz, Salomon's director of fixed-income research. The trading desk hired recent M.I.T. graduates rather than professional programmers who were experienced in writing efficient programs. The result was that the programming code written for the workstations used needed a major upgrade pushing the costs up from $7,000 per machine to $30,000 per machine.

Independent traders aside, probably the biggest problem Salomon encountered in providing an integrated trading workstation was in getting all of the software to deliver information at the speed required for a trader to make instantaneous decisions. Sometimes, the software chosen running on the hardware chosen doesn't mix well enough for the target speed to be met. This happened to Salomon. When converting the CMO databases from Prime mainframes to Sybase running on Pyramid computers, programmers found an problem in the Sybase/Pyramid software-hardware combination that precluded the use of the Pyramid machine for this function. A decision was made to switch to Sun workstations costing the firm at least $2 million in cost overruns.

Of course, as of the writing of this book, TP–21 is still a year away from completion and little more is known about this secretive project. Salomon has proven itself innovative and resourceful in moving to a more fertile and efficient downsized environment. The difficulties that Salomon is experiencing are presented to show the reader the problems that can potentially occur to an organization attempting a downsizing project of this magnitude.

In spite of these temporary traumas, there is no doubt that Salomon will successfully conclude its project.

The problems that Salomon experienced were more a result of software incompatibilities than hardware deficiencies. This stems from a plethora of software packages that "do not speak with each other" and might well be incompatible with the target hardware platform.

According to Popper, the real key to successful downsizing just might be in using the proper software tools in developing applications which will permit the company to quickly move from one hardware platform to another. By developing flexible and easily migratable software, the issue of downsizing thus becomes muted. Software developed in this manner can be on the mainframe today, on a workstation tomorrow, and back on the mainframe in a month. Software built with traditional tool sets, as Salomon and others are fast finding out, are simply not capable of this flexibility.

Avoiding Downsizing's Biggest Headaches

Amtrak received significant benefits by moving to a workstation platform. They added a flexible interface to their reservation systems, increasing agent productivity and customer service, and they reduced their expenses significantly. But it isn't always this easy. Sometimes the wrong decision is made, and as a result, costs go up while productivity goes down.

Downsizing mainframe-based application systems onto smaller, more discrete workstation-based platforms is a complex task. In order for this task to be embarked upon and concluded in a successful manner, a team composed of information technology staff and key managers in the target area(s) must be created. This team must diligently review a wide variety of issues including hardware, software, communications, people, business strategy, and functionality.

Theodore P. Klein, founder of the Boston Systems Group, has developed a rather succinct set of common pitfalls that those delving into the area of downsizing would do best to avoid[1]:

1. No Management Commitment. The decision to downsize reflects the commitment that senior management makes to accept information technology as a component of the long-term business strategy. Whether or not this is true, senior management must make a major decision. This is, in effect, a resolution of the long-standing centralization versus decentralization issue.

---

[1]Theodore P. Klein, "How to Avoid the Five Biggest Downsizing Errors," *Computerworld* (June 11, 1990).

Before the advent of personal computers there were minicomputers—today called mid-sized computers. In the early eighties, the notion of departmental computing, or decentralized computing, gained increasing popularity. The idea behind departmental computing was that, instead of one large computer which ran everything for all departments within a company, each department would have their own computer which would run only their work.

The advantages of decentralized computing were many—as were the disadvantages. On the plus side, departments could get top priority all the time on their own system. No more waiting in line or suffering from poor response time. They could finally control their own destiny. In fact, these are the factors that pushed many a user group to lobby aggressively for their own machine.

On the flip side, the early eighties was really not the time to start offloading important work onto discrete processors. In those early days, networking was simply not robust enough to support a configuration of departmental computers linked up to a centralized host. The result was a proliferation of stand-alone departmental computers. The final result was calamitous in some organizations. Data redundancy proliferated as the different departments started to create systems that tracked the same data. When systems failed, the departments who decided to go it alone were often left without backup. In sum, a whole host of problems left a rather bad taste in the mouths of some badly burned senior executives who were left holding the bill for obsolete departmental computers when the department migrated back to the security of the mainframe.

Since that time, of course, hardware, software, and networking has grown far more robust, but that bad taste still lingers on. Thus, gaining a corporate commitment for downsizing might require some pretty fancy footwork, because some of the same problems that occurred during the days of departmental computing will still be present.

One of these problems, or opportunities if you will, is that downsizing usually requires a shift in technology responsibilities and obligations. Once insulated from costs and know-how, user communities are fast finding out that in a downsized environment they do both. Perhaps for the first time, business groups are getting into the business of developing and maintaining their own software and hardware. A senior management commitment that they will have the resources necessary to assist them in this new endeavor is crucial to downsizing success. Line management must also be agreeable to taking on these new responsibilities.

Lastly, but most importantly, departmental staff members who are actually going to perform the work must be agreeable to taking on these new burdens. The best example of this not being done, and the less-than-desirable results that occurred, were at the post office. When it was decided that the clerks at the window would be given work stations, employees were never told what to expect. As a result, fear of job replacement by automation reached a fevered pitch. The system was sabotaged, delaying effective implementation of the clerk workstations for quite some time.

2. Current Information Technology Infrastructure Is Not Well Understood.   Downsizing only works when the current technology infrastructure is well-organized and structured. Adding a new component to chaos only breeds more chaos. In this vein, Klein has developed an excellent set of questions that, if answered, will determine if an organization has a good enough grasp of its environment to ensure downsizing success:

Overall Corporate Position

1. What are the key strategies and tactics already in place which will assist in achieving corporate goals?

2. How have these strategies and tactics been deployed in the various departments?

3. What are the critical success factors listed to accomplish these goals?

4. Is the company growing or shrinking?

5. Are acquisitions underway?

6. Is the company in a cost-control mode?

7. What is the relationship of the firm to its competition?

8. What are the broad technology principles that guide the firm's use of information technology?

9. Does the firm use information technology to automate? To improve effectiveness?

10. How does the firm wish to use information technology over the long term?

Distributed Use of Information Technology

1. How many functional departments now use information technology on their own?

2. What are they doing and how are they doing it?

3. What hardware and software are they using?

4. What applications have they deployed?

5. What is their cross-functional involvement?

The Applications Portfolio

1. What are the applications in use in the organization?

2. How can the application be categorized? As enterprise? As departmental? As individual?

The User Community

1. What is the experience level of the user community?

2. Can the user departments be ranked according to the following criteria: knowledge, capabilities, responsibilities, interest?

3. The Structure of the Organization Remains Unchanged After Downsizing. When downsizing is being considered, a change in the organizational structure must be considered as well. If computing power is to be downsized into the hands of divisional staff—away from the technical know-how of the information technology group—then some of this technical know-how needs to be downsized to the divisional staff level. There must be appropriate technical personnel to develop, implement, and maintain the systems that will run on the downsized platforms.

Downsizing is often more than just moving to a smaller piece of hardware. It is often a radical change in the type of software being used. Having the ability to incorporate these new software techniques into the plan is fundamental to the success of the downsizing effort. However, there is a very large risk associated with moving both to new hardware and software platforms at the same time.

Often technical personnel, whether at the information technology level or the divisional level, must learn totally new concepts such as new operating systems (e.g., instead of the mainframe system they are comfortable with they may be required to learn the UNIX operating system—as different from the mainframe environment as an apple is from a banana), new programming languages (e.g., many move from mainframe COBOL to the C language, which is more workstation–efficient), and perhaps even object-oriented techniques. Planners should be aware that this is a tall order, and plan accordingly.

Downsizing could foster even more radical change. It might be necessary, and even advisable, to reorganize the technology department down into the user group. This is, in effect, what Bankers Trust did in the middle 1980s. There are many ways to accomplish this end. The Bankers Trust model is one where each user group has its own technical staff who were not only technologists, but were fully versed in the business of the area they supported. There also exists a central group responsible for inter-communications between divisional units and global banking entities, guidelines, policies, and procedures as well as setting direction in using new technologies.

Another possibility is the one that Klein advocates. Here the Corporate Operations group manages the corporate communications network and is responsible for maintaining existing mainframe hardware and operations. The Specialized Services group is composed of a key group of internal consultants that sets up guidelines, methodologies, and development environments fundamentally providing overall leadership for distributed applications development. The Enterprise Systems Development group develops, implements, and operates systems that are considered enterprise systems. Enterprise systems are those systems that are corporate-wide and, thus, key strategic systems.

In Klein's model, there exists within each division what he terms a local facilitator and a technical officer. The local facilitators report to the technical officers, but have dotted-line responsibility to the Specialized Services Group, since it is this group that has primary responsibility for ensuring common architectures and frameworks.

4. Too Fast and Too Much. As it has been repeatedly stated, downsizing is more than just buying a smaller box. There is great danger in trying to do too much too soon. Downsizing must be planned as intensively as bringing a new product to market.

5. There Exists No Controlling Framework or Infrastructure. It is hoped that the errors of the mid-eighties will not be relived in the mid-nineties. For downsizing to be fully effective, there must be a plan to coordinate not only the work flow, but the development of applications. For, if this is not done the horrors the mid-eighties—a proliferation of redundant, incoherent, and inconsistent systems—will most certainly come back to haunt us.

Four Who Did It Right

As the prior sections suggest, downsizing requires much careful planning on the part of both the technical and business units as well as a major commitment on the part of senior management. Once accomplished, though, the benefits can be enormous. To end this chapter, let's briefly visit some companies that have adhered to the principles espoused here and who have, or will, reap the benefits of lowered costs and increased functionality.

Amtrak

Amtrak had two goals when it decided to investigate the concept of downsizing, as a way to cut costs and to boost worker productivity.

This wouldn't be easy, for the job they were looking to wrap new technology around was highly visible. The job of reservation agent is more information-bound than first meets the eye. For example, the agent might be working on a screen to make a reservation and the customer asks, "By the way, what was the departure time?" The agent then has to back out of the booking process and call back the scheduling information.

The resolution to Amtrak's problem came with the signing of a $14 million workstation contract with AT&T. Dumb Honeywell terminals used by the ticketing and reservation agents were replaced by 2,200 AT&T workstations.

The savings were considerable. Now the agents, who handle some 34 million information and ticket queries per year, have the flexibility of using the AT&T windows-based workstations to maintain views into scheduling, pricing, and booking transactions. The agents can jump around between screens at the touch of a button.

Not only has this increased the productivity of the agents significantly, but it has sliced the amount of time on each call by at least one second. When added up, across the 34 million in volume, that translates to a $250,000 per year cost reduction for Amtrack. The second, and most significant, cost savings came in the form of reduced maintenance costs. Amtrack was saddled with a $2.4-million-a-year maintenance contract when using the Honeywell equipment. Downsizing to work-stations has reduced this bill to an insignificant $500,000 per year.

Pillsbury Brands

At Pillsbury Brands, which is a part of the Food Sector of Grand Metropolitan PLC, downsizing has had some positive benefits. It has led to new applications, lower costs, and much improved management control.

Pillsbury decided to downsize after an analysis was made of its aging mainframe systems. This analysis revealed a critical need for better communication between the company's Minneapolis headquarters, plant sites, and sales offices.

Their solution was to develop a microcomputer-based, enterprise-wide network solution. This permitted Pillsbury to distribute processing power where it was needed, and to implement a company-wide electronic mail network.

Ultimately, Pillsbury downsized to more accessible LAN servers, and streamlined its operations to the point where all of these servers, are now running common operating systems and applications throughout the company. The net result was making the systems easier to support, reducing costs and managing better than before.

Social Security Administration

Even though the SSA recently overhauled its systems to the tune of $400 million, it knows that today's transaction processing rate of 6 million per week is low compared to an influx or transactions when the baby boomers get ready to retire.

Today's environment consists of 39,000 terminals hooked up to eight mainframes located at the agency's data center in Baltimore. Before automation, it used to take days to process a claim; today, it takes seconds. In fact, the new system is so robust that it has enabled the agency to eliminate nearly 20,000 jobs, reducing the work force to 64,000 from 81,000 in 1982.

Even though the IBM, Hitachi, and Amdahl computers are doing a serviceable job and capacity can be easily increased, the SSA is doing some forward thinking to the days that the baby boomers will be ready to retire. And this has led them to the conclusion that the ultimate answer is in migrating down to workstation computing.

Barnett Banks, Inc.

With the banking industry in disarray, it is little wonder that the remaining banks are doing everything in their power to cut costs and remain competitive while bringing in new business.

Barnett Banks, based in Jacksonville, Florida, has seen its assets grow from $2 billion to $32 billion since 1980. Wanting to keep this profitability amid these tough times, they have invested $100 million in a project that involved migrating from a mainframe to a workstation–based architecture.

The goal of this massive project is to cut costs and use the cost savings to invest in the bank's future. Barnett's plan is to supply each retail office with an IBM local area network with an IBM PS/2 workstation node in front of every teller and customer service representative. The user interface will be user-friendly using IBM's OS/2 Presentation Manager, which is similar to the more popular Microsoft Windows.

The bank's mainframes will still be very active in that each of the local area networks will communicate with them at the bank's Jacksonville, Florida data center. VSAT (very small aperture terminal) satellite transmission will be the form of communications used between these local loops and the mainframe at the central data center.

The downsized infrastructure consists of about 12,000 workstations within the bank's 32 retail offices in Florida and Georgia. Barnett has taken the stance that the local sites will not be responsible for the technology that they use. Therefore, the network will be managed centrally from the Jacksonville site.

A customer service representative in Georgia will be able to access a customer's account information locally on his or her local area network. When more detailed customer data is need it will be routed to the representative's workstation from a relational database running on the bank's mainframes. Credit history, available through credit bureaus, will also be available on the workstation, enabling the customer service representative to process loan applications immediately.

Pillsbury, the Social Security Administration, and Barnett Banks are three different views of the same phenomenon. Costs, functionality, and serviceability are all excellent reasons for moving in this direction. Apparently, there are now a tide of firms all going with this flow.

In fact, at the 1991 Association for Systems Management (ASM) conference, it appeared that the "small is beautiful" theme was predominant. At the conference Chief Executive Officer Charles H. Mayer of The First Boston Corporation shared this insight, "Five years from now, we will all wonder how anyone ran an organization on a centralized mainframe."

4

Infotrend #3:
From Flying Solo
to Partnering

A cornerstone of the American philosophy is, and has always been, independence. Although the founding fathers envisioned independence as a political aspect, this one tenet of our constitution has pervaded every aspect of American life. It has even infiltrated the marketplace to the point where firms act as separate islands with every other island being enemy territory.

During America's great and long period of sustained growth, independence was a sound economic principle. But in today's economy, the multiplicity of redundant and noncompeting projects funded by individual firms constitutes great waste, and ultimately siphons scarce resources from projects that are crucial to the firm's economic well-being.

Partnering Lessons
from Japan

It comes as no surprise that the Japanese are well-positioned to act as competitors, if not market leaders, in many of the industries that Americans traditionally dominated. Since World War II, the Japanese have become extremely aggressive businesspeople. Although well-known dominators of the automobile market and the camera market, they are also moving aggressively into other spheres of American influence. A case in point is the global financial industry.

The five largest companies in the world, measured by market valuation, are Japanese with four of the five being Japanese banks. The largest of these banks is Dai-Ichi. Comparatively, New York's Citibank ranks tenth after Dai-Ichi. In 1987, the Tokyo Stock Exchange became larger than the New York Stock Exchange. Around the same time period, Japan's share of the total value of major world stock markets increased from 17 percent to approximately 47 percent while the U.S. share decreased from 55 percent to below 30 percent.[1]

If there is one dominant factor in background of all financial markets, domestic and otherwise, it is the use of information technology. Although financial institutions employ less than 5 percent of the U.S. work force, they account for approximately 35 percent of information technology purchases.

Large information technology expenditures cannot guarantee market dominance. The threat to the American marketplace is very real—especially amongst those willing to give up some independence and move in the direction of resource sharing.

The Japanese are very aware of the large capital expenditures that U.S. firms are making in information technology in financial services. There is no doubt that they are positioning themselves to catch up, and then overtake, their U.S. counterparts. They just might succeed since, characteristically, they employ a collaborative approach to the development of systems.

Good examples of this collaboration are easy to find. The four major Japanese securities firms have standardized their home-computing software on the Nintendo Family Computer. In addition, they have standardized protocols, architectures and commands. This occurred at the same time that American banks moved out of the home-banking market and companies began outsourcing strategic information systems to cut costs.

The Japanese have steadily increased their market share in the world financial markets. One can deduce that at least part of this success can be attributed to their collaborative mind set. Simply, they work together wherever they are not competitive. Perhaps, individually they lose some identity in the process, but in the long run, all participating firms benefit in lower costs and greater efficiencies.

A Collaborative Approach to Technology

In the United States, this collaborative approach is beginning to catch on. Termed *partnering*, it is the process of working with external firms with the goal of sharing technological resources to reduce expenses.

[1]Richard Van Slyke, "Rust on Wall Street," *Information Strategy: The Executive's Journal* 5:10 (Winter 1990).

There are several different forms of partnering. The goal of McKesson Drug's partnering with their customers was to bind that customer to the company by providing superior service and economies. A second form of partnering is typified by Philadelphia National Bank's MAC shared network where PNB derived first mover benefits by providing various accommodating services to member banks, but solely owned the network. Confirm represents a third form of partnering where equal partners together obtain several benefits. Since Confirm is the first such network in 20 years, the partners will most assuredly derive first-mover benefits. Firms working together as equal partners have equal say in the development of the information system, giving each firm the ability to tailor the system more specifically for their needs. This gives each member firm an advantage over firms that come into the system as users of the network at a later date which are then forced to compromise.

A more significant form of partnering—especially in an era of increasing competition from all quarters—is the relationship that two or more firms forge when their perception of survival is threatened. Thus far, the first instance of this happening is in the alliance between IBM and Apple.

Even though partnering is a phenomena just now catching on, some innovators have been riding this trend for years, for instance, the major news bureaus. During the 1964 elections, many news bureaus (ABC, NBC, CBS, United Press, Associated Press) found that statistics collected when covering elections were disturbingly dissimilar. This had the effect of confusing readers. For example, one source said that candidate X was leading by 60 percent, another source said that candidate X was leading by 90 percent. These fiercely independent news bureaus decided that greater accuracy and economies of scale was worth more than independence. This decision begat the New York City-based News Election Service—a 20-year-old information technology services partnership.

Partnering comes in two varieties: competitor and client. Competitor resource sharing is a new phenomena in the United States. Although antitrust legislation precludes U.S. firms from working in the exact same manner as the Japanese in the creation of heavily funded consortiums to develop new technologies, U.S. firms are beginning to see the wisdom of shared expenses in those areas where shared resources are possible. Information technology is most certainly one resource that is easily shared.

Client resource sharing is less a phenomena than a logical outgrowth of the relationship a company has with its customers. The most common example of this is placing computer terminals on site at the office of the client so that the client may access, and even update, data.

Crossing Wall Street
as Partners

Running a back-office operation at a Wall Street brokerage firm costs an average $300 million a year. By partnering and jointly operating the same operation, there is potential for a cost savings of $50 million a year.

For many Wall Street brokerage firms, other benefits far outstrip this cash savings. By partnering their back office operations, they become better able to create economies of scale, reduce head count and even double the volume of trades.

These economies have spurred several nascent cooperative efforts, such as a plan for the building of a disaster recovery site with space for up to 1,000 traders, a joint venture of several firms that wish to share their analytics libraries, and an initiative involving a shared electronic data-interchange network.

In the bull market of the 1980s, securities firms built large data centers and hired large operations staffs. As new products were invented, more staff and more capacity was added. The rationale behind these excesses was that the introduction of the new product would more than pay for the additional overhead. Of course that all changed with the stock-market crash of 1987. Today, there are fewer new products and fewer opportunities to recoup the heavy investment costs of computers and people.

Securities firms simply built back offices for a business cycle that no longer exists. With the need to pare down these cost burdens, securities firms have increasingly looked to sharing, or partnering, of their operations.

Unfortunately, the road to partnering is not smoothly paved. Perhaps the most exciting news of 1990 was the potential agreement between Prudential Securities and Shearson Lehman Brothers to merge their back-office computer operations to cut costs. Shearson had built a state-of-the-art data center which opened in 1986. Built right before the crash, the Shearson data center had more than enough capacity to process Shearson and Prudential trade data easily. But merger talks broke down early in 1991, when American Express spun off the Shearson back office into a new company called Securities Information Group (SIG). This new involvement of American Express as a third party made the Prudential deal just too complex.

The Competitive Issue

What killed the deal was the competition bogey, an issue that the Japanese seem to have resolved. Some critics have said that partnering between competitors will never work in the securities industry. They ask, "What happens when both firms need to process something at the same time and there is computer capacity for only one of them?" These critics also question the confidentiality of data in a shared environment.

Perhaps the answer for these critics is the partnering method chosen by Kidder Peabody and First Boston. Kidder shares First Boston's data center, but uses its own operations staff as does First Boston. Still, even with the success of the Kidder/First Boston model, it is hard to persuade companies that are fierce competitors to cooperate. And even though this concept has been discussed on Wall Street for the last few years, few tangible results have been realized.

Unless some action is taken in this direction, the securities firms will remain at peak capacity. If the trading volume does not improve, too many firms will continue to compete for too few customers. These firms, having to carry the burden of the fixed costs of their computer systems, will surely seek solace in price adjustments, leading to lower margins for everybody.

Philadelphia National Bank's ATM Advantage

While the securities firms are just beginning to test the waters of partnering, a particular segment of the banking industry has already proven that the sharing of resources fosters economies of scale, reduces costs and prevents erosion of market share.

The ATM (automated teller machine) is as ubiquitous nowadays as the corner candy store. Many consumers, in fact, base their banking decisions on which bank has more, or more conveniently available, "cash machines."

There is some debate, however, over the issue of how easy or hard it is to gain competitive advantage through the use of ATMs. The debate stems from the multifaceted nature of the technology. Citibank in New York exemplifies the type of banking institution which offers what is known as a proprietary ATM network. Citibank's cash machines can only be used by Citibank customers, and are hence proprietary. The question is, did Citibank reap significant strategic advantage because of their proprietary network—or did they realize a strategic advantage because they happened to be first amongst their competitors to offer this service? The flip side of the ATM coin is the shared network, which is for the most part what this section is about.

A question often raised about shared technology is, does it offer any strategic advantage at all? Wouldn't a proprietary network—such as Citibank's—offer better positioning? These questions raise a complex issue which cannot be answered simply.

At the outset, Citibank certainly received a competitive advantage by deploying their proprietary network in advance of their competitors. But as competitors caught up, an interesting phenomena occurred. Consumers stopped thinking of ATMs as unique, and started to think of them as a commodity. To use another example, the telephone itself has been a commodity for quite a while. There is little distinction, at this point, between phones from the AT&T phone store and AT&T's rival. But still, AT&T must offer telephones for sale if they are to be competitive. This logic is similar to that of the market's newest commodity—the ATM. The truth of the ATM as commodity theory is further proven by Citibank's 1991 decision to become a limited member of a competitor's shared ATM network. Obviously, Citibank had decided that providing their customers with an extensive network far outweighed whatever advantages once were to be gained by a proprietary network.

Shared networks offer significant advantages over proprietary networks. Eric K. Clemons[2], a professor at the Wharton School, has nicely summarized this reasoning as follows:

- Necessities must be offered

- Where competitive advantage is unlikely, these necessities should be provided at the lowest possible cost consistent with desired service levels

- Shared development and cooperative operations often produce significant reduction in development costs, and often provide the least expensive means of achieving a desired level of geographic coverage

Today, the benefits of sharing now exceed the benefits of remaining proprietary. But is there another strategic, economic, or other advantage to being the owner of a shared ATM service?

The Uniqueness of MAC

MAC, which stands for money access center, is a shared ATM network provided by the Philadelphia National Bank. MAC is the only single-owner shared network among the largest ATM networks. Other shared networks, such as Yankee in Boston and NYCE in New York, have a shared-ownership structure.

When MAC was launched in the 1970s, Philadelphia National Bank was a big player in commercial and wholesale banking, but its presence in retail was not significant. In 1977, a marketing research study performed by the bank revealed two major complaints among banking customers. Bank customers indicated that long teller lines and short banking hours were their chief complaints. At the same time, Philadelphia's Girard Bank had just

[2]Eric K. Clemons, "MAC—Philadelphia National Bank's Strategic Venture in Shared ATM Networks," *Journal of Management Information Systems* (Summer 1990).

launched George, a proprietary ATM network. Philadelphia National Bank recognized in George a possible reason for erosion of the bank's market share. As a result of this market study and George, Philadelphia National Bank decided to launch MAC.

MAC's requirements would be stringent. There would have to be enough ATMs in place to be relevant and justify aggressive marketing. The system would also have to have real-time access to account balances so that member banks would want to issue cards. Because of these factors, a proprietary network was unacceptable. In choosing a shared network, Philadelphia knew that a consortium of banks sharing costs and resources would not be feasible since any bank having the resources was currently considering a proprietary network of their own. Thus, the concept of marketing services to other banks was born. In 1979, the MAC network went live with thirteen banks—all generically displaying identical advertising signs and offering identical services.

Philadelphia National Bank (PNB), in providing the MAC service, is singularly responsible for all facets of the network and the software running on the network. This includes the overall network strategy, program design and implementation, network maintenance, product development, marketing, and advertising. For banks who are members of MAC, no fees are charged for these services—a definite advantage for these same banks. Funds for running MAC are derived from the normal transaction processing charge that PNB charges.

MAC provides several levels of services to member banks. For smaller banks—with teller machines but no network and supporting software—turnkey services are provided. Here, MAC provides a complete service including start of day account balances, validation of card holder, authorization of service, and accounting deposits made and withdrawals completed. Banks with the appropriate hardware and software are provided what is known as intercept service.

MAC imposes two kinds of fees on banks sharing the network. All transactions that use the MAC switch incur a switch fee. The switch is typically invoked in those transactions where interbank accounting is required, for example where a customer of a different bank withdrawing cash from an ATM located at a PNB bank. Switch fees increase as volume increases. In addition, MAC charges an interchange fee on all on-others transactions, which are transfer payments that MAC collects from the bank that issued the card used in the transaction. MAC then pays the bank that owns the card used.

From a competitive point of view, few bankers felt that a bank gains market share by joining a shared ATM network. In MAC's case, early joiners of the network joined in a defensive posture in meeting the threat posed by Girard Bank's George. In this posture, these banks were willing to place

ATM service in the hands of a competitor. In later networks, such as New York's NYCE, member banks all use it on an intercept basis.

Even in the MAC network, more and more banks are moving into the more secured position of intercept processing. This is seen as a way to limit exit barriers to leaving the network if MAC becomes exploitive. At this point, these intercept processors can create their own alternative shared network in the manner of NYCE.

MAC's stance is now of acquisition. By acquiring competing networks, MAC has become one of the larger of the ATM networks in the United States. As the ATM networks consolidate and the industry restructures, MAC is in a comfortable position.

According to Clemons, past a certain point, both the economies of scale and decreasing network costs diminish—making the concept of a single local network or a single national interconnection network infeasible. Even though ATMs are now seen as a full commodity service, that is there is no competitive advantage to having it, but there is competitive disadvantage to not having it; PNB enjoys what is known as "first-mover" advantage.

When a system—such as MAC or American Airline's Sabre—is new, the server enjoys distinct market advantages. The marketplace is not yet cognizant of the disadvantages that a predominating server yields over the industry. For example, if airline competitors realized how disadvantaged they were, with much of their distribution channel controlled by competitors, they would have never agreed to the arrangement with American. In the case of MAC's member banks, it should be remembered that at MAC's inception the concept of ATMs was still immature—not yet a major competitive factor.

The implications are clear. For those firms which enter a market first and strongly, considerable advantage occurs. Firms entering the marketplace at a later time need an aggressive plan and sufficient resources to compete. Although PNB appears to have covered costs—and is making a modest profit—MAC is not seen as a highlight to its bottom line. It is in an intangible area where PNB has benefited the most. PNB has embellished its reputation as a banker's bank among competitors while at the same time strengthening its reputation among customers.

The McKesson Lesson

Perhaps the strongest example of an information system positively affecting the reputation of a company is Economost. In fact, McKesson Drug Company's innovative support of retail pharmacies are perhaps the best-known examples of competitive and strategic information systems. McKesson's Economost \system is, in fact, the premier system cited in this regard. It is a system often cited as affecting more than just the issuing company itself.

Economost is said to be revolutionary. Its entrance into the marketplace has affected the way business is done in the industry. This and other innovating systems have changed cost structures, relationships with customers, and even the way distributors do business.[3]

Economost is McKesson Drug Company's electronic order enter and customer support system developed for the support of retail pharmacies. The major difference between this and any other order entry system is the point of use of the system. This system is not located at a McKesson site. It is located on site at the retail pharmacy making Economost the first such customer-delivered system. The McKesson example has been widely copied, but as in Philadelphia National Bank's implementation of MAC, McKesson retains its first-mover status.

McKesson first conceived of an automated order entry system in the early 1970s. At that time, the wholesale drug industry was extremely fragmented. Over 150 distributors competed for over 50,000 customers. Customers were often shared among several distributors with it not being uncommon for a small pharmacy to order daily from two or more distributors. At the same time, McKesson felt its productivity was low. They had over 100 regional warehouses with stock laid out in alphabetic order. As customer orders arrived randomly, the process of servicing orders was slow and labor intensive. Purchasing and order staff were duplicated at each distribution warehouse—further eroding profit margins. The inefficiency of the operation encouraged direct competition from manufacturers and other sources. Economost, therefore, was a direct result of the pressure felt by the company due to these inefficiencies and competitive forces. The goals of the system were to cut costs and provide a service level and benefits to the customer that would ensure that the customer would choose McKesson as its sole distributor.

Economost is also an example of an information system that is equal parts technology and equal parts exquisite planning and control. Technology alone is never the complete answer. The functionality provided by staff employing the automated product can be either a strong link or a weak link in the chain. In McKesson's case, they provided an extremely efficient organization which was used to service the orders placed by the pharmacies.

Customer orders are automatically routed to the McKesson data center, where it is captured by one of the company's Tandem computers. The order is acknowledged using voice synthesizer units. Orders are then batched and passed to the data center's IBM 3090 mainframe.

McKesson manages quick turnaround time by employing a regional distri-

---

[3]Eric K. Clemons and Michael Row, "McKesson Drug Company: A Case Study of Economost—A Strategic Information System," *Proceedings of the Twenty-First Annual Hawaii International Conference on System Sciences* 4 (Kailua-Kona, Hawaii, January 5–8, 1988), pp. 141–149.

bution center approach. Each distribution center is equipped with a mini-computer which continually downloads orders from the IBM mainframe. These orders are then taken by staff, called pickers, who walk through the warehouse filling the orders. The warehouse shelves are ordered to correspond to pharmacy departments. The McKesson warehouse is extremely well planned. Much thought has gone into considering the most ergonomic and efficient layout. For example, the most frequently sought-after items are at the front of the warehouse at waist height while less popular items are elsewhere.

Along with the pick list, the distribution center's minicomputer produces invoices, bar-code identification labels and even a bar-code label for the tote the picker uses, which directs each tote to its appropriate location on the assigned truck. Even the deployment of trucks is well planned.

The customer experiences a model of efficiency on his or her end as well. An order is placed when the customer walks around the store with a hand-held order entry device. Several McKesson customers use bar-coding to enter the seven digit order entry number, but the majority of customers enter this manually on the hand-held terminal. This order is then transmitted using an 800 phoneline into McKesson's national data center.

Because of the efficiency in the data center and its satellite distribution centers, it is possible that a customer order can be delivered the same day. Usually, however, the orders are next day delivery. Since the order is placed in the tote in a manner consistent with aisle arrangement, no sorting need be done and the order can be placed on the shelves with a single pass. Economost also has the ability to provide price stickers with variable pricing options, as desired by the customer. Clearly, usage of the Economost system has provided greater efficiencies for the customer. In one case, it was reported that a full-time clerk was no longer required since it took this particular pharmacy only a half a day to order and a half a day to restock. An interesting side effect for McKesson's customers is that use of Economost permits them to practice what, in manufacturing, is known as JIT. Just-in-time refers to the practice of maintaining minimum stock levels and reordering only when necessary. McKesson customers view Economost as so efficient and so reliable that many keep no inventory other than what's currently on the shelves.

Aside from inventory management, Economost customers are also offered a variety of management reports. The Management Purchase Report shows what items have been ordered, price as well as profit margin.

Tangible Benefits to McKesson

The drug distribution industry is perhaps one of the more competitive with many sources of rivalry. McKesson is what is termed a drug wholesaler. Other than other wholesalers, McKesson faces potential competition from suppliers and chains, hospitals, and others who supply drugs. Since McKesson's customer base is composed of small, independent pharmacies the threat to these pharmacies from the large chains is of concern to McKesson as well. Information technology is a strategic necessity rather than a source of competitive advantage, but it is clear that McKesson needs to diversify if it is to survive.

McKesson's strategy is diversification into veterinary supplies, beverages, and other nonpharmaceutical arenas. Interestingly this move would not have been possible had the company not developed its effective order entry, customer service, and distribution system. Hence, what initially was deemed an information system to support a particular business has far overshadowed the business itself. It can now be used to move into new lines of business easily and rapidly, enabling the innovating company to meet competitive threats aggressively rather than defensively.

The benefits to the customer and McKesson alike were enormous. For the customer, use of Economost resulted in reduced costs and reduced inventory as well as management support. McKesson's use of the system resulted in even more dramatic benefits. The number of order-entry clerks employed by McKesson was cut from 700 to 15, machine-readable information provides the ability to offer more management-reporting information to their customers, as well as to efficiently manage McKesson's warehouse operations. From 1975, when the system was first introduced, to the late 1980s, McKesson's drug sales have increased over 424 percent while operating expenses have increased only 86 percent. The decision to proceed with Economost was an example of excellent foresight in planning a competitive information system. In the 1970s, there were over 150 drug distributors, but with industry consolidation, by the early 1990s, there were fewer than 90.

Probably the biggest consequence of the Economost system is that it virtually changed the stakes a new entrant must be willing to wager in order to enter the game. Since McKesson has invested at least $20 to $30 million since system inception, it stands to reason that a new entrant into the industry must be able to deploy similar resources to be able to become competitively active. Clemons refers to this investment and these systems as strategic necessities.

Both McKesson and Philadelphia National are considered first movers, that is, innovators in bringing technological solutions to marketplace problems, thereby deriving some competitive advantage from it. The McKesson and PNB case studies show flip sides of the partnering coin. McKesson partnered with customers while PNB partnered with competitors, immeasurably more difficult. Both McKesson and PNB improved their competitive position, although this increase was more pronounced at the outset. As more competitors followed this strategy, competitive advantage decreased as the commoditization of the service increased. Costs of entry serve to minimize this factor somewhat. Mimicking the McKesson system and attendant warehouse structure is at an extremely high cost, while this is less true for entry into the ATM arena. Intangible benefits, such as improved customer satisfaction and increased positive reputation, are significant and do not appear to have decreased over the years the systems have in existence.

How the Big Three in Travel Banded Together to Get Even Bigger

This issue of customer satisfaction has become one of the dominant factors in determining competitive success of companies in the 1990s. Nowhere is this more true than in the hotel business. With occupancy rates hovering around 64 percent and 66 percent, the ability to satisfy the customer and keep him or her coming back is of paramount importance. Customer satisfaction goes well beyond the porcelain tea service and mint on the pillow. Its roots are in the hotel reservation systems that virtually every major hotel chain in the world is either in the midst of development or has recently deployed.

Hotel reservation systems are becoming increasingly more complex. Few realize that only 30 percent of a hotel's reservations come into the system through travel agents or networks. The majority of bookings are made through the hotels' own central reservations number. Hotels have found that they need good technological backup if they are to make sure that adequate rooms are available through a wider range of distribution points.

These systems need do much more than just load balancing. Personalization is the watchword today. Therefore, each of these reservations systems must be able to track particular guest preferences and needs. According to a recent Andersen Consulting study of 600 lodging industry executives, 64 percent indicated that improving the quality of guest stay was a major factor in driving technology innovation in their companies. This was closely followed by improving operational efficiency and keeping pace with the competition.

The hotel reservation system that is needed today is expensive. It must be real time and be able to perform yield management. This means that the hotel knows the availability of the last room, which is a perishable commodity, and can therefore sell it to the customer at the best price. Since earnings, of late, are being squeezed the feeling of sticker shock is palpable.

Given the necessity and the constraints one of the available options to players in the industry is partnering. One group, or consortium, moving in this direction is Confirm. Confirm is a joint venture of the Marriott Corporation, Hilton Hotels, and Budget Rent-a-Car. Using an affiliate of

American Airlines, AMR Information Services, as the utility provider, Confirm is the newest partnership to be actively online. Although it is intended primarily for the use of its partners, it is being marketed to other hotel chains in the same vein that American's Sabre is marketed to competitor airlines and Philadelphia National Bank has offered MAC to regional banks.

The base technology of Confirm is AMR's Sabre customer reservation system, which is deemed the most profitable in the world. It has three components: a transaction manager, a central reservations system, and a decision enabling system. The decision enabling component will handle all historical data, customer data as well as management reports.

Even though Confirm is the first new robust reservation system to be on line in 20 years, it isn't the only one. CLAS International is a competing offering marketed by Loews Hotels and Covia which is a provider of numerous travel services including the Apollo airline reservation system. CLAS and Confirm will most certainly compete head to head. In addition, a fully funded competitor just might well go ahead and fund a proprietary system.

Of course, the market is large and choices are but the two mentioned: either develop a proprietary system and bare the large costs or compromise and join a shared network such as CLAS or Confirm.

For those that have formed the partnerships, though, the strategic advantages are many. Splitting costs is but one. Although firms that join the network at a later date complain of the necessity of compromising and accepting a product that isn't specifically tailored to their environments, that is not true for the founding partners. They are free to specify and negotiate advantageous functionalities during system start-up while the plan is still being formed. This coupled with customer perception of the hotelier as an industry innovator (if indeed the customer is aware of the hotels participation in the creation of the network) provides a clear competitive advantage over those hotels joining the network at a later date.

When Partnering Means Survival

The travel industry has been fiercely competitive for decades. So the use of technological partnering comes as no surprise to industry observers. Other industries are just finding out what real competition is all about.

The computer industry is perhaps the newest of American industries. Just a dream a mere two and a half decades ago, the computer industry shot up out of nowhere into stratospheric profitability. But as the industry matured, and the economy soured, computer hardware and software manufacturers and vendors have suddenly found themselves fighting for survival.

It's little wonder that Charles R. Wolf, a computer industry analyst at First Boston calls the IBM–Apple partnership the deal of the decade. He has forecasted that this alliance will change the landscape of the industry. Since IBM and Apple have been often bitter rivals since the inception of the personal computer in the early 1980s, Mr. Wolf's assessment of the situation is accurate.

The question is why? Although Apple is a prestigious, and profitable computer company, the reasoning behind their agreement to this alliance is less profound than IBM's. Apple was the upstart computer company where, legend has it, the idea for a generic personal computer started in a garage in the minds of two school dropouts. Although quite popular for home use, schools and in the arts industry, the Apple line of computers has never really caught on wholesale in the bread and butter business sector.

The big surprise in this alliance is IBM. IBM, a widows and orphan stock, is one of the largest and well-respected companies in this country. The general perception about IBM is that they are invincible. Their agreement to this alliance proves this perception a fallacy and clearly demonstrates the flexibility a firm must have if it is to survive in trying economic times.

Actually, IBM's alliance with Apple comes as no surprise to many who have been watching Big Blue. Over the last few years, IBM has entered into several joint agreements with other companies. Additionally, its stance over the past few years, at least on the software side of the house, has been to develop a concept and then wait as their business partners developed the actual software that would deploy that concept. This is exemplified in their CASE strategy. CASE is an acronym for computer assisted software engineering. It is the hottest topic to take the computer industry by storm. CASE is a tool for program developers. It helps them write programs better and quicker. IBM developed a strategy which they called AD/Cycle. But it is their business partners, a diverse array of firms, that has actually written this software. The Apple/IBM alliance is quite different. Apple is not, and never has been, a business partner. In fact, Apple has often been a bitter rival.

The reason behind this marriage of convenience is twofold. The industry has been so complex, so widely flung and so diverse that no company can go it alone in developing technology and winning customers. The computer industry once had only one standard—IBM's. But with the growing number of entries into the field, the number of standards has proliferated. This has occurred both on the hardware and the software side.

An Example of Fragmentation

Perhaps one of the better demonstrative examples of this industry fragmentation is in the CASE market. Since the idea of CASE was conceived, dozens of vendors have flooded the marketplace. Each of these vendors brought with them their own CASE tool. Customers, who bought these CASE tools, are just finding out that many of these disparate CASE tools simply do not speak the same language.

Sometimes connecting one CASE tool to another is similar to connecting that three and one quarter-inch pipe into the three-inch hole. According to Howard Rubin, President of Howard Rubin Associates in Pound Ridge, New York, "A lot of energy being wasted right now in constructing systems is worrying about the binding process versus worrying about the individual components. The binding should be less of a headache and we should be focusing on what are the right components to assemble."

In order for this vision of full-scale tool integration to take flight, one all-consuming issue must be resolved. This is the issue of standards. If plumbers hadn't developed, and adhered to, a set of standards, then building a house today would be even more of a nightmare than it already is.

Building the technology for today's IT shop is very much like installing the plumbing for a new house: mixed vendors and services. Given the increasing predilection toward becoming mixed vendor shops, information technology groups are very interested in heterogeneous solutions. Therefore, we must look at the set of services that has to be pervasive across all kinds of operating systems and different types of hardware to be really useful. This heterogeneity requires strict standards.

The real problem is not a lack of standards. The problem is too many standards leading to mass confusion and fragmentation of the marketplace. How confused *is* the marketplace? The world is dividing up into two camps. There's IBM and what is referred is as open systems. HP, Unisys, DEC, NCR, Siemens, and Bull are all in open systems along with some of the CASE vendors.

The migration of vendors into either one of these two camps is evidenced by the current consolidation of the CASE industry. Although there are plenty of market niches where a good CASE vendor can take root, the problem is one of distribution and perhaps user confidence. As more and more users are moving into the CASE marketplace, they are searching for some level of standardization, and looking to the bigger vendors for support, training, and stability. Because of this, some of the smaller players with good technology are finding themselves being shut out of the market. In order to survive, vendors must take the consolidation route by forming strategic alliances with other vendors, or even merging with other vendors as in the Index/Sage merger into the company now known as Intersolv.

Losing Control of the Market

The alliance between Apple and IBM is clear proof of the fact that IBM has lost control over the very market that it helped create. IBM has become, in effect, just one more cog in the wheel competing with hundreds of lower-priced but equally capable companies. Even IBM's own machine has little that is IBM in it: An IBM PC's chips are Intel's and its operating system is Microsoft; much of the profits go to these two firms.

Therefore, many see the alliance between IBM and Apple as a merger with the specific purpose of jointly gaining control over the diversity of design and standards issue as well as the proliferation of the marketplace issue.

Apple and IBM's letter of intent calls for the formation of a new, independently managed company, whose goal will be to create an advanced operating system. This new operating system will be used in both new and existing Apple and IBM computers and will be marketed to other companies. In the choice of an operating system as the prime vehicle for this alliance can be seen the underlying reason for this partnership. In a word—Microsoft.

It will come as no surprise to readers of the business pages that the relationship between Microsoft—the maker of the most popular operating system for the PC—and IBM has gone astray. What may be surprising is the level of acrimony between the two giants. It is perhaps in the deteriorating relationship between IBM and Microsoft that can be found the real reason for the IBM and Apple partnership.

Microsoft was the first business partner that IBM squired in the PC world. At the time, Microsoft was a young start-up company, so the partnership agreement between the two was nowhere nearly as significant as this most latest partnership between IBM and Apple. IBM was just entering the PC market and needed an operating system for that PC. Microsoft was the chosen partner. It appeared to be a relationship made in heaven and, in fact, did prove beneficial to both for quite a number of years. What IBM didn't count on was Microsoft's aggressive entry into more segments of the software market and their growing market share. Today, Microsoft is one of the most profitable, and dominant, computer companies of all time.

As Microsoft grew, it also grew more independent. The war with IBM over its newest operating system was the blow that broke the partnership apart, pushing IBM into the comforting arms of another. IBM's newest machines run under an operating system called OS/2. IBM's relationship with Microsoft called for Microsoft to develop a newer and more robust version of OS/2. But Microsoft had a different agenda. Instead of OS/2, Microsoft spent its resources on developing newer versions of their original operating system, DOS, and something called Windows.

Windows is a software program that mimics the look and feel of the popular Apple computer operating system. But Windows placed this functionality on an IBM PC. Since Windows runs under DOS, Microsoft had no desire to move ahead with the IBM OS/2 agreement. Instead, Microsoft aggressively pushed Windows. Given the popularity of Windows, this was a good strategic business decision for Microsoft. But it did have the side effect of stirring great controversy in the industry—and destroying the long-term relationship with IBM.

When IBM finally understood that Microsoft would never fulfill its agreement to develop the OS/2 operating system for the IBM PC, they finally began to understand that their onetime business ally had turned aggressive rival.

In situations such as these, one is often pressured to choose what is perceived as the lesser of two evils. IBM must have surely been in a quandary. On the one hand, Microsoft had most surely severed its relationship with IBM by its actions. On the other hand, IBM viewed Apple as a prime competitor. But in considering its options, IBM must have realized that its only chance for survival in the personal computer wars would be to develop a partnership with its once most fearsome competitor—Apple.

The alliance is actually more extensive than the development of an Apple-based operating system for both the Apple and IBM platforms. The companies will develop products to make it easier for Apple Macintoshes to communicate and share information with IBM machines that are now widely used by corporations. The two companies will also develop a version of IBMs UNIX operating system (this high-end operating system runs on advanced workstations) that will run programs written for the Macintosh. Apple will begin using an IBM microprocessor in future versions of the Macintosh. Finally, the two companies will develop common approaches to displaying images on displays and reproducing sounds.

The benefits that Apple derives from this partnership are perhaps even greater than those that IBM will enjoy. Once viewed as a loner, Apple will now take its place among the prime contenders in the IBM PC arena. It will be able to sell more computers to large corporations who, presently, have shied away from the Apple configuration and standardized on the IBM PC. Since the alliance will provide the ability of easily merging Apples computers into an all IBM environment, the floodgates should open for Apple sales.

The IBM Apple alliance is not the first alliance in the computer industry. Digital Equipment, Compaq, and Microsoft also have an arrangement. What is significant in the Apple IBM partnership, though, is that two of the biggest names in the computer industry, and the two who were originally the most competitive, have joined forces in order to survive.

The Computer Industry Leads the Way in Strategic Partnering

Three months of 1991 provide an excellent overview of how partnering is changing the shape of the computer industry. It is presented here in calendar format:

April 9, 1991:	Compaq, along with 20 other companies, launches the Advanced Computing Environment Consortium to establish a new standard to compete with Sun, Hewlett Packard, and IBM.
April 12, 1991:	Federal Trade Commission widens its investigation into Microsoft for possible antitrust.
May 1, 1991:	CompuCom purchases Computer Factory (both companies are retail computer stores).
May 6, 1991:	NCR (National Cash Register) agrees to be purchased by AT&T.
June 4, 1991:	JWP buys Businessland (both are computer retail chains).
June 13, 1991:	Tandy, reversing its stance on independence, agrees to carry products from Apple, Compaq, and IBM in its stores.
June 18, 1991:	Wang forges agreement with IBM to resell IBM products.

The computer industry shakeup is a portent of things to come in most American industries. Markets are so fragmented and competition so aggressive that even the strongest of firms are increasingly finding that they cannot survive in isolation.

Partnering, however, requires a great deal of effort from those firms which agree to join forces. The lines between these participating organizations tend to blur at contact. Being able to cope with the new rules of the game can make the difference between a successful partnership and one that ends in acrimony (i.e., IBM and Microsoft) and possible market repercussions.

Many in the computer industry, although lauding the IBM and Apple alliance, are taking a wait-and-see attitude. The question these critics raise is, "Can IBM and Apple put their differences aside and work together in unison to develop their line of products?" Only time will tell.

Negotiating the Sharing of Information

Information partnerships between corporations may be the next wave of the future, running the gamut from links between suppliers and customers (such as McKesson) to joint ventures between companies in the same industry to collaborate on R&D or marketing (such as the Apple–IBM venture).

In all of these partnerships, the common entity will be a shared-information resource. Sharing of information will require exacting managerial efforts as widely dispersed companies, out of necessity, must provide a commonality in the areas of data definitions, relationships, and even search patterns.

Even into the 1990s, companies are having difficulty in creating an internal information resource, common to all divisions within a single company. Thus attempting to develop an intercompany information resource will be even more difficult. Flexibility, cooperation, and computer power seem to be the keywords of a workable, and mutually profitable, partnership—as exemplified by Corning. Corning's approach to strategic alliances is one of adapting to great change. This ability to accommodate is, perhaps, the deciding factor between success and failure. A partnership is only as successful as the partners' abilities to make it work, which requires that each partner changes more than just the way business is performed. The partners may have to change corporate culture as well.

Corning is no stranger to this phenomena, since it has a large number of strategic alliances and joint ventures. For an information services department bearing the brunt of development for the new relationship, it means having to accommodate clients who are external to the company. For Corning's information services department, this has meant determining costs, negotiating rates, and sending out bills. These are activities that Corning's internal information services group never had to do before.

The way Corning's information services group works with partners is directly related to the nature of the partnership and the needs of the various participants. In one notable instance, 50 percent of a Corning division had divested into a joint-venture company. The new company's information services group had to be apportioned from the central group. In addition, the new joint venture decided to purchase some services from the central group as well requiring the central group to begin monitoring the new company's usage in order to calculate billables.

Just like Corning, other developers of intercompany information resources will have to overcome multiple political problems, priority problems, and jargon problems. Developing a negotiating game plan can be of invaluable assistance. Here's how to avoid the pitfalls and achieve successful cooperation:

Standardize the Terms That All Companies Use. Greenwood Mills, located in Greenwood, South Carolina, found that standardization of jargon was a necessity if they were to successfully implement a system which linked the textile company to its customers and suppliers. Greenwood was used to keeping track of material using standard sizes such as 36 or 48 inches. In reality, those measurements represented the minimum size on the bolt. In essence, a 36-inch bolt of material might very well be 37 inches wide. This was a big issue to Greenwood's customers, as many of them were using numerical control equipment which was sophisticated enough to take advantage of this difference requiring them to remeasure the fabric.

Greenwood also found that they had a jargon problem in the naming of colors. Greenwood designated names for shades while their customers used a value that described the amount of variance from a standard color.

Choose a Board of Directors.   In joint venture partnerships, all partners are created equal. This, of course, is just theory. In practice, it is possible that the information services group will find itself beholden to several masters. Since the partnership is being formed around a joint goal, an insistence on a many master approach to the information services group will most surely result in lowering efficiencies. Information services must serve one master only. In joint partnerships, this can be accomplished through election of a Board of Directors, the function of which is to oversee information services efforts.

The Board of Directors should have equal representation from all partners. Their function is to determine both the short- and long-term plans of the information services group. This includes the determination of priorities of all development projects as well as resolution of any political confrontations.

In situations where a firm has formed an alliance with one or more companies in which that firm permits utilization of a proprietary information system to those companies, it is reasonable to expect requests for modifications to that system. All too often in these situations, those external companies are handed a phone number of the technician in charge of that system who is then confronted with having to fit these requests into an already filled agenda. On many occasions, these requests for change are not desirable to the owner company. A better control of the situation is desired.

In these cases, a user liaison should be appointed to run interference between these external companies and the owner company. This liaison will be responsible for taking requests for change, and then working with the user team as well as the information services group to determine if the change is desirable, and when and if it can be accommodated.

Determine the Boundaries of Exchange.   Data links between two companies can be unidirectional or bidirectional. A supplier posting new product information may require only a one-way link. McKesson's system typifies a system with a two-way link. Not only was McKesson able to provide information to the pharmacy, the pharmacy was able to transmit order information as well.

Eliminate Redundancies.   In a joint venture, separate firms, each having its own information services department, join forces for a common goal. In cases such as these, there may be a desire for each firm to retain its own independent information services group.

Efficiencies are lowered when a processing function is performed more than once. In addition, redundant data often becomes inconsistent. For example, a group of three firms uploads market data to its respective marketing research departments for analyses. Each market research department has its own computer system. It is possible that three different results will be obtained due to the differences in data processing. Additionally, the longer the raw data sits in diverse databases, the stronger the chance that the data will be altered and, thus, differ from those in its sister databases.

It is recommended that all data be processed in one location to negate these potentialities. This calls for the creation of a joint processing center servicing the legitimate needs of the partnership. If this is not possible, or desirable, then one location should be chosen as master with the ability to update. The remaining locations should have the ability to download in a read-only mode to prevent the data from becoming redundant and corrupted. To ensure that data analyses are performed singularly, software should be located on a network for shared use or the same analytical programs should be made mandatory.

Allow for Varying Levels of Sophistication. In building information systems for multiple partners, it should be remembered that each partner will exhibit a particular level of sophistication, with its own set of requirements.

In building the Economost system, McKesson had to deal with the fact that its pharmacy customers lacked the degree of sophistication that its own internal staff had. In providing hand-held terminals as well as scannable inventory labels, McKesson recognized, and provided for, its level of sophistication.

Many firms develop a joint system with multiple interfaces. One for the least sophisticated user, one for the average user, and one for an extremely knowledgeable, or power, user.

Be Ready to Compromise. In a single-user system the user can tailor the system for a specific purpose. This is usually not possible in jointly held systems. Although many of the problems of partnership systems can be resolved through the use of a Board of Directors, companies involved in process should be ready to compromise some of their specific requirements.

5
Infotrend #4: Integration—The Buzzword of the 1990s

Most organizations structure their information technology endeavors in the same way that they structure their corporate hierarchies. These hierarchies have traditionally been nested deep in multiple levels, reflecting a rather severe segmentation of tasks between departments. Each department views itself in isolation, ceaselessly protecting its turf from invasion and takeover by other departments. Lines of communication between the separate departments are often marked by political infighting and only a modicum of cooperation. From a technology point of view, this has led the typical organization to create a wide diversity of often overlapping, redundant, and nonintegrated systems.

This assessment of the large American corporation is, unfortunately, all too accurate. Of course, the level of severity of this malaise that any particular corporation endures varies. Even if a firm experiences full and willing cooperation among its working departments, its corporate hierarchical structure has worked against it in producing discrete, stand-alone work environments. This, in turn, has been reflected in the creation of automated systems as stand-alone as the departments in which they run.

This organizational model has been the status quo of many organizations for the last 25 years. At the same time, there has been an absence or paucity of productivity payoffs from information technology, despite massive investment over the same 25-year time period.[1] It may be theorized that one of the reasons—though not the exclusive reason—for this paucity of productivity gains is the rigid organizational model to which firms traditionally adhere.

The Case for Integration

It has been shown that a more flattened organization—and one marked by fluid interdepartmental boundaries—has the ability to react more readily to market forces, making firms with this organizational structure more competitive than firms with the structure described above. When this organizational structure is coupled with an emphasis on teams which, in turn, have a keen interest in quality and productivity, competitiveness is then enhanced.

In growing numbers, the tide has been turning from rigid and closed hierarchies to a more open team approach. With the integration of business units, technologists are finding a need to create more cross-departmental systems. Movement of firms from one model to the other has been heavily dependent upon competitive forces in the market, with those firms sensing the greatest threat moving into integrated software environments faster than those firms complacent in their competitive position in global industry.

Two industries that come readily to mind as examples of industries with the highest concentration of firms moving into an integrated software environment are the financial services industry and the manufacturing sector, which have been hit hard by aggressive competition.

Integration of software environments in the financial sector was the result of new product development. In restructuring its businesses to offer more competitive products, the financial services industry found that it needed computer systems to support this strategy. Flexibility and innovation became important assets in this strategy and is was quite necessary, as a result, to redistribute information technology to make it accessible to naïve end-users, as well as to the knowledge users who could make the most of it. The Travelers, a financial services company based in Hartford, Connecticut, exemplifies those that have moved into diverse financial instruments from the security of one product. Originally, the Travelers was an insurance company, and to this very day, most associate The Travelers with insurance. But during the last decade and a half, The Travelers began to restructure themselves to be competitive in the emerging market for integrated financial services. In this market, there is only a blurry distinction between commercial banking, investment banking, and insurance. The financial services industry

---

[1] Paul Attewell, "The Productivity Paradox." White paper and talk. State University of New York at Stony Brook, (New York: Feb. 1990).

lines of demarcation became even more blurry as securities was factored into the equation. The only deterrent to a complete amalgamation of separate instruments into one financial block is the Glass-Stegall Act which effectively blocks banks from trading in securities. Banks are pushing to repeal this—with much opposition from the securities industry.

In the manufacturing sector, the path to integration came about somewhat differently. Integration was not the result of new products, as in the financial services industry—integration itself was the product.

Manufacturers have been hit hard by a number of economic variables. Intense competition from overseas, the cost of labor in the United States are but two. Perhaps what has hit manufacturers the hardest, though, is aging plants and equipment. U.S. industry was among the first to automate, and over the years, this equipment has aged. Retooling of plants is expensive, but the threat of possible extinction has forced these firms to dig deep into their pockets and invest in newer and more innovative plants.

The major thrust today is toward building manufacturing plants that exhibit computer-integrated manufacturing (CIM). As opposed to the financial services industry, where new products have fostered an integrated information technology infrastructure, CIM itself is seen by many to be the solution to the manufacturing industry's pressing problems.

Integration as the Cure

In both industry examples, integration is seen as the key to the cure of inefficiency and waste. Joseph T. Brophy and Rod F. Monger[2] have put forth a framework which harnesses this principle. They quote recent studies that have found that communications is the largest component, almost 50 percent, of the average white-collar worker's time. Intellectual work (e.g., reading, analyzing) occupies less than 33 percent. They contend that if information technologies fail to achieve economies in that communications component, it is doubtful that they will produce significant benefits overall. For these benefits to be achieved, all aspects of administration must be in the system through system-wide integration.

Brophy and Monger use the term computer-integrated offices to describe the effects of integrating all aspects of the office through computerization. It is this computer-integrated office that will have the ability to react readily to dynamic markets with quick-hit solutions—something not possible in traditionally configured companies.

In traditional companies, by contrast, managements identify objectives and then develop a strategy for reaching these objectives. Often one of the

[2]Joseph T. Brophy and Rod F. Monger, "Competitive Capacity from an Integrated IS Infrastructure," *Information Strategy: The Executive's Journal* (Winter 1989).

resources called into force at this time is information technology. This presumes that during the period in which systems are designed and then implemented—often years—the dynamics of the market will not change. This is simply not true.

Many firms would do better to reverse the traditional ends-ways-means logic to means-ways-ends.[3] In other words, these firms would do better to develop capabilities and then encourage their exploitation than to develop a plan and then wait for the strategy to be implemented some time later.

Brophy and Monger's framework is a methodology to create a technology infrastructure that exhibits a great deal of integration.

Senior management must constantly align the technology infrastructure to balance the future general capacity development with medium- and short-term exploitation. The framework provides for three phases, all occurring simultaneously, which will accomplish this end.

The Assessment Phase can be thought of as a watch on the environment. In this phase, the changing business environment is surveyed as is the potential of emerging information technologies. The key is to determine the potential changes in industry structure and the basis for its competition. Matching up business needs to technologies, future or otherwise, is the real goal here.

The second phase of the framework has been termed Position Taking. This is the phase where senior management theoretically understands, and invests in current technology requirements as well as mandates discretionary funds for future research. In practice, this seldom occurs since most firms practice a financial accounting approach to allocating monies to information technology. This approach fails to take into account benefits versus gains, making some technology investments difficult to justify. Senior managers should manage information technology as they would an investment portfolio that is constantly being reevaluated for performance on the basis of risk, return, and time-horizon.

The third phase is termed the Policy Formulation phase. It is in this phase that senior managers work though the changes necessary to implement an appropriate integrated technology infrastructure. Many factors come into play here, including organizational issues such as structure and culture, work-force issues including restructuring the work force, and external factors such as accounting and education.

What Brophy and Monger have shown is that creating a technology infrastructure to support the integrated office that is required to compete requires careful planning and can be greatly assisted by putting a methodology into place.

[3]Robert H. Hayes, "Why Strategic Planning Goes Awry," *The New York Times* (April 20, 1986).

The Role of Systems Integrators

The majority of companies do not wish to dramatically alter their organizational structures. They do, however, wish to integrate their systems. Whether one will work without the other can only be determined by the company and the circumstances surrounding the integration process. Most companies, whether they change their organizational structure or not, have found the task of integration to be arduous. A cache of hundreds of systems, many of them linked, and many of them carrying hard-to-trace redundancies need to be analyzed and sorted into neat little piles. As a result of the complexity and difficulty of this process, many firms have turned to the use of systems integrators to assist in the process.

An Enterprise Approach to Integration

The most successful systems integration starts out with a proper enterprise model. This is a model of the entire organization—its data and its processes. After the enterprise model is created, it is then possible to parcel out the project into smaller tasks that are easily handled. Spending more than three to four months on a strategic planning level for each of these projects implies a level of complexity that is a sure road to failure.

In studying case histories of systems integration, a common thread among the success stories was that the firms had taken an approach similar to the one that Charles Popper recommends. Enterprise modeling and its complementary data modeling, are two processes with which technologists should be familiar. Despite the numerous books and magazine articles written on this topic, it is surprising to find that many firms pay only lip service to use of the techniques.

There are several definitions of enterprise modeling. Some vary only in semantics, while others are fundamentally different in terms of scope and approach. While some view it as a model of a business from a strategic perspective, others view it as a formal representation of the business that includes planning, control, and operational views as well as the strategic view. Those that are more technologically oriented view the enterprise model as a subset of data modeling or information-flow modeling.

The major purpose of enterprise modeling is to understand a company's technology in terms of its business. This requires the building of a model of the important components of the organization. Once a strategic-level enterprise model is completed, the flow of information through the enterprise is charted—an activity usually referred to as "data modeling." Since integration is heavily dependent upon organizational as well as informational flow, both must be understood if an organization is to be truly successful. What follows is an overview of the major steps required to successfully create a working enterprise model.

Develop an Approved Working Team

If enterprise modeling is performed at all, it is usually performed by the information technology department independently of the business units. This is an egregious error since few, if any, information technology departments understand enough about the business to be able to adequately represent its different layers of strategy.

The most effective way of creating the model is to first get senior executive support. Creation of the model should be directed and funded by senior management since they are the ones that will need to buy into any resulting integration plan at the end. Their inclusion from the outset assures at least a knowledgeable decision at the end.

Teamwork is the operative word here. There are two levels to the activity of creating an enterprise model. On the strategic level, a team should be formed that is composed of representatives of the various business units as well as a highly placed official from the technology department. Starting with the organization's mission statement, and then proceeding downward through the various business units' mission statements, the team should prepare a common document that captures the gist of the organization.

Model the Business Functions

Modeling is often performed diagramatically. A model of an entire organization often looks like a typical corporate hierarchy chart. A corporate mission statement should encompass the stated objective and goals for the entire organization. It follows then that the business units' missions, when taken together, should fit neatly into the stated objectives of the corporate mission. Sometimes, this is not the case. When this occurs, having a team composed of players on the strategic levels of the organization, would have the capability to rectify the situation.

Those involved in the creation of the enterprise model should be aware that there are automated tools that can assist in preparing the documentation that will result from this exercise. It is expected that this documentation will include a written narrative, including an executive summary, and a set of hierarchical diagrams that will capture the essence of the model. Some of the automated tools that can assist in this rather laborious documentation task are listed in the appendix at the back of this book.

Missions and goals must now be followed by describing the functions that each of the discrete business units perform. It is at this point that some firms realize that more than one business unit is performing a similar task, or it might be found that one business unit is performing functions that would be better handled in another unit. In Chapter Two, we discussed Carmine Vona's findings that the combination of the money transfer function and the foreign exchange function in one business unit created difficulties at Bankers Trust. By careful analysis, Vona determined that the Foreign Exchange Operation would be better served if parceled out into two discrete units. This same sort of analysis needs to be applied at this point if the team is to develop a successful enterprise model. It makes no sense to model existing deficiencies.

More than likely, the team members will need the cooperation of the individual departments of the business unit to gather a complete set of functionality attributed to that business unit. It may be a revelation to find that functions are being performed that are not charted on any list and other functions, which were assigned, are not actually being done. Business corrections need to be made at this point as well, if any deficiencies or deviations are found. A list of business functions for each business unit should be accompanied by a list of activities that are performed in order to achieve this function.

At the risk of delaying the completion of the model, this juncture appears to be a good opportunity for each department to reassess its own strategy in terms of the activities it performs to accomplish its mission and its goals. Are these activities complete enough? Is there overkill? Can any activity be enhanced?

Tie In Information to the Business Function

It is more than likely that each activity requires one or more pieces of information for successful completion of that activity. At the time, the department is preparing its list of activities, it should also be preparing a list of germane information items. This list should be composed of information that is available internally as well as information that is obtained externally, such as through clients, suppliers, and competitors.

This information list should be annotated by the individual departments such that it captures prioritization of each information item as well as the source and ownership of each information item.

For illustrative purposes, let's say that one particular business department uses 10 information items. It is decided by the strategy team that information priorities should be rated on a scale of one to three with one being the most important and three being the least important. Each of these 10 information items will, therefore, have to have a prioritization level assigned. In addition, an item needs to be tracked according to source and ownership.

For a hypothetical department, for example; item one's source is client-owned not resident on any in-house computer; item two's source is The Morning Report with an ownership of corporate; item three's source is the finance department with the ownership being the finance department; and item four's source is an on-line system with the source being self-ownership, and so on.

Since we're working on a strategic level, it is not necessary to get bogged down at the detail level. Information items should be referred to at the group level. For example, The Morning Report is 10 pages long and prints several hundred items, or fields, of information. It is only necessary, at this point, to refer to The Morning Report rather than breaking it down into its component parts.

Model the Information That the Business Function Produces

Business functions usually produce information which then is sent to other departments. This needs to be described in detail as well.

It is at this point that participants may uncover a paper flow that is not efficient. Departments often produce reports which then are broadcast to closely aligned departments. Not all of these reports are used or wanted. Most of us are familiar with the ploy of ceasing the distribution of a particular report to see who complains, in an attempt to eliminate that report. If enough departments complain, the report is then reinstated.

The strategy team should take a hard look at this paper flow to make sure that all of it is needed and useful.

Model the Points of Interaction

D&B Software, a merger of MSA and McCormack & Dodge, create what they call a data-ownership matrix. This matrix illustrates how a business function owns information. It shows the integration "touch points" between business function.

This step is extremely important, for it is here that the diagram of the information flow becomes clear. It will also become clear, through viewing this diagram, whether or not information is flowing logically through the organization as detailed by the functionality of the respective business units.

Develop a Data Model

The strategy team develops a complete list of business functions and their associated information inputs and outputs. Each piece of information is tracked to the degree of knowing if it is sourced from in-house or obtained externally, whether it is owned by the business unit using it or it is "borrowed" information. All information is also labeled with its prioritization level.

One of the by-products of this process is that organizations come to the realization that much of the data important to the firm is actually obtained from outside rather than generated and stored in-house. At this point, the organization might wish to begin planning to bring some of this external data in-house.

Next, the second level team comes into play. The realm of data modeling is purely the domain of the information technologist.

The goal of generating a data model, within the context of this exercise, is to produce a logical representation of the data elements contained in the information flows from an information technology perspective. Up until now, the process of enterprise modeling has been extremely business driven. But it's now time to put the shoe on the other foot, and let the technical team turn the information model into a data model which can serve as a baseline for creating not only the enterprise model but the integration plan as well.

There are several modeling methodologies that stand out since they are common components of CASE tools. Warnier-Orr diagrams are useful for both data structure and program architecture design. Entity-relationship diagrams are well-suited for describing relationships between data elements and data-flow diagrams show the path of information routing through the organization. Each will be summarized to give the reader a flavor of the techniques available for this purpose.

Warnier-Orr Diagrams.   This is a simple and straightforward tool for representing the structure of data within an organization. The basic component of the Warnier-Orr diagram is the bracket or brace.

Warnier-Orr charts look much like corporate organizational hierarchy charts. They are, in a sense, but they are a hierarchy of data rather than people as shown in Figure 5-1. The Warnier-Orr chart is a diagrammatic tool that permits the developers to expand or collapse parts of the structures to reveal or hide levels of detail and refinement.

The example shows the structure of the Inventory Database. This database is composed of two different types of records: a vendor record and a warehouse record. The vendor record, in turn, is composed of two different types of information: vendor description and stock items. As we move progressively to the right of the Warnier-Orr diagram, the level of detail becomes more decomposed. We move from database to record to data field.

Entity-Relationship Diagram.   While a Warnier-Orr diagram is extremely useful for depicting a specific data structure, it does little to depict the flows

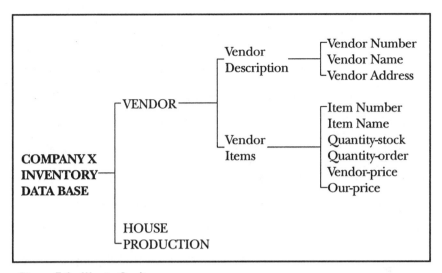

Figure 5-1. Warnier-Orr diagram.

of information between data structures. Entity-relationship (ER) diagrams are probably the most popular methodology for this purpose and a basis for many of the more robust CASE tools.

Entity-relationship diagrams are simply constructed. They consist of only two components: entities and relations. Entities are the objects being defined. Entities may be data, such as that which is represented by the Warnier-Orr diagrams in the last paragraph, but they may be people as well. An entity might even be an abstract notion such as a service.

Relationships are the associations or links which show how one entity, or group of entities, relates to another entity or group of entities. Figure 5-2 depicts an entity-relationship diagram of the relationships between a customer and an invoice.

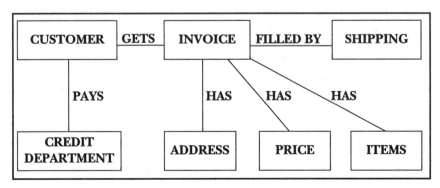

Figure 5-2. Entity-relationship diagram.

Entity-relationship diagrams are extremely handy in diagramming the relationships between information flows in the corporation. However, again it should be noted that performing these by hand is tedious. Entity-relationship notation is widely available in CASE tools, the use of which should be seriously considered.

Data-Flow Diagrams.   Data-flow diagrams graphically depict the different items in a computer system(s) and their movement from process to process. They depict a system from the data's viewpoint only. In some ways, the data-flow diagram is the best interpretation of the way the user views a system, and thus might be used as a first step by the technical team in interpreting the work of the strategy team.

Data-flow diagrams consist of four components as shown in Figure 5-3. Data flows are the individual data items that are sent and received by the processes. They are represented by arrows on the diagram. The direction of the arrow indicates the direction of the data flow. *Processes* are represented as bubbles on the diagram which lead some users to call data-flow diagrams bubble charts. Data flows in and out of these processes. Processes transform data. In other words, processes are the procedures that are performed on the data. Square

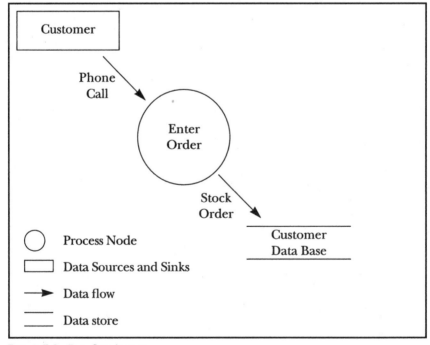

Figure 5-3. Data flow diagram.

boxes on the data-flow diagram represent data sources and sinks. Data sources can be thought of as inputs and sinks can be thought of as outputs. *Files and databases* are represented by horizontal bars on the data-flow diagram.

Warnier-Orr, entity-relationship, and data-flow diagrams are by no means the only methods of developing a data model. Developers' choices are many and run the gamut from state-transition diagrams to decision trees to flow charts. The three discussed in this chapter, however, are the most usable in the context of developing an enterprise model for use as a baseline for the integration plan.

Create a Data Dictionary (Repository)

Since data dictionaries form the underpinnings of the data-flow diagrams, the creation of the data dictionary will be more or less automatic as the process proceeds.

There has been much discussion about the necessity of the data dictionary. Most data base managers come with them. But it has long been recognized that individual data dictionaries as components of database managers do little to assist the organization in the development of an enterprise-wide data dictionary. Individual data dictionaries track data within a database, but ignore data stored in different file structures and located on different hardware and software platforms.

Information technology groups have long realized the need of a global data dictionary which would have the capability of storing information on every element of data the organization utilizes, regardless of location or type of data structure. These global data dictionaries have come to be known as the corporate data repository.

Even though automated tools for the generation of enterprise-wide data repositories have been available through several leading edge firms for quite some time, it wasn't until IBM announced their entry into the CASE marketplace that data repositories really have taken flight. AD/Cycle (short for application development cycle) is a set of integrated tools and techniques that encompass the entire application development cycle—from enterprise modeling to implementation of the system. Central to AD/Cycle is the Data Repository. Since it captures and stores all the data for an organization, regardless of the system it is utilized in, it is here that a business is able to document objects, and its relationships, which will describe the business's critical success factors.

Availability of a central data repository is a key factor in any successful integration plan. Knowing what database, files, reports, and fields are being used in common can greatly expedite integrating and then streamlining systems.

Make the Integration Decisions

Once the enterprise model is finished and a complete picture of the organization is available, it becomes possible to compare the interrelationship between business functions from the perspective of the interrelationship between data. There can be several possible, and simultaneous, conclusions to this study.

There Are Business Functions That Require Data That Is Not Now Being Obtained from Other Business Functions. Modelling the business functionality of the enterprise clearly shows a relationship between two or more business functions. Source data from these business functions should be made available to the related business functions but is not currently available. There may be more than one reason for this omission. The business unit that the business function is sourced in may not have this data flow automated. A second reason might be that the business unit that requires the data feed may not have an automated system to receive the data. Finally, both the sending and the receiving business unit may be automated, but it was not realized that the data flow between the two was beneficial.

There Are Business Functions Sending Data to Other Business Functions Which Is Not Required. Although there is a smaller possibility of this event occurring than the one discussed above, it is still possible. The idea of integration has been bandied about for years inside the inner sanctum of corporate data-processing departments. These groups have sometimes overzealously integrated systems which had no business being linked. The caveat here is not all systems require linkage for an effective integration plan to be in place. Linking extraneous systems is obviously not cost effective since the links cost to run and cost to maintain. Linkage of systems should never occur unless the business functions between the systems are linked. Information technology staff should not be the sole arbiter in this decision-making process.

Redundancies Exist Between Business Units Where the Same Data Is Being Tracked and Stored. From a review of the various models built in the previous steps, it should have become apparent if certain types of data are being stored redundantly at more than one corporate location. A common problem is the tracking of customer data. In most organizations, the customer has multiple points of entry into the company. It is entirely possible that each of these points of entry, or business units, stores its own record of customer information and interaction. Customers often interact directly with marketing, public relations, accounts payable, and sales departments.

Therefore, it would not be surprising to find that each of these departments had a database called customer master. Each customer master file stores somewhat similar information, with an emphasis on tracking those data elements that are necessary for that business unit. The potential dangers here are obvious. First, storing the same information in multiple locations increases the risk of data error when one file is changed and not another. Secondly, there is no global view of the customer available virtually eliminating any strategic use of the data. Finally, from a customer service perspective, it should be maddening for the customer to have to constantly repeat the same information to any number of people.

One industry where the redundancy problem has proven especially bothersome is the banking industry. Customers who open checking accounts oftentimes are required to fill out customer information anew when they apply for savings accounts or CDs or other financial instruments. Many banks today realize the potential problems and limintations of unlinked accounts, and have opted to build what they refer to as relationship banking systems. In banking systems such as these, the customer is tracked as a unit regardless of the number and types of accounts being held. This is advantageous for a number of reasons. From a customer service perspective, the customer sees all of his or her holdings on one integrated statement and more than likely can communicate with one banking representative about all of these accounts. From a marketing perspective, having all of the information on a customer available in an integrated file setup provides excellent marketing opportunities.

Global Data Exists Within the Enterprise That Is Not Being Adequately Transmitted Down to the Business Unit Level. It might become apparent that there exists data, either already automated or not as yet automated, that should be required viewing for all organizational staff. One example of this may be communications material that should be transmitted from senior management down to the middle-management level, but invariably gets lost in translation between hierarchical rungs on the ladder. In Chapter Seven, on Info-marketing, much room is given to the discussion of EIS (executive information systems). Many firms use the electronic mail function of EIS systems to transmit "morning report" type data which can consist of everything from late-breaking relevant news to profitability figures to project status reports.

In building the enterprise model and the related integration plan, it is important that the strategy team fully understand that information is more than just the data elements found on a file or a report. Information can take the form of notes jotted from a telephone call, senior staff meeting minutes, board meeting minutes, news wire information, and virtually anything else that an organization uses to become more competitive.

Plan and Prioritize

Deficiencies in the way the organization is currently integrated will, by now, have become readily apparent. It should also have become apparent by now that tackling the appropriate integration of business units is a massive undertaking, and one that will not be completed as a single project.

The strategy team should be reconvened at this time to consider alternative project plans that will serve to divide the integration plan into manageable units. Recalling Charles Popper's advice, it is necessary that these units be evolutionary as well. In other words, project B should logically follow project A in a sort of building-block approach to integration.

More than likely, a number of projects will be charted on the integration plan. Since it is doubtful that any corporation of the 1990s will have the capital needed to complete all projects, a priority should be assigned to each project listed. It is important to perform this task with the building-block principle in mind since it would be fruitless to assign a low priority to a project on which 10 other higher priority projects rely.

Finalize the Plan

Working their way through the steps in this plan will take the strategy and technical teams in the range of six months to a year, depending upon the size of the company and the complexity of the information flow.

Along the way a series of milestones will have been accomplished as a result of the analytical review of the business functionality of the organization:

1. A revised mission and statement of goals for the organization.
2. A revised mission and statement of goals for the individual business units.
3. A plan for the reorganization of business units, if appropriate.
4. A plan for the reorganization of business unit functionality, if appropriate.
5. An information (data-flow) model
6. An enterprise model synthesizing the business information captured in items one through four with the information tracked in item five.
7. A list of inadequacies of current systems in terms of:
   - redundancies
   - information not available in an automated mode
   - information available but not provided
   - and information provided but not required.

8. The integration plan encompassing items one through seven; project prioritizations and schedule.

There are many approaches to creating an integration plan. This last section describes a general approach which can be modified to fit with the individual organization's perspectives. Some companies might choose to use CASE tools, others might not; some companies might use data modeling, others might use some other technique. How this task is performed is not as important as the fact that it *must* be performed if the company is to reap the benefits of a streamlined, integrated approach to providing the technological underpinnings of the business.

Smart Companies Integrate to Compete

John Rockart, head of the Center for Information Systems Research at M.I.T.'s Sloan School would more than likely applaud the use of an integrative software framework such as Computer Associates. He is in the unique position to truly understand that the old methods of nonintegrated, nontalking systems aren't good enough anymore for an organization to compete, "The buffers of space, time, people, and inventory are gone, so you have to have the lubrication of information to get the flow going."

Ingersoll Milling Machine Company

One of the first companies to seize upon this principle was Ingersoll Milling Machine Company of Rockford, Illinois. Back in the 70s, Ingersoll was an extremely competitive machine tool producer, but increasing threats from outside were worrisome. That's when the head of systems and planning, George Hess, sold the chairman of Ingersoll on what was considered then a risky business. It was the business of integration.

Ingersoll's system was completed in 1982 at a cost of $5 million. It has helped. While half of American machine tool companies folded since the 1970s, Ingersoll's shipments multiplied over tenfold over the same period. They shipped nearly $500 million in 1990.

Ingersoll might have been the first of the manufacturing companies to make the push to integration, but it certainly wasn't the last. And the trend has caught on even outside of this country. Sony is looking to use integration to cut the time it takes to make and distribute products from 50 days down to 20 days.

Du Pont

Du Pont is probably one of the largest of companies jumping on the integration bandwagon. They have made a business decision to tie all of their 80 business lines, located in some 50 countries, together into a uniform information network. Du Pont expects this project to take about five years at a cost of $200 million dollars. This is a considerable expenditure, and risky, since the $200 million represents more than 25 percent of their annual information system budget.

Du Pont's requirements are trickier than most, since theirs is to be a global integrated system. For example, if a Du Pont salesperson in France wants to sell O rings to an auto company today the salesperson must look it up in a French catalog. When the Du Pont integrated system is on line by the mid-1990s, this same salesperson can look into a worldwide database and find not only what O rings are available, but also what products are being developed in the future and when they will be ready for delivery.

Du Pont started down their long road to integration about ten years ago when the company made the momentous decision to standardize all divisions to a standard of IBM mainframes and DEC and Hewlett-Packard minicomputers. Over time, Du Pont put into place other pieces of an integrative architecture such as a worldwide network linking 80,000 of its 146,000 employees and an executive information system that supports some 300 top executives with key numbers that are updated on a daily basis.

The plan over the next half decade is to merge each of these systems into a much expanded network, standardized on hardware and software. The move to standardize on IBM mainframes and DEC and HP minis was part of an effort to scale back on the proliferation of hardware and software that threatened to bog down the company. Another example of this was Du Pont's use of 40 different types of distributed control systems. These are the microprocessors that run the continuous processes such as refining oil and other sensing devices used in process control. Du Pont cut the 40 down to two.

Saturn

Perhaps the easiest way to integrate a company is from the ground up. That's how they did it at the Saturn plant. But then again, they had the luxury of building that plant from the bottom up. Saturn is General Motors' new small-car subsidiary. It had the luxury of being conceived as a computer-integrated enterprise. At Saturn, everything from designing to purchasing to manufacturing is tied together into one single corporate-wide database. The pieces that make up a Saturn car are designed on computers. The system then tells other Saturn departments what they must do for that part to be made. The Saturn system then goes on to schedule production.

This sort of integration goes a long way towards successful implementation of another trend, which is partnering. The Saturn plan is to link up with their top suppliers. This will enable a electronic path for orders and payments. In this way, once a car is built, a computerized record will follow it to the dealer and through its life until the car is junked. As long as the owner of the car continues to service it at a Saturn dealer, each service visit will become part of the Saturn database.

The real goal behind Saturn's ambitious plans are twofold: to run on slimmer inventories and to hang on to more customers. Saturn hopes that by providing good service at good prices, they will hang on to two-thirds of its customers for regular service and repairs after the warranty period. The norm is one-third. By keeping track of sales and customer preferences, as well as fine-tuning production, Saturn hopes to operate with a leaner 30- to 45-day supply of cars as opposed to the conventional supply of 60 days.

Mayday

Probably the key objective behind computer integration is speed. Getting products out there faster and better. A good case in point is Mayday, a $5-million-a-year machine tool shop. This Lewisville, Texas-based company specializes in the manufacture of bushings which are the metal sleeves that protect moving parts on aircraft.

Jim Nelson, Mayday's president, well understood the need for something to push his business ahead in an industry where everyone uses the same type of production equipment. His first step was to buy large-scale automated Japanese lathes for his plant. But as the plant became more productive, Nelson realized that he needed to automate some of the back-office processing so that the orders could be processed faster to keep up with the machines.

Mayday's integrated computer system today can quote prices when a customer calls in for an order. The customer need only give a specification and the Mayday computers can figure the costs of materials and machine time and quote a delivery date and price within a 30-second time period. The system works even if the part requested has never been made before. If the client places an order, the Mayday system automatically sends that customer a confirmation by fax or by mail. The system also begins the production process by automatically ordering materials and scheduling machine time. At every step of the production path, the Mayday system tracks the progress of the order. At the end, the system produces the shipping labels and invoices.

Integration or Re-engineering—Two Sides of the Same Coin

Mayday, Du Pont, and Saturn are at the opposite ends of the ease to integrate spectrum. According to Lynda Applegate, a Harvard Business School professor, the companies that can expect to have the hardest time integrating are the large ones that set up massive computer rooms back in the 1960s and 1970s. Their systems are often obsolete, but replacing them is costly and complex. It follows then that small companies such as Mayday are easier to integrate than such big companies as Du Pont; New companies, such as Saturn, are easier to integrate than old ones.

Some companies that are experiencing problems in pursuing a successful integration strategy have turned their attention to re-engineering. According to several surveys and polls taken by Computerworld, Andersen Consulting, and CSC Index, re-engineering is a *hot topic* for the 1990s. The question is: What is re-engineering and how is it different from what we are doing today?

Re-engineering is similar in goals to integration in that it hopes to improve speed, service, and quality through use of information technology. But where integration strives to utilize a somewhat longer term, evolutionary approach, re-engineering pushes for a dramatic, revolutionary change in the status quo. In fact, in some corners, the battle cry of re-engineering teams is, "Don't automate, obliterate."

Re-engineering couples the redesign of the information technology environment with the redesign of the business process. According to Tom Davenport, a consultant at Ernst & Young in Boston, "the organizational changes involved in re-engineering are both wrenching and difficult." It's also expensive. Because the tactic of re-engineering is a dramatic overhaul of the way business is done in a short period of time, costs are all up front. The bills for in-house resources and outside consultants can easily reach the seven-figure range.

Progressive Insurance Claims the Re-engineering Title

The list of movers into re-engineering is prestigious. Ford Motor, AT&T, Kentucky Fried, and Digital Equipment Corporation have all ventured forth into this technological no-man's land. While most are secretive about re-engineering cause and effect, Progressive Corporation has been very forthright in explaining their foray into this area.

Progressive, located in Mayfield, Ohio is an insurer who shares with the rest of the insurance industry the problem of skyrocketing expenses. Their goal in moving towards re-engineering was to increase profits and cut costs.

This was done by tackling one of the largest automation projects ever undertaken at Progressive. Their re-engineering goal was to build a claims processing system. Pacman, Progressive's Automated Claims Management System, got its start back in 1986 when senior executives realized that they had to make revolutionary changes if they were going to survive the often cutthroat competition in the automobile insurance industry.

As in many of the firms discussed in this book, Progressive saw the answer to their problems in building a system that would better service their customers. The system—which ultimately cost $28 million and took five years to build—was implemented in conjunction with a change in policy that dictated immediate response to all accidents—no matter how small.

Ultimately, the goal of the system was to automate every piece of paper involved in a claim to reduce the number of days it takes to move from claim to check. The first phase of the system was rolled out in July 1989. Underwriting for each policy is accomplished at the work-station level. An expert system is used which accurately assesses cost estimates and detects possible fraud.

In January of 1991, phase two of the system was implemented. The "immediate response" program began in selected test areas. In this program, adjusters are dispatched immediately to the scene of an accident often handing out a check right at the accident scene.

In Atlanta, adjusters work out of 12 vans which are equipped with personal computers and modems to link into the Pacman system back at headquarters. These roving vans are also equipped with a fax machine and a cellular telephone, permitting them to easily take claims information and then issue checks. They even make tow-truck calls and hotel reservations for stranded policy holders.

The use of Pacman and its tentacles out to those roving bands have dramatically altered the way Progressive runs its business. In the past, adjusters were tethered to a desk for most of the day. Today, they are out in the field with current and prospective policy holders. The changes felt by the adjusters were felt by the entire company as well. For the first time, the insurance agent was not in complete control. Some accommodation to power sharing with the claims adjuster had to be made. The rest of the company had to change gears as well, in moving from the traditionally slow pace of the insurance industry to a more reactively paced, aggressive survivor.

Who Should Re-engineer?

Some of you who read through the Progressive description of their foray into re-engineering might be somewhat confused. You might ask yourself, "If this is re-engineering, just how is it different from what we've always been doing?"

According to Jon Turner, director of the Center for Research on Information Systems at New York University, "There's not a great deal new here. More consultants will sell re-engineering services—the same services they sold before, only painted white."

So how is re-engineering different from traditional development? The answer is that it's not really different, in spite of all the hoopla. Re-engineering uses much the same techniques that a good developer uses when developing a new system or redeveloping an old one, except that the emphasis is different.

Emphasis on Work Flows. According to NYU's Turner, "Enlightened companies have always injected questions about work flows early in the process." This is right on target. The problem here, and the reason for the push to "re-engineering" is that this "enlightenment" really didn't happen until the middle of the 1980s. Through the 1970s and the early 1980s, hundreds of thousands of systems were built that did not reflect the *right* way of doing business. These systems merely automated the current paper flow. For the vast majority of companies these systems now constitute the information baseline that, collectively worth several billion dollars, is the basis of Paul Attewell's productivity paradox. Remembering what Harvard's Applegate advised about integration is equally true here. The older a company, the more stock it has already invested in information systems, the harder it is to design competitive systems. Perhaps the easiest approach, then, is to simply throw out the old and bring in the new.

Emphasize Business over Technology. Some who attempt to re-engineer by emphasizing work flows will fail miserably. Why? Because these organizations probably threw the ball into the information technology court. The process of re-engineering is business driven rather than technology driven. In fact, in those organizations that have successfully undergone this sort of radical transformation, IT executives rarely led the effort. Information technology's role is important to the process, but it is not at the center of it. This point was borne out when Xerox Corporation tried their hand at it. An eight-person team was created to define cross-functional processes ripe for re-engineering. These Xerox managers started the project thinking that the Information Technology department would play a large role in the work, but, as they progressed, they realized that they had overemphasized the role of technology in the process that they were performing. As Judy Campbell, director of Xerox's corporate business process puts it, "Originally our vision was more IT-focused. We began by thinking about the information flow. But we quickly found that the steps that come before automating are more critical. You've got to understand the strategic vision." One of the biggest of the re-engineering companies is Andersen Consulting based in Chicago. Bruce Johnson, director of Andersen's Center for Strategic Technology Research adamantly agrees that this process should concentrate its efforts on the business at the expense of technology, "IT assumes that if we share information, we'll get business integration, and that if we give information to top management, they'll make rational decisions. But passively moving information is insufficient for business integration."

Emphasis Is on Culture Change. Perhaps even more important than ensuring that work flows are adequately represented by computer systems is the emphasis on changing the culture of the organization to accommodate the changes that computerization brings. Progressive is a good example of this. The company spent an extra $1.3 million on training. This included videos, computer-based training, a 40-hour live training class, two user manuals, and support documentation. Progressive fully understood that the use of the new system, and the new policies surrounding the system, would dramatically alter the way each employee did his or her job. Progressive wanted these employees to be prepared.

Emphasis on Solutions in Reaction to Perceived Crisis. Perhaps the common denominator to most of the case histories one reads about in this area is that the push to re-engineering is precipitated by a perceived crisis. A sort of wolf at the door syndrome. According to Tom Davenport of Ernst & Young, "Companies with problems to solve invented re-engineering." Progressive's crisis was stiff competition, slow processing times, and increasing costs. They are fairly typical of the insurance industry which is moving aggressively towards re-engineering. The insurance industry is part of the larger financial services industry which is beset by the same problems. Deregulation, coupled with infiltration of vertical marketers and foreign competitors have forced the entire financial services industry to take a good long look at its aging portfolio of computing systems and consider new, and often radical, options.

The reason why re-engineering is being discussed within the context of this chapter on integration is because, in essence, the goal behind re-engineering is to better integrate the companies manpower to its computer power to achieve speed and profitability. In nearly every case study of re-engineering, you will read the description of a system built to integrate diverse functions, together with the data required to do the job. Hence, re-engineering can be thought of as one avenue—though not the only one—an organization can take to integration.

6
Infotrend #5: Outsourcing (The Inside Story)

Few other trends have attracted as much controversy and garnered as much publicity as outsourcing. As there are always two sides to an issue, each side has its own perspective and its own—often aggressive—spokespeople. On one side are the yea sayers who firmly believe in outsourcing as a way to reduce costs and gain the strategic advantage of a higher-caliber staff. On the other side, there's a growing legion of nay sayers who are convinced that outsourcing is an absolute admission of failure.

Outsourcing is not a new concept. Before the term was coined, the practice was referred to as "using a service bureau." In fact, this practice has been around for about as long as there have been corporate data centers. In the days before PCs, mainframe computers were—as they still are—expensive. Companies lacking the capital and/or technical skills to house their own information technology shops opted to "buy time" on a third-party computer. Once the price of computers dropped, and the PC became ubiquitous around the corporate landscape, the practice of buying time began to lose favor. In order for these service providers to survive, chameleon-like, they had to change their colors. Many began to specialize in a particular industry, not only delivering computer time, but also delivering specific application programs tailored to their clients' exacting needs.

The securities industry is a good example of this development. Not all securities firms are as big as Merrill Lynch. The vast majority of the several thousand securities firms have no computer, no computer expertise—nor do they want any. What they want to do is to concentrate on the business of making money. These firms rely on the service bureaus of companies such as ADP, located in Newark, New Jersey which has developed a stock of securities industry applications that rival, in terms of functionality, the largest of the blue-chip investment firms. Many firms rely on such service bureaus as ADP to better concentrate on obtaining the strategic objectives of their respective firms.

If this sounds vaguely like the current definition of outsourcing, you're right—but with a twist. Many of today's firms are considering outsourcing to better leverage their technical skill set and to better concentrate on the business of doing business.

The Yankee Group, a Boston-based consulting firm, estimates that by 1993, outsourcing will become a $50 billion dollar market. IBM, EDS, Andersen Consulting, among others, have jumped into what they consider to be an extremely lucrative market niche. This adds another side to the issue, making some insiders wonder whether this is another case of the cart driving the horse. Has demand for outsourcing been pumped up by these aggressive marketers looking for a niche and finding one in a sea of shrinking budgets but increasing expectations? Or is outsourcing a genuine, solid good idea whose implementation can lead to rich rewards for those who embark on its straight and narrow path? The answer is yes to both of these questions. Yes, aggressive market leaders are pushing mightily to create demand. And yes, outsourcing can lead to a greater reward. But not for all firms, only for those firms who understand that outsourcing should be only part of their information technology strategy, not all of it.

The ranks of the outsourced read like a who's who in business: Southeast Banking Corporation, located in Miami, with $13.4 billion in assets goes to IBM; First Fidelity Bancorp, of Lawrenceville, New Jersey, makes a $450 deal with EDS. The best case, however, is the very first case to make headlines. This honor goes to Kodak.

Eastman Kodak Puts IBM and DEC in the Picture

Kathy Hudson, Chief Information Officer of Eastman Kodak, is the eye at the center of the outsourcing storm. Voted CIO of the year in 1991 by *InformationWeek*, Hudson has been labeled savior and traitor in turn by her colleagues. Her decision to outsource much of her vast empire was the unleashing of the dam that let the outsourcing waters flow free.

In 1989 and 1990, Hudson signed three contracts that assigned Kodak's data center operations to IBM for 10 years, telecommunications operations and management to Digital Equipment Corporation and IBM for five years, and PC systems and services to Businessland for five years. Before Hudson's brave move, outsourcing was thought of as a last-ditch strategy taken by

companies feeling the stress of a severe financial bind, or ones so misman-
aged that outsourcing was seen as the only way out of a quagmire. Eastman
Kodak was none of the above.

There's more to Hudson's story. Unfortunately, many executives read only
about this far, with the result that some organizations moved into outsourcing without actually considering the ramifications. Hudson did consider the
ramifications. Her reasons for recommending an outsourcing program were
not financial. Her reasoning was that she didn't consider information systems as a business that Kodak should be in. "We're trying to get out of the
day-to-day, nitty-gritty technology choices." Instead, Hudson intends to concentrate her resources on better understanding technology in general, so
that information technology can be brought to bear on business issues.

Hudson sees outsourcing as the first step in the road to developing a
technology platform for doing business on a global basis. She wants to build
an information technology infrastructure with the communications ability
sufficient to permit Kodak to do business on a global basis.

Hudson's plan is to develop a two-pronged infrastructure: a worldwide
telecommunications network to act as a corporate backbone; and a second
network to be composed of large-scale computing facilities. This latter network will link together the new Kodak data center, being built by IBM, with
two existing facilities in Europe.

Hudson's grand scheme calls for a total overhaul of Kodak's business
processes vis-à-vis information technology. Project Nova (for novel approach
to applications development) will eventually see the complete refitting of
Kodak's aging stock of software with totally new software and an emphasis
on interactive systems, relational databases, and working in real time.

Hudson will accomplish this feat in several ways. Her first task is to search
out a set of common, integrated software that will serve to speed the development of those interactive systems. Secondly, Kodak is "focusing on high
value-added systems." This means concentrating on software for manufacturing processes and operations that directly affect customers. Finally, Hudson
hopes to accomplish this large list of deliverables with the help of experts.

This help runs the gamut from re-engineering to redefining business
processes. To help Kodak redefine Kodak's business processes, Hudson has
brought in a team of prestigious consultancies including EDS, Price
Waterhouse, Andersen Consulting, CSC Consulting, and Coopers & Lybrand.

Hudson might outsource much of information technology-related work,
but one thing she would never outsource is the responsibility for making decisions. Responsibility for this massive change is couched in councils, cooperation, teams, committees, and consensus. She has created an information technology executive council that does most of the actual planning for innovation.
In fact, outsourcing was one of the many decisions on which Kodak employees
voted.

Hudson well understands that outsourcing is only one of many strategies that an organization can synthesize to gain the competitive upper hand. In some organizations, outsourcing is seen as an all-or-nothing proposition. Since executives in these organizations have never seen real value in information technology, outsourcing is used as a shield to dispense with it entirely. Kodak doesn't see it that way. They want to be able to control their information technology resources to be able to better leverage them. This doesn't mean that they intend to throw the baby out with the bath water. In spite of DEC, IBM, and Businessland involvement, Hudson is still very much in control of information technology—as well as the benefits of information technology.

Weighing the Risks of Outsourcing

Should a company outsource its marketing department? Most executives would vehemently answer, "By no means!" To that, Charles Popper asks a second question, "Why, then, would a company outsource its computer resource?"

In spite of all the brouhaha about this latest trend, and in spite of Eastman Kodak's much discussed launch into this area, the final figures are not in—not even for Kodak. Whether outsourcing turns out to be the panacea it is heralded to be won't be known for another few years, when all the results are tallied. So, those who are considering this option should be well aware that outsourcing is certainly not risk-free and, in some situations, might even be disadvantageous.

Since outsourcing is not for everyone, it is important to carefully weigh the advantages and disadvantages of this dramatic change for each individual corporation. To help you through the process, we'll go through a series of thought-provoking questions which just may help you make up your mind—one way or the other.

What Is the Real Objective Behind the Push to Outsourcing?   There are several reasons why organizations make the move to outsourcing. Perhaps the most popular reason is to save money. But other reasons are equally valid. The outsourcing vendor might possess a level of skill not able to be duplicated by the organization in question. A third, and equally valid, reason might be that the organization wishes to dispense with that part of the information technology unit that provides no added value. Whether or not the information technology unit can be split apart in this manner can only be decided on a case-by-case basis. Organizations which rely on heavy strategic analysis might consider dispensing with the "computer room" facility but maintaining their talented development staffs. On the other hand, a company such as NSCC (National Securities Clearing Corporation), whose sole function is to process the trades of the largest securities exchanges in the world, would have a hard time justifying the dispensing of their computer operations facility.

Will the Company Still Be Competitive After Outsourcing? Will the company be able to react fast enough to a competitive threat? Will it be able to react fast enough to take advantage of a perceived opportunity? These are the two questions that must be asked if a company is to ensure that, after outsourcing, it will still have the wherewithal to seize new opportunities and crush competitive threats. American Airlines experienced a competitive threat of this nature that required it to build a better mousetrap in an extremely short period of time. Reacting to heavy advertising from a competing airline, American Airlines used artificial intelligence to build a system that deals with over 10 million customer frequent flyer records. Had they outsourced their information technology unit, this coup de grace would not have been possible.

Can the Chosen Vendor Really Do All That It Says? For this most important decision on information technology, a quickie study and sign on the dotted line will not do. There is more than one vendor out there, so look at them all. Questions to ask: What kind of track record do they have? Have they serviced other clients in your industry? What kind of references do they have from the clients already using their services? Will they be able to run your systems the same as, or better than, you can run them? What kind of response time do they have on their equipment? What kind of turnaround time do they have in addressing problems? How user friendly are they? How responsive to the remaining, if any, technology staffers are they?

Can the Chosen Vendor Really Do All That It Says at a Lower Cost? If the vendor says it can do it all, then find out the cost—for the current year and for five years down the line. If possible, it would be wise to get them to commit to this projected budget. One great fear in the industry is that once a firm is outsourced and dismantles its internal operation, it just might find itself on the receiving end of higher prices—and with no bargaining chip.

What Kind of Checks and Measures Can Be Put into Place to Make Sure the Vendor Is Doing a Good Job? Just because a vendor is large, well-known, and generally does a good job doesn't mean that, in your case, the service will be satisfactory. There are several measures that can be taken that will ensure that your company gets the most value for the money. First, a vendor firm should never be left on its own. At least one member of the original technology team should remain behind at the company to provide a set of checks and controls. Second, an extensive checklist of these checks and controls should be created, and agreed to by all parties—*before* the lights are dimmed in the corporate data center. Factors to include are such things as response time, uptime, bug-defect rate, bug-correction rate, and customer service.

Will You Be Locked into Using Only Products That the Vendor Offers?

If you choose IBM as an outsourcing vendor, can you use DEC—or vice versa? If you want to start using a new software or hardware tool, will the vendor support it? In other words, will you retain the flexibility that you had when you were master of your operational universe?

What Part of the Operation Will Be Outsourced?

Will you outsource both data-center operations and development? Or only data-center operations? Will you be able to react fast enough to the competitive environment if you outsource one, the other, or both?

How Many Outsourcing Vendors Will You Use?

Eastman Kodak used three: DEC, IBM, and Businessland. Should you? Do you have the wherewithal to manage three interconnecting vendor relationships? Henry Pfendt, director of corporate information services for Eastman Kodak, admits that the biggest challenge in its outsourcing effort is the coordination of efforts among outsourcing vendors and different parts of the company. In addition to the hurdle of managing multiple teams, one must consider the ramifications of having to port applications from one hardware base to another.

If You Decide to Stop Outsourcing, Will You Be Able to Get Back on Track Quickly?

This is probably one of the most important questions a company can ask itself. Unfortunately, it is seldom asked. As mentioned, outsourcing is very much a new phenomena. No one yet knows whether or not outsourcing will, ultimately, prove beneficial to the firm over the long-term. Even though the idea of outsourcing certainly seems like it could boost a firm's competitiveness, if done thoughtfully and properly, the final tally is not in. Therefore, it is important to have a contingency plan that the company can use to jump-start its internal operations if it has to. This might mean keeping technical staff on board, perhaps, as advisors. These advisors would serve a double purpose. During the length of the outsourcing agreement, the advisors can work with the vendor(s) to ensure a smooth transition to outsourcing and then a smooth running outsourced operation. If the outsourcing arrangement is terminated, these same advisors would form the nucleus of a newly reconstituted internal technology department.

If You Outsource, Will You Be Able to Hire the Technology People That You Need Internally?   If the company entirely outsources its technology group, it will more than likely have a tough time recruiting experienced and talented technology staff at a later date. Technology people are attracted to technology environments, not companies. If no technology department exists in a company, officials will find it a hard sell to try to lure qualified candidates to what these candidates consider a technology desert.

What Recourse Do You Have If the Outsourcer's Equipment Fails with Resulting Damage to Your Business?   The contract between vendor and client must have a clause imposing stiff penalties on the outsourcer in this eventuality. Some clients even require vendors to take out insurance policies. Even if neither of these options are taken, it is strongly recommended that a formal, and documented, backup procedure be in place for each of the outsourced systems.

Perhaps the best tack for a company considering outsourcing to take, is to leverage the best of what a vendor offers with what the company itself offers. Eastman Kodak exemplifies this approach. They outsourced the dirty work of data-center operations while at the same time maintaining a skilled staff with which they are planning to implement CIO Hudson's vision of a global network.

Outsourcing Catches On

In spite of all the risks, outsourcing is catching on rapidly at a wide variety of U.S. organizations. The details of some of the agreements make for interesting reading and show a clear trend toward displacement of entire information technology groups. Reading through the plethora of case studies, including those highlighted below, it is possible to discern some interesting subtrends.

Many of the firms described below outsourced because they really had no alternative. The vast majority of early participants to this trend outsourced simply to reduce IT expenses. However, the severe recessionary state of the economy, at the start of the trend in the late '80s and early '90s, may account for this. Another notable subtrend is that the companies who seem to derive the most benefit from outsourcing are the financially solvent, mid-sized companies.

Mid-sized companies, no matter how solvent they are, usually do not have the funds to invest heavily in IT; therefore, the competitive advantage that

IT can offer is minimized. But if these same companies can "jump on the bandwagon," so to speak, of a high-tech service provider, then advanced IT tools and techniques, not available to the mid-sized company before, are now instantly available. Thus, in an outsourcing environment, it is quite possible for a mid-sized company to bypass the growing pains that, historically, other firms have had to go through before they were able to derive competitive advantage from their stock in IT.

A third subtrend involves such large, solvent companies as Eastman Kodak, which appears to be leveraging its own internal IT expertise with that of one or more outsourcers so that the company can actually "have the best of both possible worlds." That is, such companies can invest their time and resources in developing strategic IT applications, while the outsourcer takes care of the daily business of running the corporate data center. Most large companies understand how beneficial this is, since they constantly bemoan the fact that they are too busy "putting out fires" to spend any time on the creation of strategic systems. Let's look at several real-life experiences with outsourcing.

Continental Airlines

Continental Airlines, in desperate need of cash, recently signed a 10-year systems management agreement worth at least $2.1 billion to the outsourcing vendor. The agreement called for the outsourcer to assume responsibility for all of Continental's information technology services.

This particular outsourcing agreement is particularly significant because Continental outsourced more than its in-house data-processing department—it outsourced its airline reservations subsidiary as well. Continental's System One is a computer automation services company which provides worldwide information management as well as data processing and telecommunications services to the airline and travel-related industry. As one of the world's largest suppliers of computerized reservations, flight operations, and passenger-handling systems, System One serves nearly 8,000 travel agency and airline customers.

Outsourcing such an important part of a company's business might be beyond comprehension in light of the risks already discussed. This transfer of power only becomes understandable when one remembers the financial bailiwick in which Continental found itself. In fact, the outsourcing papers were only signed after Federal Bankruptcy Court Judge Helen Balick issued a court order authorizing the companies to proceed with their relationship. This reason for outsourcing would appear to lend credence to the belief that the only firms engaging in it are either poorly managed or in financial jeopardy.

Meritor Savings Bank

When Meritor, the nation's oldest savings bank and seventh largest thrift, signed a 10-year outsourcing agreement, its grand plan was to find a third party that would handle all of its systems development and maintenance. As was Continental, Meritor was sagging under a huge load of debt. With the country just beginning to come back from a recession and the S&L industry facing some particularly tough times, outsourcing looked to be one way to improve stability and build a stronger capital position. In Meritor's case in 1989, the bank was sinking fast. It had 83 branches in the Philadelphia area, $21 billion in assets, and $10 billion in deposits. But its capital position was well below the 6.5 percent federal regulatory requirements. The warning signs were ominous.

The vision, back in 1989, was to trim costs and boost capital assets and profitability. Andersen Consulting, which at that time did not itself offer outsourcing services, recommended outsourcing as a solution since there was no possible way that Meritor could further scale back its in-house information systems operation. It seemed, at the time, that the only possible solution was outsourcing. But there would be some caveats to the competitive request for proposal that Meritor placed out into the marketplace. First of all, the numbers had to look right. Outsourcing would have to dramatically pare the budget to be able to boost Meritor back into a stable financial position. Next, the vendor chosen for outsourcing would have to find positions for each of the technology staffers eliminated in the process. Third, the vendor would have to have prior experience in banking.

Meritor took the right steps to keep alive. Outsourcing of the Meritor development group was only a first step. Meritor followed this dramatic move two years later with a movement of its Philadelphia data center to a regional site supported by the outsourcing vendor.

As a result of outsourcing, over a two-year period, Meritor actually achieved its goal, saving nearly $9 million and showing greater profitability on their annual report.

Zale Corporation

Zale Corporation, famous for its mall jewelry stores, is another of the debt-laden companies which have sought solace in the arms of an outsourcer.

In the spring of 1991, Zale signed a 10-year outsourcing contract with IBM's new outsourcing subsidiary, Integrated Systems Solutions Corporation (ISSC), worth somewhere in the vicinity of several hundred million dollars.

Zale's problems began in 1985 when a leveraged buy-out of the privately held firm left it looking at $970 million in long-term debt by December of 1990. Zale's move to outsourcing was seen, by some observers, as an attempt to get some cash up front to pay off some of that debt. This "cash" arrangement is possible if the outsourcing vendor pays a premium for the equipment it buys from the company.

In Zale's case, ISSC is most certainly making some sort of payments to Zale, but the company insists that their long-term debt wasn't a primary factor in moving to an outsourcing arrangement. What really attracted them, according to David Karney, VP for IS at Zale, "was the financial side of their proposal and the future benefits from a partnership with IBM."

ISSC's responsibility will be to oversee Zale's IBM mainframe and six local area networks as well as a multimillion dollar contract with AT&T for point-of-sale computers at Zale's 2,000 stores.

Consistent with most other outsourcing arrangements, someone will remain behind at Zale to oversee applications development and manage the contract with ISSC. The 90 Zale employees who manned the data center were offered jobs with ISSC.

Sun Oil

As did many other companies, Sun Company had expanded mightily during the early '80s. It had even created a subsidiary, Sun Information Services, with the express notion of selling information services. During the oil industry's downturn, however, Sun needed to find a leaner image of itself—which included selling off Sun Information Systems as well as another subsidiary, Sun Exploration and Production Company. The net result was that the Dallas data center was left with just too much capacity.

As a result, Sun Company, Inc., worth about $11 billion today, decided that it would turn over control of its mainframe systems to Andersen Consulting. This $200 million contract calls for Andersen, over the next 10 years, to manage Sun's computer processing and network services.

To accomplish this, Andersen purchased Sun's Dallas computer center for $15 million. Consistent with many other deals, Andersen also agreed to hire on the 70 employees working at the Dallas site.

The Reasons for Outsourcing

EDS is *the* largest vendor of outsourcing arrangements. It's also been in the business the longest, so of all the vendors, its perspective is perhaps the most notable. In analyzing its customer base, it has noted that there appear to be four main drivers of outsourcing[1]:

---

[1] This section is excerpted with permission from a speech given by Gary J. Fernandes, Senior Vice President EDS, at the INPUT executive conference, "Outsourcing of Information Systems," (Washington, D.C., June 8, 1990).

1. The gap between the expectation of IT that's been created in the minds of the executives and the value that's been achieved

2. The "demystification" of the computer in particular and IT in general

3. The trend toward focusing on core business issues

4. The increased legitimacy of outsourcing as a function of the number of major providers who have come to the market

The first driver of outsourcing is the considerable gap between the expectation of IT that has been created in the minds of the executives and the value that's been achieved. Here's how IT is all too often positioned in the mind's eye of a senior level executive:

> I know that information technology is integral to the success of my company. Accordingly, every year I, along with my colleagues, decide to increase our IT budget so that we can create bigger and better IT systems for the good of our enterprise. In return for this annual budget increase (sometimes disproportionate to the rest of my cost structure), I expect to likewise increase the competitive advantage that I gain through the use of IT.
>
> To my chagrin, I've found no real increase in productivity, no real reduction in my cost of goods or services, and no marked increase in quality over and above that of my competitors that I can attribute to these budget increases. Rather than delivering the promised competitive advantage, this technology investment has given me, at best, competitive parity.

These, and other unrealized expectations of a technological promised land for the corporation, bring to light the fact that technology, in and of itself, cannot and should not be expected to create competitive advantage.

The second outsourcing driver mentioned is the demystification of technology. Twenty years ago, information and communications technologies were the province of experts and experts only. But today the doors have opened up, effectively demystifying this once enigmatic and arcane technology. We now have an everyman's approach to technology—or at least every man can access and use technology.

This gradual demystification of IT eradicated fear about the technology and increased its acceptance by both the leaders and employees of the corporation. This, in turn, meant that the benefits of IT could become more readily apparent, and more readily available to the prevailing mass of non-technocrats in the corporation.

Once the use and the benefits of IT became comparatively easy to identify and understand, the emphasis on IT changed. Companies began to view IT not as a mysterious yet necessary evil, but as a strategically important element of their business.

The third driver, or catalyst, of this outsourcing issue is the current trend toward turning valuable management resources away from support functions and focusing them instead on core business issues.

Frank Borman, in trying to diagnose the many problems driving Eastern Airlines into a gradual descent of megacompany malaise and ultimate bankruptcy, determined that one of the contributing factors was a lack of focus on core business issues. He found that Eastern had diverted such a high degree of attention and resources to catering, to turbine engine reconditioning, and to other ancillary activities, that it had lost sight of its primary mission: transporting people from one city to another.

The fourth, and final, driver of outsourcing is approached with a large degree of reluctance—and perhaps even some amount of skepticism. The increase in outsourcing is, in part, a reflection of the number of major companies which have recently entered the market as outsourcing suppliers—hung out their outsourcing shingle, so to speak.

We should also be aware of an issue that's sometimes mistakenly labeled a driver of outsourcing. An issue that, when used as the basis of an outsourcing decision, often creates more problems for, than solutions to, the outsourcing dilemma. This is the attempt to use outsourcing solely to reduce costs of an enterprise's information technology operations.

The problem is that all too often this approach masks the true strategic value of outsourcing, in serving the true business needs of the enterprise. At worst, it ignores, and at best thinly veils, attempts to direct outsourcing toward improving one of the three critical competitive elements of any business: quality of goods or services, cost of goods or services, and customer responsiveness.

Perhaps the truth—that everybody knows but nobody speaks—is that while cost might be a reason to outsource, it's never the only reason. A louder truth, though—that more and more industry leaders as well as IT users are growing bold enough to speak—is that competitive utility is a reason to outsource. Decreasing cost of goods or services is a reason to outsource; and improved customer responsiveness is another reason.

This focus on the strategic application of IT yields us yet another benefit, bringing us perhaps one step closer to the panacea so often promised by IT. The message to outsourcers is clear: Our success can only be achieved through our customers' *business success.* And that is as it should be.

Insourcing and the Value of People

A success factor most often cited by those traveling along the outsourcing route is that of eliminating in-house data processing; the organization benefits from higher-tech hardware and software at the provider's site. Even though rarely verbalized, the fact is that most companies are also buying the higher-caliber personnel at the outsourcing provider's site as well.

Most of these case histories are representative of outsourcing agreements in general, in that the outsourcing provider agreed to hire on staff that was being displaced by outsourcing. This presents somewhat of a paradox since it raises the question of, "How can a higher-caliber staff be secured if outsourcing providers continue to indiscriminately hire on those that would be displaced?"

This rather thorny issue has several side issues as well. Don Winski, as CIO of Time Warner, has said that the only jobs worth having in the future—for people in the information technology field—would be with the manufacturers of hardware and/or software and with systems integrators (which is an euphemism for outsourcing providers). With all the merger and acquisition activity taking place today and the industry's aggressive push towards outsourcing, the only remaining interesting technology jobs would be in these quarters.

Andersen Consulting reportedly hires its technology staff right out of the hallowed halls of academia. These young college graduates are then sent out for intensive Andersen-type training, where they learn the methodologies and tools that will enable them to participate fully in Andersen's consulting practice. The "green" skills of these junior consultants are made more palatable to customers by leveraging them with inclusion of a partner into the mix. Thus, on any given project run by a consulting firm, what you usually find are many inexperienced but exceptionally bright consultants, one or two experienced managers, and one senior level partner. This mix of people may not always reflect the expectation of obtaining "higher-caliber" people when an operation is outsourced.

On the other end of the spectrum are those staffers that are being outsourced. These staffers, unlike Andersen recruits, usually do not have (advanced) degrees from prestigious universities nor the benefit of Andersen's expert intensive training program. These are the people who, to put it bluntly, are often blamed for the sorry state of a company's technological infrastructure. In the paradox described above, what is questionable is whether or not it is actually possible to obtain higher-caliber staff if the outsourcing providers are being inundated by the lower-caliber staff.

To pursue this line of tricky reasoning, consider this: since outsourcing, these hungry new providers have been quite agreeable in hiring on those the company considering outsourcing would have to otherwise let go. In fact, outsourcing providers are benefiting from hiring these people since: (a) these staff have the experience level to run the systems the outsourcing provider is taking over, and (b) these outsourcing providers are taking over so many contracts at this time that they need to staff up. But, eventually, the rule of diminishing returns will set in. This can happen in several ways. Eventually, the outsourcing provider will learn the business of the organization being outsourced. With experience comes a diminishing need for large numbers of staff. Once the outsourcing provider becomes expert in a particular industry, the need to hire any additional staff at all is negated, since the provider already has the experience level needed and is fully staffed. If one projects over time, it is clear that a time will come when outsourcing providers will no longer accommodate the wholesale hirings of these displaced staff members.

Of course, over this same time frame, the experience level of an outsourcing provider necessarily becomes generic. Economies of scale for these providers will preclude them from continuing to specifically address the needs of an individual client without that client paying a premium price.

Since outsourcing is so new, we don't know exactly what we're in store for 10 years down the line. Outsourcing could indeed be the panacea the industry has long sought, or it could turn out to be a huge mistake in which the industry is replacing tailored systems run by experienced pros with generic systems run by those with generic experience.

It is clearly an anomaly that so many companies who push for outsourcing blame their technology staffs for nonproductivity in-house, and then laud these same people as more productive as soon as they're on board with the outsourcing provider. Interestingly, it turns out that they are, indeed, more productive.

If an outsourcing provider can turn staff considered unproductive into productive and valued employees, then why can't those firms considering outsourcing? Perhaps this is a viable alternative to the outsourcing trend. In fact, it has a name—insourcing.

Insourcing is a new term in the industry and, because of this novelty, has taken on several meanings. On one hand, insourcing is an expression used by those who vehemently oppose the concept of outsourcing. In this context, insourcing means retaining the data-center operations, development, and everything else related to technology "inside" the organization. A second meaning aligns itself more closely to the gist of what an outsourcing provider supplies its customers. In this context, insourcing means setting up an organization within the company that acts as an internal service bureau—functioning in much the same way as an outsourcing provider.

Whichever way insourcing is brought to bear in an organization, it does have its benefits. Systems run are tailored specifically to the organization and staff is truly experienced in the very business of that same organization.

However, insourcing requires a changed view of technology staff. Few organizations put its technical staff through as intensive a training program as Andersen and other such service providers do. In fact, over the last 10 years, there has been a marked decrease in the training expenditures per staff member that an organization is willing to invest in its technology staff. This follows the decade-long decline in employer-employee mutual commitment, which reached a nadir in the wholesale layoffs of the late '80s and the early '90s. Productivity will continue to decline as long as the employee does not sense a loyalty or commitment to his or her future in the organization. With increasing commitment comes increasing productivity, followed by increasing competitive advantage.

Thus, insourcing would appear to provide a route to increasing competitive advantage. By committing to the well-being and, especially, the training of an employee, the organization will reap advantages in excess of its expenditures in this direction. Nowhere is this truer than in technology jobs.

It is particularly distressing that a company that expresses a need to better leverage its assets by moving into more high-tech areas, would prefer to hire experienced staff than train staff already on board. This leads to a problematic dichotomy. On the one hand, the company is investing in a staff of higher-priced (Andersen-like), advanced technology gurus. On the other hand, this same company is spending millions of dollars a year on employing able-bodied workers, ignoring their abilities for self-improvement, all the while shunting them off to do less stimulating maintenance. The dichotomy is that those high-end staff members by no means make up for the lack of skills of the low-end staff members. In creating a split of this sort, the company can never hope to be truly competitive. A company must leverage all of its resources if it is to take advantage of technology—not just some of them.

This is a rather roundabout way of saying that a company must be prepared to invest in its technology staff. While there will always be people who grow so comfortable in their environments that they wish to stay stuck in it forever, the vast majority of technology people love to learn and want to learn.

The "skilling" of employees requires a certain amount of managerial planning and influence. Project Leaders and Project Managers are the ones often held responsible for training. But these same people are often left out of the communications loop when long-term plans are laid out. If the skilling of technology staff is to be done in such a way as to impact the firm then the following items should be taken into consideration.

The Managers Involved in Setting Up Training Programs Must Be Included in the Long-Term Planning Loop.   In this way, if it is decided that three years down the line a new process control system will be initiated, training can begin at an appropriate time for the technology staff to develop the skill set necessary for this project.

It Is Recommended That at Least 10 Days of Training Be Provided Every Technology Staff Member, Every Year.   This is not unreasonable.

A further refinement would permit technology staff members to accrue training days over the course of one or more years as they do now with sick days. An extra bonus could be factored in, if a certain number of sick days can also be used toward this end.

Technology Staff Should Be Reviewed on Their Participation in Training Programs.   To motivate those who have reservations about taking additional training, an section of their yearly performance appraisal could be given over to training involvement.

Institute Mentorships.   Most company's technology staffs are clearly split between the "advanced technology" groups and everybody else. Joining these two groups together through a mentoring program can provide two-way advantages. In this scenario, the mentor is the staff member from advanced technology who meets with a staff member from the traditional IT group on a periodic basis for a transfer of skills. This is a two-way process, since the advanced-technology staff member reaps some benefits as well. Usually, these types are set apart from the rest of the business. As a result, they know little about the business. This is a service that the traditional IT staff member—usually well-steeped in the business needs of his or her clients—can provide to the advanced-technology staff member.

Incentive to Use.   This is the technology manager's equivalent of the salesman's premium. Let's look at an example of trying to provide incentive to programmers to become more productive by using the techniques of reusable code. If you talk to the average programmer, he's going to shrug his shoulders and say, "Why should I bother trying to achieve high levels of reusability—it doesn't buy ME anything." In fact, in some organizations the programmer will get penalized because he only gets measured on the number of lines of new code that he writes. NASA took a different stance. To foster reusability—and ultimately a lower-cost end product—NASA contractors are being paid to develop quality software. They're also being paid to develop software that can be put into a library, and paid again to take things out of a library to use them. Other organizations pay programmers a royalty on reusable modules that they've put into a library.

Although it is true that many U.S. organizations, during the '80s, went out on a hiring spree which needs to be corrected, the level of consolidations today appears excessive.

Industry after industry is being hit by shutdowns, layoffs, mergers, and a general downsizing. Analysts have usually lauded these moves as necessary for a firm, the main allegiance of which should be the shareholder rather than the employee.

Since this is a very new phenomena, however, nobody can predict accurately where we will ultimately end up—as leaner, meaner, more competitive organizations? Or as organizations whose productivity rates plummet in parallel to overzealous attempts to jump aboard the downsizing bandwagon?

Downsizing—meaning in this case cutting down the number of staff—is not always done in the most expeditious manner. In many organizations, political clout and personalities get in the way of performing this exercise in a manner consistent with achieving the desired result of that leaner, meaner organization.

As the payroll plummets and staff are asked to take on more responsibility (many take on these additional burdens due to fear of the same fate that befell their teammates), what have we really achieved? What can we expect to achieve in the future? And finally, have we helped or hindered our competitive edge?

7

Infotrend #6: Info-Marketing Using Information Technology to Gather Intelligence

The term *competitive intelligence* is very much on the tip of the tongue in today's economic maelstrom. The majority, if not all, of American companies collect some sort of information about the direction that their competitors are taking. What few realize, though, is that competitive intelligence is really only part of a larger view of the business world we live in. This view is called business intelligence.

Competitive Intelligence is a subset of Business Intelligence—and, as a subset, it is not the complete picture. Herbert E. Meyer, noted author and consultant, as well as past vice-chairman on the U.S. National Intelligence Council, calls business intelligence the corporate equivalent of radar. As with radar, the business environment must be continually scanned to avoid danger and seize opportunities. Meyer describes business intelligence as the other half of strategic planning. Once a plan is completed, business intelligence monitors its implementation and assists in making strategic course corrections along the way.

Business intelligence is not just looking at your competition, but seeing all the changes around you, including politics, consumer affairs, and even environmental issues. All of these influence the long-term future of the company. Any company. In any industry. The use of competitive intelligence transcends industry boundaries and, if used correctly, provides the organization with an immediate advantage.

No two companies will implement a competitive intelligence system in the same way. The rest of this chapter will be split between case studies of the best of these systems and explaining how to build your own competitive intelligence system.

Quaker Oats Marketing
Sword Slays a Paper Dragon

Perhaps the department with the biggest need to digest huge amounts of information is corporate marketing. Aside from the product or service being marketed, it is the efforts of the marketing department that will make the biggest impact on the profitability of a company. It stands to reason that providing marketers with the appropriate tools and techniques will most certainly enhance their efforts, and in doing so—the bottom line. These tools and techniques make up the foundation for a trend that I like to call *info-marketing.*

The Quaker Oats Company is one of a growing legion of companies that see the relationship between smart marketing and increased profitability. The Quaker Oats marketing decision system, built specifically for use by the marketers to assist in making marketing decisions, is indicative of the company's understanding of the importance of the role of technology in their marketing efforts.

The Quaker Oats Company, located in Chicago, Illinois, is a leading multibillion dollar international food manufacturer of cereals, pancake mixes, snacks, frozen pizzas, and pet foods. Over the past several years, Quaker has embarked on an aggressive acquisition campaign, resulting in the establishment of several new sales forces and the introduction of new product lines.

From a marketing perspective, this diversity of products makes it difficult to perform the necessary marketing analysis. All of these forces led Quaker to build an automated decision-support tool. With its plethora of functions and ease of use, *Mikey* makes a good first example of the first level of info-marketing tools—the executive information system.

Mikey

Quaker Oats built a PC-based system that they dubbed "Mikey." The system gets its name from the famous Quaker Oats commercial where a finicky little boy finally tries a Quaker cereal and likes it. At corporate headquarters, and at sales offices around the country, Mikey is currently being used for on-line access and ad hoc query capability of large corporate marketing bases. Due to its distributive nature, Mikey has become Quaker's central coordinating facility for the creation and distribution of marketing plans, production requirements, and financial estimates.

Using pcExpress and Express MDB, from the Chicago-based marketing tool vendor Information Resources, Quaker built a robust marketing system the components of which include business review reporting, marketing planning, ad hoc reporting, general information, and utilities. The business review reporting component produces standard reports based on the company's historical sales and comparisons with competitors. The 10 standard reports can be generated for an extensive range of market, brand, time and measure selections, or time aggregations.

The ad hoc reporting component allows marketing users to essentially write their own marketing analyses programs. This permits them to look at data and create their own brand or market aggregates.

The market-planning module permits the marketing department to review the marketing performance of any particular product. Data stored, and able to be analyzed here, include such things as package weight, cases, the cost of the product to the company, price, and advertising budget. Mikey understands the relationships among all of these items. In a planning mode, if marketing staff decides to alter one of these variables—for example, package weight—the system will automatically change the other relevant components in the mix.

The Value of Executive Information Systems

Executive Information Systems (EIS) are hands-on tools that focus, filter, and organize information to make more effective use of that information. The principle behind these systems is that by using information more effectively and more strategically, a company can ultimately increase profitability.

The goals of an EIS should be:

- to reduce the amount of data bombarding the executive.
- to increase the relevance, timeliness, and usability of the information that reaches the executive.
- to focus a management team on critical success factors.
- to enhance executive follow-through and communication with others.
- to track the earliest of warning indicators: competitive moves, customer demands, and more.

Comshare is an EIS-vendor located in Ann Arbor, Michigan. Their executive information system tool—appropriately named EIS—is used by hundreds of companies involved in info-marketing. Since Comshare's EIS is representative of this class of info-marketing tool, we will spend some time in discussing its attributes.

Comshare's EIS is actually a series of tools, the first and foremost of which is the Briefing Book^{tm}. Basic to many paper-based executive reporting systems is what is known as the monthly briefing book. Some companies call this the monthly project control report, while others call it an executive summary. Whatever the semantics, its purpose is the same—to advise the senior executives of critical issues and the status of key projects within the organization. The problem with the paper reports is that it usually arrives too late for preventative or corrective action. In addition, the format of the report is too rigid for an in-depth investigation. The worst problem is that the executive can't ask it questions to get more detailed information. Thus, the briefing book is supplemented in most companies with monthly status meetings, just to respond to these deficiencies.

This lack of information results in an organization's executives spending approximately 80 percent of their time in attending these status meetings. If one adds in the trickle-down requirement of rolling information down to the staff level, then these additional "one-on-ones" and roll-down meetings add overhead to a firm that forces it to spend more time *meeting* about being competitive than actually *being* competitive.

In many companies, at least part of this problem is being addressed by automating the briefing book. Comshare's Briefing Book can be implemented in a couple of different ways:

As a menu of items corresponding to tabs in a paper briefing book or goals in a budget write-up; or

Starting with a top-level executive report using the system's color-coded exception reporting facilities. With this approach, "bad" variances can be colored red. Touching the red variances results in another screen being displayed—either of component variances, textual explanations, trend graphs, or a combination of any one or more of these.

There are many advantages to an automated briefing book. Each executive can receive a personalized selection of reports and charts, reducing the amount of irrelevant information he or she sees. In addition, each executive can set up variances responding to acceptable tolerances. For example, an automobile executive wishes to flag any line of car in which the company's market share falls below 25 percent. Since executives often like to see facts in context, automated briefing books should have the capability of comparing information on a competitive or historical basis. For example, looking at current sales data as the latest event in a continuum indicates whether sales volume is heading up or down. Similarly, executives usually want to compare information with goals, budgets, and forecasts as well as with information stored on the competition.

Perhaps the biggest obstacle to upwards reporting is that the senior executive is only privy to information on a monthly basis. In an age of stiff competition but easy access to distribution channels, a fast reaction time to an event may make a major difference to the bottom line. This "information float," as it is sometimes called—the time it takes for information to wend its way up through the channels to senior management—can be nearly eliminated by use of an automated system.

Comshare's Execu-View^{tm} runs in conjunction with the Briefing Book. Once a significant variance is identified within a Briefing Book report, the executive must be able to investigate the variance with much more detail and from multiple perspectives. It's not enough to know that at the consolidated level, profits have deviated from goal by 7 percent. Some business units might be over goal and others well under goal. The executive must have some facility to answer questions such as: What makes up the deviation? Is it a faltering distribution channel? Are there competitive problems in an established product? Is it a failure in a particular geographic area? In a particular product line? Or in one customer grouping?

To do this, a multidimensional information base designed to support the managerial perspective of financial performance must be made available somehow. Execu-View permits the encoding of definitions of economic behaviors tailored specifically for this viewpoint. For example, in taking sales and expense data from the general ledger into a product profitability model, allocation rules are used to prorate cross-product costs, such as sales and overhead. The result is financial data with a layer of strategic perspective.

In addition to this filtered information flow, the Comshare model of an executive information system comes equipped with a calculator which permits the addition of new columns, calculation of ratios, trends, and even variances. Add to this a connection to the Dow Jones Newswire through Comshare's Newswire^{tm}.

Sun Goes for the Golden EIS

Few realize how large a company Sun Company is. As a major domestic refiner of oil and natural gas, Sun has been a supplier of fuel needs to Americans for over 100 years. But this $11.1-billion-dollar company also produces and markets petroleum products worldwide.

With five major refiners and six divisions, senior management's goal is to get this wide range of products to market while being as flexible as possible to maximize their service and profits. To do this, Sun's steering committee, consisting of the top executives from its six divisions as well as executives from Finance, Planning and Systems, and Administration understood that they needed to develop a common model of the entire enterprise so that division executives could be aware of the impact of their decisions on other divisions.

Sun built their "Enterprise Information System" using Comshare's EIS. Sun's EIS, which allows cross-functional sharing of information across organization boundaries, is a veritable fountain of filtered information. It includes sections showing operational information for each of the six divisions; daily operational information supplied by the general manager of each of the five refineries; analysts' interpretations combining competitive, market, and internal information. There is also an information feed from external information including commercial listings of oil prices, and news summary stories about the industry containing insights not likely to be found in a general trade journal.

According to Ken Fulmer, Manager of Product Management in the Planning and Systems Group, "The ability to compare ourselves to the competition in the external world is absolutely a key part of our system. In order for our executives to stay abreast of rapidly changing market conditions, they want to see not only the company's internal data, but also industry data that's external."

The biggest benefit of the EIS and the whole enterprise concept at Sun has been that the executives have a better understanding of what is going on in their business. Because each executive sees the same information, including the reports used by the top executives in each of the other divisions, they have better trust, greater communication, and a more complete understanding of the situations that exist in the other parts of the company. As a group, management can better identify which challenges to react to and how best to deploy resources for the greatest efficiency and profitability for the organization as a whole.

Du Pont Uses EIS to Go Global

With over $35.5 billion in revenues generated outside the United States alone, E.I. du Pont de Nemours has recognized early on the need to operate effectively in global markets. Thus, globalization has become a major objective for the entire company. Part of that push has been the development of global information systems. "Key to Du Pont's management philosophy is the belief that the effective utilization of global information technology is fundamental to maintaining a competitive position today, and even more so in the future," says Pete Trainor, Manager of Du Pont's Global Financial Database Project.

Most companies, Du Pont among them, store information in departmental databases. In a company such as Du Pont, this compartmentalizes, or fragments, information in a way that renders it unusable as viewed from a global perspective. This is where Trainor's Global Database comes in.

Trainor devised a three-pronged approach to develop Du Pont's global system. First, was developing the infrastructure; that is, establishing the networks necessary to support the global system. Perhaps the hardest task was to get the house of information in order. This meant setting standards to achieve data consistency and information resource management. The third component was to develop an interface that was insightful and easy to use.

The very first system put into production was Du Pont's Executive Information System (DEIS). Using Comshare's EIS this global system is now in use by over 150 managers, directors, vice-presidents as well as the CEO. DEIS provides global access to over 18 critical areas of information, including key new strategic plans. As was the case at Sun, executives at Du Pont began to think on a organizational level rather than at a departmental level.

Frito-Lay's Hand-Held Decision-Support Miracle

Quaker Oat's use of a powerful decision-support tool is indicative of a trend that is catching on in the competitive arena of packaged goods. Although Quaker is probably one of the first companies to have introduced the concept of info-marketing, others are quick on their heels. Kraft USA, Proctor and Gamble, and RJR Nabisco are reportedly installing massive systems to track sales. But among all of these Goliaths, it is a David that has produced one of the most innovative info-marketing systems.

Frito-Lay, a subsidiary of Pepsico, makes corn chips, potato chips, and tortilla chips. This is an extremely competitive market, with much of that competition coming at the local and regional level. With 100 product lines in 400,000 stores, a mountain of data is produced on a daily basis. In order to get a leg up on the competition, Frito-Lay needed to be able to collect, digest, and then act on that mountain of information quickly.

Frito-Lay's solution was a combination of advanced technologies. This includes scanner data from Information Resources (IRI) combined with sales information from field staff all combined on a sophisticated network, encompassing hand-held computers, the newest of IBM PC computers and even a private satellite communications network connecting the 300 distribution sites, and ultimately accessible through a decision-support system developed by the Ann Arbor-based, Comshare Inc.

The idea of electronic data entry from the sales force dates back to the late 1970s; but it wasn't until 1989 that Frito-Lay saw their vision become a reality. By then, the company had equipped more than 10,000 sales representatives with hand-held computers developed with Fujitsu at a cost of more than $40 million.

These hand-held computers, called "bricks" by Frito-Lay, are used to track inventories at retail stores as well as to enter orders. The bricks are connected to miniprinters in all delivery trucks. The sales reps use these printers to prepare invoices which indicate which items are to be restocked at each stop on their route, as well as indicate current prices and any promotional discounts.

At day's end, the bricks are connected to an IBM minicomputer at a Frito-Lay distribution center, and all sales data collected at the stores that day are sent to the central data center at the company's Plano, Texas headquarters. Here the central computers digest the information, run it through a series of edits, and, finally, put it in an understandable format. Next, the data is shipped out to the regional and divisional levels for further analyses by marketing and other staff. At the same time, the central computer sends pricing and promotional updates back to the hand-held computers. Finally, each Monday it gives the sales reps a review of the previous week's results on their routes.

A Micromarketing Approach

Frito-Lay built a total information system that could be customized at every level of the company. As the network developed, the company realized it could shift from a national marketing strategy to one that targeted local consumers. This is known as micromarketing.

Employees using the system run the gamut from marketing support to the chief executive officer, Robert Beeby. On one occasion, Beeby noticed spotted red numbers on his Comshare EIS screen. This indicated that sales were down in the central region. Quickly calling up another screen Beeby located the source of the problem in Texas. Continuing on his hunt, Beeby tracked the red numbers to a specific sales division and finally to a chain of stores. Apparently, a local company had successfully introduced a new white corn chip which was eating into Frito-Lay's market share in that location. Frito-Lay immediately put a white-corn version of Tostitos into production which appeared on shelves a few months later.

Mary Ellen Johnson typifies the Frito-Lay sales manager. In order to do her job, Johnson was often required to pull together sales information from a variety of sources that sometimes took many weeks to assemble. In some cases, the information had to be obtained from telephone calls, in other cases the data was simply not available.

With Frito-Lay's info-marketing system, Johnson now is able to get reports on her accounts by brand, by type of store or package size. She is also able to obtain results from the best and the worst of the 388 sales representatives in her territory as well as pricing moves by competitors. She can compare the results of her sales reps' performance with the previous week, the previous year, as well as with current targets. She can even compare a product's sales in different markets, such as supermarket versus convenience stores.

The original motivation behind Frito-Lay's unique marketing tool was to cut down on the amount of time it took sales representatives to keep their records, thus freeing them up to make new sales calls. In reducing this overhead, Frito-Lay also realized a benefit of minimizing the accounting discrepancies between the sales force and headquarters which had risen to $4 million annually.

The significance of these systems is that they achieve positive returns on a multitude of levels. Frito-Lay's info-marketing system has affected every level of staff, and every layer of the corporate hierarchy. What originally started out as a mechanism to reduce the overhead of the sales rep in the field, has turned into a bonanza of information for marketing staff back home, has cut down on administrative overhead at the home office, has fine-tuned the production cycle by providing timely information, and has even provided an executive information system for the 40 or so senior executives in the company. This system is pervasive.

The executive information system allows key executives to retrieve status reports by region or product. Using Comshare's EIS, these executives merely touch the computer's screen to obtain desired information. For example, by pressing an image of a book labeled "Briefing Book," executives can select maps and charts which will provide them with more detailed information. The image of a green monster calls up information about competitors.

Using this system, Frito-Lay has been able to maintain a prestigious annual sales growth, about 6 percent, which is twice the industry average. Their earnings are impressive as well, currently at the double-digit level.

The Science of Gathering Business Intelligence

Frito-Lay and Quaker Oats use a first-class set of business intelligence tools and procedures to collect, collate, and reassemble internal and external data to provide enough information to perform competitive decision making.

Frito-Lay and Quaker info-marketing systems, which have been refined to the point of providing these companies tailored, filtered, and usable information, required an intensive two-level effort to create. On the first level was the development of the underlying technological infrastructure, permitting the information to be distributed to and analyzed by the appropriate parties. On a higher level was the effort required to determine the depth and the breadth of the information that would be required.

Sitting a hundred people in a room with access to every newspaper, journal, magazine, and book that has ever been produced will produce only disconnected tidbits of information.

Virtually every piece of information in those journals, magazines, books, and newspapers is available on line through any of a myriad of "information vendors." With merely a PC and a modem, it is possible for a farmer in Idaho to dial up long-term weather conditions and for a businessman to dial up and download information on products, competitors, or trends.

The list of what's available on line covers everything from Who's Who to Soviet news. Even with easy access to this wealth of information, however, you still don't have intelligence. Take the case of a major pharmaceutical company. Over a one year period they spent $12 million dollars in on-line downloads. According to the CEO, virtually all this expensive information was worthless. That's because they didn't have the ability, or know-how, to turn this plethora of information into intelligence. It is a discipline that requires the use of tools and techniques to be able to coordinate and correlate discrete bits of information into intelligence.

Perhaps the biggest stumbling block to the process of creating business intelligence is where it is done. Since the creation of this intelligence relies on the downloading of information, the task is often assigned to the information technology department. This was the case with the pharmaceutical company mentioned. It turned out to be an expensive mistake for them.

A profile of a department most likely to succeed in this endeavor would include the following abilities: being able to work with technology to gather the raw information; having the writing talent to present it in an understandable fashion to management; and possessing the sociopolitical skills to draw conclusions from those analyses accepted by the diverse, and often conflicting, groups that make up a modern corporation.

This is the tact that Herbert Meyer, and his partner Mike Pincus, take when advising their corporate clients on how to build an intelligence gathering department. They look for people with library skills, technical skills, and familiarity with the company's business. They also look for someone who has an "in" with the CEO, so the results don't get politicized.

According to Pincus, "Part of the problem with intelligence is when it's done well, it tends to offset bad judgment which often comes from executive support people. These executive support management people feel threatened by intelligence since it tends to offset their own bad opinions.

Where you have bad management advice, you have to bring someone into the unit who has the social/political/corporate capability to be able to move around in that environment without upsetting people or causing them to feel threatened." In other words, the role of this person is internal public relations.

The first step involved in building an intelligence unit is to build a profile of a company. This is really a needs analysis which will document the products and services that a company manufactures or performs, its goals and priorities as well as requirements for competitive information. Basically, this will be a comprehensive list of categories of information that the company must monitor in order to be competitive. Examples of categories are suppliers, markets, customers, and so on. The profile also uncovers irrelevant information that the company is tracking. In addition to all of these, an assessment must be made of the cultural climate of a company. How is information passed up and down the corporate hierarchy? What political machinations are in place that could possibly affect, or even impede, the information flow?

With profile in hand, Pincus and Meyer perform what they call an "intelligence audit." This is the process that determines if the right people are getting the right information. It is really a two-step process. First, as one would expect, the information needs uncovered during the process of developing the profile are satisfied by locating the proper on-line source that contains that piece of information. As already demonstrated, virtually anything ever written can be located in an on-line database. The trick is in being able to first locate it—which is what Pincus and Meyer do—and then being able to download it and, finally, process it. This is where the second step of the intelligence audit comes in. Pincus and Meyer examine the company's "technological mentality." What kind of technical expertise does the company have? What are they comfortable with? From the information collected in this process, Pincus and Meyer are able to develop a technological solution that would best satisfy the needs, and capabilities, of their client.

Probably the most crucial step in this entire process is in training selected personnel in how to convert the information obtained to business intelligence. This is actually done on two levels. On the technical level, one or more people must be trained to develop skills in correlating information which supports the staff that will ultimately turn this raw information into intelligence. This top tier of staff are the ones who will need to develop and hone, skills to coordinate, correlate, analyze, and ultimately convert raw streams of information into useful business intelligence.

A Checklist for an Information Audit

Information audits are tailored to specific companies and their individual needs. The goal of this process is to pinpoint the information requirements of a company, and then proceed to recommend solutions to satisfy these requirements.

Basically, the process, if one follows the Meyer approach, is composed of four steps:

1. Selecting what needs to be known

2. Collecting the information

3. Transforming this collected information into finished product

4. Distribution of the finished product to appropriate staff

Selecting What Needs to Be Known. According to Meyer, figuring out the right things to know is one of the trickiest, least understood, and most underrated jobs. To perform this feat requires not so much of an expertise in one or more fields, but the ability to recognize what factors will influence that particular issue or area of concern.

The process is begun by reviewing the objectives that have been outlined by the CEO, or management committee. Meyer provides an example of this process in a business environment[1]:

The CEO of an aluminum manufacturer wants to improve sales of the company's pop-top beverage cans. To do this requires an assessment of the prospects for growth in the beverage industry. This is the obvious information that would be required. A person experienced in performing these audits would most certainly look beyond the obvious to, say, assessing the prospects of third-world aluminum producers into the canning business. Even this might be obvious to some, so we need to go deeper into the assessment and evaluate producers of other materials that could perhaps replace aluminum cans.

In essence, this example demonstrates the need to think about issues in a multidimensional way.

Collecting the Information. Once it has been decided what needs to be known, one can begin to collect the appropriate information. There are several categories of information.

First, there is *information that is already available in-house* either residing on some corporate database, on a distributed database (perhaps on some PC), and paper files. The next category of information can be referred to as *public information.* This is information that is on the public record, available in the form of magazines, newspapers, and information from public agencies.

---

[1]Herbert E. Meyer, *Real-World Intelligence.* (New York- Grove and Weidenfeld, 1987).

The next category is *private information.* This is information that is not publicly known, but is available for a fee. Much of this information is available on line through one of the many sources listed in the appendix of this book. But Meyer goes one step further in this category. He suggests that a lot of this information can be obtained through old-fashioned legwork. If a company wants to know whether Singapore or Taiwan would be a good place to locate a manufacturing business, someone should be sent to scout around Washington, New York, London, Zurich, and Tokyo, meeting with consultants and political figures who could share their keen understanding of Singapore's and Taiwan's economic and political prospects. Meyer goes further in suggesting that this person also seek out universities to try to locate an expert on the topic. Ultimately, this person will visit the countries in question and talk with as many people, from as many walks of life, as they can to find out what is likely to happen in these countries years from now.

The final category of information is what is known as *secret information.* This is information privately held by competitor companies. Unfortunately, most of this information is impossible to obtain legally.

Transforming the Collected Information into Finished Products. Deciding upon and then collecting the information is only half the battle. For the information to be truly useful, it must be presented in analytic reports which provide, according to Meyer, "The best judgments, conclusions, and projections based on this information."

Transforming this data into useful information is a multistep process. These steps require a team to study the material and then debate what the material actually means, whether it is accurate and whether it harbors any inconsistencies. It is this first step where all facts will be verified, experts consulted, and theses developed and tested.

It's in this step that we depart from the Meyer approach. Although Meyer actively uses technology in this process, his multistep approach relies on manual efforts of intelligence officers. These people argue over the facts, and then make a decision as to the correct interpretation of the data to be delivered to the CEO or other staff member.

In the info-marketing approach, this step is replaced by loading all collected information into a technological toolset by automatic analysis and distribution. The tool sets described in this, and other, chapters in this book have the power to make these types of judgment calls.

Distribution of the Finished Product to Appropriate Staff. Information should be presented to the staff members appropriate to that staff members level within the organization. Certainly executive information systems, as described in a previous section, provide this capacity.

The Metamorphosis of Lincoln National

Lincoln National Corporation is a $23 billion insurance and financial services company located in Fort Wayne, Indiana. As is the case in any company of Lincoln's size, the process of collecting, interpreting, and disseminating information was time consuming at best and hit-and-miss at its worst.

As is true for nearly any financial services company, one of the most demanding business problems Lincoln National was experiencing was their need to digest large amounts of information. In the past, this had been done by issuing a daily news digest—as is done in the majority of companies. This paper report formed the baseline of information around which Lincoln executives and managers made their strategic decisions.

Understanding that the method of creating this daily report left large gaps of business intelligence unaccounted for, the Information Services group began development of a corporate-wide information retrieval and telecommunications system, using information auditing techniques known as the Office Productivity Network. Today this network is used to collect and disseminate business intelligence company-wide.

Consisting of word processing, spreadsheet, database management systems, desktop publishing, financial modeling, and more, the Office Productivity Network's most important component is its electronic mail feature. This is the software that actually disseminates business intelligence to appropriate staff members.

Given the proliferation of productivity software (i.e., word processors, spreadsheets) on the network, one would suppose that a large part of the business intelligence disseminated to staff was internally generated. This turned out not to be the case. Lincoln discovered that most executive needs were not for information in the corporate database. In general, the executives at Lincoln got their business intelligence from the various news sources. This, then, was what they wanted in their Morning Report.

The Information Services group has been able to create an automated morning report that retrieves, searches, and correlates textual external data to assist staff. The Morning Report's intelligence comes from a variety of external sources, including *The New York Times* and *Business Week*. It has given Lincoln the ability to analyze information from a wide variety of other sources as well. At times, data in an automated format is not available. This is especially true for information from internal documents, paraphrased documents, and anecdotal information. These are all obtained using high-speed scanners which can convert printed material into the automated format that is required.

The Morning Report is viewed, by Lincoln, as a business intelligence gathering tool that feeds information into their executive support system.

Even at this preliminary level, Lincoln has seen some significant productivity improvements. Prior to attending meetings, staff members can review the pertinent information—negating the need to brief meeting attendees so that meetings can move forward more quickly. Perhaps the greatest benefit of all is improved communications within the company, permitting key executives to make better decisions and facilitating the company's avoidance of the inevitable filtering effect that so often happens as information makes its way through the corporate hierarchy.

Lincoln uses their executive support system for strategic planning and competitive analyses. Along with external information, Lincoln management can analyze internal sales data, competitor activities, field reports from sales staff, as well as competitor's financial data to determine the best way to compete.

Electronic mail forms the basis with which Lincoln can collect and disseminate data. It is used to communicate with the sales force in the field. The sales force, in turn, collects competitive data and enters it onto preformatted screens providing quick feedback to the strategic planners.

Competitive analysis is a major component of Lincoln's planning process. Using the information entered by the salespeople in the field, Lincoln builds a profile of each competitor's strengths and weaknesses. This is done by identifying the factors that are considered critical for each line of business, and then ranking each competitor's capabilities in the same area. At the same time, the same criteria is used to rank Lincoln's own capabilities in those same areas. Using a side-by-side comparison of competitor versus itself, Lincoln can evaluate whether or not they are weak in the critical factors needed for success in any particular product line. If a perceived weakness is noted, Lincoln formulates a plan to strengthen the company in that particular area. At the same time, their marketing plan is modified to focus on their key strengths—while minimizing their weaknesses, as uncovered during this competitive analysis.

This marketing plan, as well as plans from the other eleven lines of businesses, is sent through the electronic mail system to the corporate office, where it is consolidated and then sent to the CEO for final approval. One of Lincoln's greatest strengths is the ability to track and process competitor's data and then relate it to their own data, further strengthening their own product and marketing plans. Being able to monitor what a competitor is up to requires a combination of technology and techniques.

What's the Competition Up To?

For those that wish to embark on a program of gathering competitive intelligence, luckily, one innovation permits even the smallest of companies to drag important information out of hiding. This was the invention of the PC. For along with it came a plethora of information services that can potentially offer a firm all of the competitor intelligence it needs.

In order to perform the task of searching for competitive intelligence alone, it is worthwhile to first review several techniques performed in industry to assist in putting the found information into perspective.

Combustion Engineering's Competitor Analysis

The philosophy behind Combustion Engineering's technique[2], is that information coupled with the experience of a seasoned industry manager is more than adequate to take the place of expensive experts in the field of competitive analysis.

The goal behind Combustion Engineering's technique is to analyze one competitor at a time to identify strategies and predict future moves. The key difference between this technique and others is the level of involvement of senior managers of the firm. In most companies, research is delegated to staff who prepare a report on all competitors at once. Combustion Engineering's method is to gather the information on one competitor, and then use senior managers to logically deduce the strategy of the competitor in question.

Combustion Engineering uses a five-step approach to performing competitive analyses. Each will be discussed in turn.

Step 1—Preliminary Meeting. Once the competitor is chosen, a preliminary meeting is scheduled. It should be attended by all senior managers who might have information or insight to contribute concerning this competitor. This includes the CEO as well as the general manager and managers from sales, marketing, finance, and manufacturing. A broad array of staff attending is important to this technique since it serves to provide access to many diverse sources of information. This permits the merger of external information sources—as well as internal sources—collected by the organization, such as documents, observations, and personal experiences.

At this meeting, it is agreed that all attendees spend a specified amount of time collecting more recent information about the competitor. At this time, a second meeting is scheduled in which to review this more recent information.

---

[2] The Conference Board, "Calculating Competitor Action: Combustion Engineering's Strategy," *Management Briefing: Marketing* (October–November 1988).

Step 2—Information Meeting. At this meeting each attendee will receive an allotment of time to present his or her information to the group.

The group will then perform a relative strengths/weaknesses analysis. This will be done for all areas of interest uncovered by the information obtained by the group. The analysis will seek to draw conclusions about two criteria. First, is the competitor stronger or weaker than you company? Second, does the area have the potential to affect customer behavior?

Combustion Engineering rules dictate that unless the area meets both of these criteria, it should not be pursued further either in analysis or discussion. Since managers do not always agree on what areas to include or exclude, it is frequently necessary to appoint a moderator who is not part of the group.

Step 3—Cost Analysis. At this point, with areas of concern isolated, it is necessary to do a comparative cost analysis. The first step here is to prepare a breakdown of costs for your product. This includes labor, manufacturing, cost of goods, distribution, sales, administrative as well as other relevant items of interest as necessary.

At this point, compare the competitor's cost for each of these factors according to the following scale:

Significantly higher

Slightly higher

Slightly lower

Significantly lower

Now, translate these subjective ratings to something a bit more tangible, such as slightly higher is equivalent to 15 percent. By weighting each of these factors by its relative contribution to the total product cost, it is now possible to calculate the competitor's total costs.

Step 4—Competitor Motivation. This is perhaps the most intangible of the steps. The group must now attempt to analyze their competitor's motivation by determining how the competitor measures success as well as what its objectives and strategies are.

During the research phase, the senior manager (and/or his or her staff) gathered considerable information on this topic. By using on-line databases, it is possible to collect information about promotions, annual reports, press releases, and the like. In addition, information from former employees, the sales force, investment analysts, supplier, and mutual clients is extremely useful and serves to broaden the picture.

Based on the senior managers' understanding of the business, it is feasible to be able to deduce the competitor's motivation. Motivation can often be deduced by observing the way the competitor measures itself. Annual reports are good sources for this information. For example, a competitor that wants to reap the benefits of investment in a particular industry will most likely measure success in terms of ROI.

Step 5—Total Picture. By reviewing information on the competitor's strengths and weaknesses, relative cost structure, goals, and strategies a total picture of the firm can be created.

Using this information the group should be able to use individual insights into the process of running a business in a similar industry to determine the competitor's next likely moves.

For example, analysis shows that a competitor is stronger in direct sales, has a cost advantage in labor, and is focused on growing from a regional to a national firm. The group would draw the conclusion that the competitor will attempt to assemble a direct sales effort nationwide, while positioning itself on the basis of low price.

Phantom Analysis. Combustion Engineering has also devised an approach to dealing with the situation in which an outsider enters the market place. Here, the strategy above obviously wouldn't work.

Using the same group of people gathered to analyze competitor strategy, this exercise requests the group to look at the market as an objective third party would. The task is to design a fictitious company that would be able to successfully penetrate the market.

Compare this fictitious company with the competitor firms in the industry to see if any of the traditional competitors can easily adopt this approach.

When Combustion Engineering's phantom analysis uncovers a strategy that traditional competitors might adopt easily they adopt this strategy as a preemptive move. When this same analysis reveals that an outsider could penetrate the industry by following this strategy Combustion Engineering attempts to create additional barriers to entry. This includes forming an alliance with an outside company to pursue the phantom strategy itself.

Missing-Piece Analysis

A complementary strategy to Combustion Engineering's competitor analysis methodology is one developed by F. Michael Hruby, founder of the Society for Competitor Intelligence Professionals.

Hruby's Missing Piece Analysis[3] also attempts to anticipate competitor moves, but it does this by identifying key weaknesses in the competitor. By concentrating on the competitor's weakness, the great wealth of information on that competitor can be turned into usable, action-oriented intelligence.

The methodology for performing Hruby's missing-piece analysis is to analyze the strengths and weaknesses of a competitor in six areas. In each of these areas, the competitor in compared to the company doing the analysis.

1. *Product.* Compare the strength of the competitor's product from the consumer's point of view.

2. *Manufacturing.* Compare capabilities, cost, and capacity.

3. *Sales and marketing.* How well does the competitor sell the product? Compare positioning, advertising, sales force, so on.

4. *Finance.* Compare financial resources and performance. How strong are these relative to a requirement for launching a strong competitive thrust?

5. *Management.* How effective, aggressive, and qualified are the competitor's managers?

6. *Corporate culture.* Examine values and history to determine whether a competitor is likely to enter or to attempt to dominate a market.

The goals of this exercise are to identify weaknesses in each of these areas, as well as to see whether any one of these weaknesses stands out as a major vulnerability. According to Hruby, most companies have a key weakness—or "missing piece"—that can be exploited.

To perform this technique requires that the competitor be rated in each of the six areas listed. Ratings are done on a scale of 1 to 5 with a 1 being very weak, 2 is weak/uncompetitive, 3 is adequate/average, 4 is very strong/competitive and 5 is excellent/superior.

Hruby summarizes these scores in a competitive-strengths matrix as shown in Figure 7-1. This matrix lists the names of the competitors down the right-hand side and the competitive areas of interest across the top. Scores are entered in the appropriate cells. The worst score for each competitor should be highlighted. This is their weakest point and should be monitored accordingly.

In our example, Company A and Company B are both weak in the finance area. This means that they do not have enough strength to launch a major advertising campaigns to bolster a new product. What this means is that if the company doing this analysis is ready, willing, and able to spend a lot of money, a new product launch would most probably be successful.

Company C scored a 1 in the product category. This means that its prod-

---

[3] F. Michael Hruby, "Missing Piece Analysis Target's the Competitor's Weakness,"*Marketing News* (January 2, 1989).

Competitor	Competitive Areas					
	1	2	3	4	5	6
Company A	5	3	4	2	4	3
Company B	4	4	3	2	3	4
Company C	1	3	3	5	2	3
Company D	4	5	4	4	5	4

Area 1 = Product   Key: 1 = Weak to 5 = Excellent
Area 2 = Manufacturing
Area 3 = Sales & Marketing
Area 4 = Finance
Area 5 = Management
Area 6 = Corporate Culture

Figure 7-1. Hruby competitive strengths matrix. (*Source: Hruby*)

uct is not as good as the company doing the analysis. In this case, an advertising campaign emphasizing product differences would serve to grab some market share from Company C.

Company D, on the other hand, scored strong in all matrix areas. Given a strong product and an aggressive management team, this company is likely to make an aggressive move—perhaps a new product launch or major advertising on an existing product. It might even reduce costs. Company D certainly bears watching.

Company C, on the other hand, has a weak product but a good financial position. It just might launch a new product. However, its weak management structure might defer any product launch.

In summary, upon analysis of the competitive strengths matrix, one would deduce that a combination of a strong financial position and competent management are a mix that indicates a strong likelihood of aggressive action on the part of the competitor. By using this analysis on information obtain from various sources—particularly information obtain through the use of information technology techniques—it is quite possible to keep tabs on what the competition is up to.

Monitoring the Competition's Moves Through Information Technology

These and other techniques rely on information. Although some information can be obtained through salesmen, ex-employees of rivals, suppliers, and customers, this is but a trickle compared to the wealth of information available to a information-savvy company.

Meyer and Pincus's firm, Real-World Intelligence, described in one of the sections above, performs the intelligence audit to make sure that the right information is retrieved and delivered to the right person. Then it proceeds to modify the stream of information already retrieved by the company— adding new data streams and deleting inappropriate or useless streams.

With the proliferation of PCs and access to some of the hundreds of databases a savvy company, however—which perhaps cannot afford the services of a consultant specializing in this business, or wants to do it on its own— one can learn about the competition's sales, size, profit and loss, credit history, officers, organization, R&D efforts, intellectual property, and a host of other informational tidbits.

A word of advice is warranted here. Having a PC and subscriptions to half a dozen on-line services does not guarantee good intelligence. Before embarking on this journey solo, a company should make sure that the person doing this work is practiced at searching the on-line database(s) in general. Searching for information through any of the subscription services is often expensive. Spending time on line "playing" around with the information—trying to find some meaningful intelligence—is even more expensive. Most professional on-line searches spend more time off line than on line in performing their research. Off-line time, i.e., free time, is spent in determining which of the on-line databases should be searched. Then they spend some time in formatting queries so that precious and expensive on-line time can be spent in being productive immediately.

To cut down costs, a company should not perform research against all the competitors in the field. Choosing the top three to five is usually sufficient. Next, determine what the most relevant areas of competition. For example, car-rental companies compete on several factors, including pricing and location. Performing a search on the types of cars that they are buying yields intelligence of little use; however, finding out that a rival just obtained counter space in hotels in major cities is invaluable.

The following steps are recommended by Kirk Tyson, president of the Competitor Intelligence Group. Tyson recommends a tiered approach: daily intelligence briefings; profiles of your competitor's essential finances, market and product lines; and focused data, such as sales strategies.

Daily Briefings.   There's probably few managers who don't know what a clipping service is. Before computers, these services would scan thousands of newspapers, magazines, and journals, literally clipping out anything of interest to a particular customer. The customer in question usually indicated his or her parameters of choice—say all information about the aerospace industry—and the clipping services searched for this information daily.

With the advent of on-line subscription services, clipping has been automated. Not only can this information be viewed on line, it can be printed on your PC printer and even downgraded into a variety of PC software.

Kirk Tyson thinks of this as the bedrock of a competitor intelligence program. Luckily there are a host of easy-to-use services out there to assist the company who decides to go it alone.

Probably the most popular of services is CompuServe's Executive News Service. CompuServe is one of the oldest and most popular of on-line services. Used by consumer and businessperson alike, it is both economical and easy to use.

Once logged onto CompuServe, the simple command, GO ENS, gets you access into this service. CompuServe's eminently readable manual makes it easy to get into the service. In general, the Executive News Service puts the resources of The Associated Press, Reuters Financial Report, The Washington Post, OTC NewsAlert, and McGraw-Hill News to work.

There are several options for the user. One is to simply review any of the stories from the wire. There are many. For example, the Associated Press database carries over 7,000 stories a day. Since the purpose of this exercise is to target the exact information needed, and to bypass irrelevant details which save time and money, the best way to approach the situation is to create a clipping folder.

Under CompuServe's Executive News Service, that is exactly how it is done. Here, the thousands of stories are scanned on the company's behalf, and only the ones that meet the specific criteria preset by the company are stored in an automated clipping folder.

Specifying areas of interest is usually done by entering keywords. For example, if a company were interested in saving all information about Apple Computer, the keywords might be Apple Computer.

Since there are other on-line clipping services, such as GEnie's NewsGrid Executive News, time must be spent on each one honing the keywords for the most effective, and economical, use of computer time.

Although automated clipping services are for the most part alike, they differ in their strengths. For example, it has been said that GEnie's NewsGrid covers the international business market slightly better than does CompuServe. On the other hand, Dow Jones/Retrieval offers the widest range of business wires in a single package.

For the most part, most companies will soon discover that variety is indeed the spice of life, and will sign up for several services simultaneously.

Rival Profiles.   Clippings will provide the raw news required to keep abreast of competitor moves. At some point, though, some analyses must be done to predict competitor moves. To perform these analyses, it will be necessary to collect information of another kind to create a rival profile.

The profile should contain information to track trends in market share, profits, management information, products as well as other criteria desired by the company.

CompuServe's IQuest is known as a gateway to hundreds of databases. Dialog also provides a similar array of information. BRS, Dow Jones, Nexis and NewsNet are also good bets.

Knowing what information to search out is an art unto itself. It pays to study carefully the manuals that each service provides. In each, a list of databases and the type of data contained within is spelled out. For example, a good place to find out information about a public competitor is through its filings with the Securities and Exchange Commission (SEC). Through the 10Ks and various other filings, it is possible to uncover such things as officers, ownership, income statements, and even a five-year business summary.

Private firm information can be obtained through Dun & Bradstreet. Through Dunsprint, available on CompuServe, it is possible to track information on sales, balance sheets, and even credit on some 2 million private companies. Additionally, through NewsNet, it is possible to access TRW's Business Profiles for the same information. Information on foreign firms is available through many of these services as well.

Perhaps the key database in researching a true market picture is the Investext database available through CompuServe. This database stores over 200,000 securities analyst's reports on more than 12,000 public companies—including some foreign firms. Investext reports come from more than 90 of the most well-regarded securities analyst firms, and includes such information as market share, gross margins on sales, research and development expenditures, cash flow, and other important financial statistics.

Industry newsletters are available on line through NewsNet. Also available through NewsNet is the PR Newswire, which tracks press releases. These two sources will assist in tracking trends and releases of newer technologies into the industry.

Sharp Focus. The information obtained so far was general competitive data. How can you use these on-line services to answer more specific questions such as "is your competitor going to launch a new product?"

Several databases are available which provide more in-depth coverage of a particular firm's actions. One of these is Insider Watch, which is available both on Dialog and Dow Jones. This database gives up information concerning open market sales as well as purchases and stock options exercised by over 100,000 corporate insiders in more than 8,500 firms.

Dialog also offers a wealth of biographical information about a competitor's officers. The Biography Master Index contains more than 7 million references for over 40,000 companies. It also provides information such as number of employees and corporate structure.

Since corporate structure is such a tell-all concerning how a firm is organized, this information is also available on Business Dateline and Corporate Affiliations. It is available through Dow, BRS, Dialog, and Nexis. Other databases that tell all are Financial Industry Information Service (FINIS) on Dialog as well as Nexis and BRS. Those interested in merger and acquisition activity would best consult M&A filings on Dialog. Of course, no research would be complete without looking at Standard & Poor's Register— Corporate.

Uncovering the Gold in the Corporate Database

While executive information system tools provide a baseline for analyzing business intelligence, there will come a time when higher-order software tools will be required to sift through collected data and uncover relationships that can be mined into profitability. When developing an information technology infrastructure, these tools should not be overlooked.

While choosing an architecture for the company's corporate database standard is important, and should be funded as well as supported by management, this process should not overshadow the more important issue of being able to navigate effectively through the data contained within so that corporate data can be turned into competitive gold as in the case of Lincoln National.

Standard database query languages easily retrieve information—but only if the user knows specifically what he or she is looking for. If the request for information is vague, one needs to use a more heavy-duty tool.

A more difficult class of information to deal with is what can be termed unknown information. Upon analysis of a large database, it is possible to discover patterns, rules, and unexpected relationships between data items that were previously unrealized—the hidden gold in the corporate database.

This is an intriguing possibility, but not one that on which many companies are embarking. This is unfortunate, since these same companies would most certainly benefit from discovering some interesting correlations between sales data and customer financial data. Before we launch into a discussion of how this technology works, a simple example of how useful this technique is warranted.

The New York Stock Exchange's regulatory department is charged with ensuring that the brokerage firms that are members of the Exchange are financially sound. This is accomplished by requiring these firms to file huge amounts of financial data which financial analysts, working for the Exchange, then review.

The preeminent tool for this purpose is a software program called the Exception Disposition Report (EDR). This report is produced by comparing the data filed by the brokerage firm to a set of statistical algorithms such as, *"If the firm's excess net capital is greater than 25 percent of its profits then flag this exception."* These exceptions, in the form of rules, were developed by the financial analysts by comparing and reviewing one item of information against another item of information. The rules, called EDRs, were actually coded statements concerning the relationship of financial data item to financial data item. The financial analysts were continually meeting to improve on these rules. Since these rules were developed manually, there was always a chance that the relationship, as defined by the rule, was incorrect. A worse problem was omitting a rule about a potentially volatile financial situation altogether. What if software could be used to determine these rules automatically? Wouldn't the Exchange's product be a better one? A more competitive one?

An Automatic Discovery Program

The number and size of operational databases, such as the Exchange's, are increasing at a progressively quickened rate. Because of the number of these databases, their size and complexity, there is a tremendous amount of valuable knowledge locked up in these databases that remains undiscovered. Since the tendency of most modern organizations is to cut back on staff, it follows that there will never be enough analysts to interpret the data in all the databases.

Fortunately, information technology has spawned a new concept that has the ability to perform automatic analysis of large databases. This name coined for this technology is automatic discovery.

IntelligenceWare, located in Los Angeles, California, is the market leader in automatic discovery software. IXL, an acronym for Induction on eXtremely Large database, is a unique system which analyzes large databases and discovers patterns, rules, and often unexpected relationships. IXL uses statistics and machine learning to generate easy-to-read rules which characterize data providing insight and understanding.

The president of IntelligenceWare, Kamran Parsaye, coined the term *intelligent databases*. The goal of intelligent databases is to be able to manage information in a natural way making the information, stored within these databases, easy to store, access, and use.

The prototypical intelligent database, according to Parsaye, would have some robust requirements. An intelligent database would need to provide some high-level tools for data analysis, discovery, and integrity control.

These tools would be used to allow users not only to extract knowledge from databases, but also to apply knowledge to data. So far, it is not possible to scan through the pages of a database as easily as it is to flip through the pages of a book. In order for the label intelligent database to be valid, this feature is necessary. Users should be able to retrieve information from a computerized database as easily as they can get it from a helpful human expert. Finally, an intelligent database must be able to retrieve knowledge as opposed to data. To do this, it needs to use inferencing capabilities to determine what a user needs to know.

In developing the theory behind intelligent databases, Parsaye enumerated three basic levels in dealing with a database[4]:

1. We *collect* data, e.g., we maintain records on clients, products, sales, etc.

2. We *query* data, e.g., "Which products had increasing sales last month?"

3. We try to *understand* data, e.g., "What makes a product successful?"

In general, most current database systems passively permit these functions. A database is a static repository of information which will provide answers when a human initiates a session and asks a set of pertinent questions.

IXL attempts to change this point of view by turning the database into an active repository of information, automatically posing queries to the database and uncovering useful, and sometimes unexpected, information.

This was the case for a well-known computer manufacturer who suffered sporadic defect problems in their disk drive manufacturing process that they just couldn't locate. Using the IXL program against a database which consisted of the audit logs of the manufacturing process, this company was able to pinpoint the particular operator who was causing the problem. The defect was then traced back to a lack of proper training.

An even more interesting case study deals with lead poisoning data from the University of Southern California's cancer registry. Analysis of this data, using the IXL program, uncovered a relationship between gender and the level of lead in the blood leading to kidney damage. Before IXL's analysis, this relationship was unknown and potentially deadly.

Software such as IXL amplifies our ability to navigate and analyze information so that it can be rapidly turned from discrete and disconnected pieces of data into intelligence. But tools such as these address only one side of the competitive coin. As much as we would like to rely purely on analytics, the truth of the matter is that creativity provides a counterbalance that we cannot dispense with. Is there perhaps a way to make people more creative?

---

[4] "IntelligenceWare. What Can IXL Do That Statistics Cannot?" Internal paper 1990.

Computerized Brainstorming

Human performance. Maybe that's what it all boils down to! Enabling a person to perform at his or her full potential. In the beginning, we developed technology appliances to make the drudgery of clerical work less burdensome—and even to replace humans. Later, technology began to be used to help humans sort through the massive information datastores. The age of the personal productivity appliance, the PC, began in the early eighties and during that decade, and on into the nineties, spurred an avalanche of productivity-enhancing tools that nearly boggle the mind. But still, the emphasis was on productivity-*enhancing*. What's readily needed by companies searching for that elusive silver bullet of competitive leadership is some sort of tool that is productivity-*producing*.

Marsh Fisher may just have found that silver bullet. You may have heard of him. Fisher was the original founder of the Century 21 real-estate empire. Any businessperson would take advice from Fisher. After all, his real-estate business was worth billions. But Fisher wanted to offer more than advice. He wanted to offer ideas. Actually, he wanted to offer competitive advantage through creativity. Fisher calls this type of software Human Performance Technology.

Fisher got the idea for creativity boosting back in the days when computers were large, monolithic, mainframes stuck away in the basements of office buildings, providing only a smattering of the functionality that has become available as a matter of course in the 1990s. In 1964, Fisher was studying comedy writing. But he noticed that most of the other students in his class were much better at being fast on their feet that he was. They seemed to ad lib a lot better than he did. So he started looking for some sort of crutch with which he could at least become competitive.

He began to study the art of ad libbing, and comedy in general, and found that there is a unique association between the punch line and the set-up line. Related to both of these phrases is an assumed word or phrase. It is this word or phrase that associates the set-up line to the punch line.

When Fisher retired from Century 21, he began to study cognitive sciences, which is a combination of linguistics and computer science. One of the goals of cognitive sciences is to determine whether the mind can be mimicked in the mysterious task of problem solving.

Fisher describes problem solving as the 3 R's: recording, recall, and reassociate. Recording of information is done spontaneously. Everything we see, hear, smell, or touch is stored in the grandest of all databanks—the human brain. Of course, once it's stored inside, it's sometimes quite difficult to get it back out. This is the task of recall or remembering. We have this massive warehouse of information stored in our subconscious, and trying to find something buried away is usually quite difficult. Once an item of information is recalled, the third R is deployed. We reassociate, or recombine, one or more items of information to produce an original creative idea.

Of course, if we had instant access to everything tucked away in our memories the road to creativity would be much less arduous. Unfortunately, as we're reminded time and time again as we search in vain for the name of the person that we just met in the hallway, this is usually not the case. Even if all humans were possessed of the gift of instant recall, there's still that third R to contend with: Reassociation—the creative R, the R that gives us creative leverage.

In the sixties, Fisher wanted to give humans a creativity shot in the arm by publishing a book of associations. By the time he was ready to do it, the PC had become so ubiquitous that he decided to write it in software. This is when IdeaFisher was born.

IdeaFisher claims it can help us make something quite novel out of fragmented, and seemingly useless, bits of information. Here's how it works:

In this example, we'll join the Product Planning Group of a Sock Company. They're developing a plan to sell more socks in the summer months. In undertaking a challenge of this nature it is important that the strategy team understand that this process actually consists of four processes: understanding the goal, defining the strategy, naming the product, and finally identifying the key attributes of the product for advertising and product positioning. We'll take a quick tour through IdeaFisher to show how software of this type can assist the creative process.

Understanding the Goal

Our first step is to fully understand the specific challenge. In order to do this, we'd normally get a group together to brainstorm. To pick the goal, and the resultant ideas, apart and piece them back together into a solution. Brainstorming relies on a series of questions and answers. But what if you can't come up with the right questions? Fortunately, IdeaFisher comes with a question bank, called the QBank, preloaded with some 3,000 questions to spur the process on. Questions are categorized along several lines including developing a story or script, developing a new product or service, developing a name, title, theme, or slogan, and developing a marketing strategy or promotional campaign. Since our goal is to develop a new line of socks, we'll choose developing a new product or service. Here we look through a series of questions and pick the ones most appropriate to our goal. Questions such as: Does the audience or customer fit a particular category—a distinct type of thought and behavior (a stereotype)? What are the customer's relevant physical traits in addition to age and sex? List the person's relevant pyschographic traits. What product or service characteristics are most important to this customer?

After each question is selected, the strategy team enters its responses directly on line. The team brainstorms answers such as adult males and females of all ages, people at home and outside, likes to be outdoors, gardening, bird-watching, socks should be fashionable, socks should be useful in outdoor activities, socks should be in a fabric that does not hold moisture or is hot.

What we have in our automated note pad, called the Idea Notepad in IdeaFisher, is a set of rather prosaic responses to some very well-directed questions. Once this prose is filtered into a series of key concepts through the Filter Question process, the team is ready to target the most relevant key concepts and move on to the next step.

After much debate, our team finally targets the key concepts of bird watching, color coordination, gardening, moisture, and useful in outdoor activities. This then, is the breakdown of the key elements in their marketing strategy. Defining a specific strategy is the next activity.

Defining the Strategy

To develop a feasible strategy to sell more socks in the summer, our team will use IdeaFisher's IdeaBank. This is a fascinating repository of 28 major categories broken down into 387 topical or subcategories containing over 60,000 words. By associating these word and phrases, it is possible to wind up with a staggering 705,000 direct associations. Our team wants to begin with the socks key concept. Upon highlighting this word in the note pad, the program will display all of the topical categories that contain the word socks. Apparently, IdeaFisher has 10 topics that deal with socks including black/gray, cleaning/dirty/clean, clothing/fashion/style, and push/pull/attract/repel. This last topic intrigues one of the members of the team, so it is highlighted to see the section titles on the next level. It turns out that there are 945 idea words or phrases associated with push/pull/attract/repel neatly categorized into 11 groupings such as things/places, things that repel, things that attract, and abstractions/intangibles. The team decides to pursue things that repel. Highlighting this they find 26 intriguing items such as anti-icer, body armor, car wax, and mosquito repellent. Certainly, these are things that repel.

Marsh Fisher describes the act of creativity as one that involves coming up with new ideas whose revelation excite the creator so much that he or she exclaims, "A-ha!" He calls this the "A-ha experience." Our fictitious team experiences this feeling when they realize the interesting possibilities in mosquito repellent on socks.

Naming the Product

Now that the team has decided upon their novel product, they need to come up with a good name for it—a good hook. Selecting a name for a product or service has many elements: It must be easily remembered; It must be descriptive; and it must tie in with the customer's perceived needs and values.

The team decides to compare two topical categories using IdeaFisher's Compare feature to create a unique name for the socks. It wants to associate disparate ideas to merge them together into a single word or phrase that creates a novel hook for their new product. Picking socks as the first key concept to compare, the team is prompted to pick one of the many topical categories containing this word. The head of the team recommends that the team pursue limbs/appendages. Outdoors is the second word that the team wants to use in the comparison. Again, a list of topical categories containing the word outdoors is displayed. This time the team picks camping/hiking/mountaineering. IdeaFisher takes over at this point and produces a listing of words and phrases found in both of the topical categories selected. This list serves as a jog to creativity. The team looks through the list bypassing blister, footing, footpath, and 50-odd other words and phrases. One word on that list jumps out at them as the perfect name for the new line of socks; Surefooted.

So far, all in one sitting, the team has brainstormed the meaning of their challenge, defined their strategy, and named their product—in a space of hours, rather than days. All that remains of their task is to identify key attributes for advertising and product positioning. In order to do this, the team decides to explore the key concepts stored in the automated note pad in greater detail.

Identifying Key Attributes

The team decides that the key attribute they want to emphasize is summer uses of socks. So they select and highlight the word summer—listed in the automated note pad. Ultimately, the team winds up with a host of summertime activities and hobbies that people in the target market might enjoy more with Surefooted socks.

The final results of the IdeaFisher session, which began just a scant few hours before, is as follows:

1. Socks that keep bugs away

2. Color coordination with current athletic clothes and incorporation of reflective material in some models

3. Lightweight material that doesn't hold heat or moisture inside

4. An insect-repellent fabric that could be used for clothing, sleeping bags, and tents

Computerized Brainstorming in Use

When Pabst Brewing Company customers began calling out PBR when ordering Pabst Blue Ribbon Beer, Pabst knew it was on to something hot, but it needed more than just "PBR" to create a hot jingle—it needed some inspiration. That's when it turned to IdeaFisher to assist in writing a jingle that is based on abbreviations. This is what its fishing caught, "I'm gonna give my thirst some TLC, just PBR me ASAP." Pabst is not alone; IdeaFisher has been used to write proposed copy for everything from Bud Beer to the Discover card.

Even the world's foremost advertising agency uses IdeaFisher. Saatchi & Saatchi Advertising rarely runs out of ideas. But sometimes, even in the most creative of firms, the well just runs dry. That's when this New York City-based company turns to IdeaFisher, which Saatchi's Perry Davis calls a "creative springboard."

One way in which Saatchi uses IdeaFisher is as an idea generator for focus groups. The traditional method of conducting a focus group is to get 8 or 10 people around a table and go through a structured session of key ideas or seminal words that people will react to. The problem with this method is that it's very possible to travel down a path and ultimately lose sight of the forest because you keep examining the trees. In other words, it is quite possible to reach a very dead end. Using IdeaFisher changes all that, and permits Saatchi to create the most rigorous of focus sessions—and at the lowest possible cost for the client. According to Davis, "IdeaFisher gives us the broadest range of opportunities to wrap one's hands around. It's one of the all-time great tools."

Info-Marketing Redux

Without information, technology organizations would be reduced to searching for the proverbial needle in a haystack. In fact, without information technology, many of the products or services companies offer for sale today simply would not be available.

Mauna La'i guava drink is a case in point. When Ocean Spray Cranberries performed test marketing for this tropical fruit drink, initial results were less than promising. What this translates to is that the product would not meet Ocean Spray's sales objectives. But it decided to recheck these results through Information Resources' electronic test-market service. Surprisingly, the IRI analysis showed that the depth of repeat purchases would make up for lack of volume in the trial.

A plethora of package-goods companies are finding that the use of information technology to assist in uncovering golden nuggets amid an avalanche of data is key to expanding market share. At Cadbury Beverages, much of this market information comes from scanner data sold by companies such as IRI. Using IRI's decision-support software, Dataserver, Cadbury wafts through the data for a first pass. More information technology is used for a refined view of the data under the guise of IRI's Coverstory. Not only do these innovative software tools permit Cadbury to find new openings in the competitive marketplace, but they enable Cadbury to perform intra-prospecting.

By far, the perfect "new" product is one that exceeds sales projections *and* whose time to market as well as developmental cost are low. In Cadbury's case, it first looks for new opportunities in their own product categories(i.e., intraprospecting). In these analyses, Cadbury scrutinizes subcategories of products that perform better than average. For the most part, though, new opportunities are found outside of current product boundaries.

Holland House cooking wines is a case in point. Upon researching the marinade category, Cadbury discovered that this was a market niche that was underpopulated by the competition. This was discovered by subjecting the data to intensive analysis in hopes of finding potential buyers. When the market researchers combined this information with information on product sales and competition, Cadbury management gave the green light.

There are few companies that are seriously interested in being competitive that are not using one or more of the techniques described in this chapter. But the techniques of info-marketing can assist the savvy organization in more areas than just marketing. Once these tools and techniques move into the mainline corporate environment, info-marketing just might become the pinnacle of ideas upon which corporate success relies the most.

This entire chapter was based on the use of information technology. From becoming more innovative to tracking a competitor's moves to tracking your own company's progress in bringing a product to market, there is no area left untouched by the use of technology. It simply couldn't be done any other way.

8
Infotrend #7: Turning Data into Knowledge

The Strategic Use of Information

For the most part, in spite of great advances in technology, most organizations are using the same tired old methodologies that we've been using since the dawn of the computer age. These antiquated formulas and systems for data processing are ill-equipped to deal with the complexity of information we must assimilate today.

1. A regulatory agency automates a system that displays a profile of the entities that it regulates. The profile pours so much information on line that it tops out at over 91 display screens for each firm.

2. The Securities and Exchange Commission must process thousands of free-form financial filings on a daily basis, far exceeding the capacity of human reviewers.

3. The process of entering insurance underwriting data into the company computer is so difficult, it takes one Midwestern insurer six months to train each new employee.

The problem is not in getting the information; computer systems solved that problem years ago. The problem is that once you get it in, it is difficult to get it out in a manner that permits rapid, strategic decision making. In this chapter, we will explore artificial intelligence techniques for turning data into knowledge.

Accessing the Net Worth of Organizational Information

Most organizations suffer from a proliferation of data that is either redundant or underutilized. These same organizations often suffer from not recognizing the true value of their data.

Calculating the Value of Information (VOI), is a useful exercise that assists an organization in determining the true worth of its investment in information.

The following exercise is not meant to be performed by the technology group in a vacuum. Assessing the worth of a company's data is very much a group exercise that cuts across the organization. This is also not an exercise that can be rushed through and, in fact, can even harm the organization if hastily prepared.

Preparing the Field. Before any meetings are held to debate the relative worth of data, a data dictionary should be prepared that describes all automated systems as well as systems to be automated but still on the drawing board. This task is not as onerous as it sounds if the technology department employs an automated dictionary. In those shops where an automated dictionary is not employed, a bit of work will have to be done to uncover this information and organize it logically. One of the key tasks of this assignment is to track all data elements that are being used by more than one system. The reason for this will become clear as we proceed with this exercise.

At a minimum, a chart should be prepared that looks similar to the one in Figure 8-1. Although it is common, from a data definition perspective, to break down each data element into its component parts, this should not be done in this case. For example, a customer address may be composed of four individual data elements: street address, city, state, and zip. For the purposes of the VOI exercise, we will be interested in customer address as a single entity only. A corresponding document should be made available that carries complete explanations of the rather cryptic system names contained within the chart.

Custfile	Customer file
Cust_name	Customer name
Cust_addr	Customer address
Cust_phone	Customer phone
Cust_credit	Customer credit score
Cust_line	Customer credit line
Cust_last	Customer last order number
Cust_date	Customer date of entry

Figure 8-1. Creating the data dictionary for the VOI process.

A Monetary Value of Information. The ultimate goal of this exercise is to assign a monetary value to each unitary piece of information. In this way, an organization—used to assessing relative worth based on bottom-line statistics— can instantly recognize the value of information in terms that it understands.

With this in mind, a team should be assembled that is composed of representatives from the technology and user groups. Bear in mind that since this task is somewhat judgmental, a senior manager who is in the position to act as corporate tie breaker should be in attendance at the assignment of relative worth to any individual data element.

The team is now ready to evaluate each data element and apply a weighting algorithm that will ultimately tie the data element back to the organization in a monetary sense. The steps that should be taken for this assessment follow:

1. Assign each system a weighting relative to the importance to the organization. Permissible weights for the entirety of this exercise are one for a low relative value, two for a middle relative value, and three for a high relative value.

2. For each data element within a system, assign a weighting that indicates that data element's importance relative to that system. Again, use the weightings one through three.

3. Multiply these two numbers together to get the total weighting of a data element relative to all data in the organization.

4. Each data element should have an annotation next to it, indicating the number of systems in which this data element is cross-referenced. For example, it is possible that customer name is used in the sales system, the inventory system, and a marketing system. This would give us a total of three systems. The product calculated in instruction 3 is now multiplied by the number determined in this instruction.

5. Convert this number to a percentage.

6. Using the last audited net income amount for the organization (this could be a quarter or for an entire year), calculate the VOI by multiplying the percentage calculated in instruction six by the net income amount. A completed chart is shown in Figure 8-2.

The Tools of Strategic Systems

The seemingly gradual evolution from data to information saw some marked advances in the tools and uses of technology. This was the era of fourth-generation languages as well as the personal computer. Personal productivity through the use of inexpensive hardware and software was freely at hand.

Custfile	Customer File	Corp. Weighting	System Weighting		Cross References		VOI
Cust_name	Customer Name	2	3	=6	5	=30	$1.5M
Cust_addr	Address	2	2	=4	2	=8	$.4M
Cust_phone	Phone	2	3	=6	1	=6	$.3M
Cust_credit	Credit score	3	3	=9	3	=27	$1.35M
Cust_line	Credit line	3	3	=9	1	=9	$.45M
Cust_last	Last order	2	2	=4	3	=12	$.6M
Cust_date	Date of entry	1	1	=1	2	=2	$.1M
			=Total Weighing				In millions

Figure 8-2. VOI calculation based on net income of $5 million.

At the same time, companies began to utilize new methods to be able to strategically sift through their massive corporate databases. There are a host of filtering methodologies for serving up relevant data to the tactical manager. For the most part, they are classified in three different ways.

The *monitoring method* serves up data to the user on an exception basis. This can be variance reporting, where the system produces only exceptions based on programmatic review of the data, for example, to review credit-card payments and display only those accounts where the payment wasn't received or the payment is below the minimum amount.

The advent of the fourth-generation language (4GL), a tool enabling the end-user to access the corporate database with an easy-to-query syntax, has thrust the *interrogative method* of system tailoring to the popular forefront. This method takes into account the many occasions when the user cannot identify the set of information necessary to handle day-to-day, ad hoc analyses in complex decision-making environments. In these cases, all of the data elements need to be resident in an accessible database. A tool needs also to be in place to permit the user to easily and quickly develop queries and variations on these queries against the data.

When Bankers Trust decided to get out of the retail business in the early 1980s, the data-processing effort to achieve this feat was enormous. One area that Bankers spun off rather quickly was the credit-card subsidiary. The

4GL in use at the time was FOCUS (by Information Builders located in New York City). Staff used this tool to great advantage to ensure a smooth transition of accounts to the many final resting places. Some accounts spun off to a bank in Chicago, some to Albany, while the high-rollers were deposited in privileged checking accounts.

A *model-oriented approach* is really a series of methodologies. Human resource or facilities departments are good candidates for *descriptive models*, which can be organization charts or floor plans. On the other hand, a *normative representation* of data is a good fit for budgeting when the goal is to provide the best answer to a given problem. Economic projects are a good target for modeling methodologies that have the ability to handle uncertainty. Operations management aficionados often apply game theory to those problems where there is a requirement to find the best solution— in spite of a profound lack of information. An example of a problem that would use this type of strategy would be a competitive marketing system where data about the competition is scant or unknown.

However, information technology is more than just software. Gradually, companies began to realize that the value of information was being enhanced by improvements in hardware as well. The age of the Big Iron mainframe system, long a staple of the seventies and early eighties, was giving way to a more efficient approach, using the localized power of the PC (i.e., workstation), perhaps accessing a distant computer. With distributed architecture becoming the norm, information systems was no longer a descriptive term for the phenomenon taking place in the mid-late eighties. Thus, the era of Information Technology was born.

Are Information and Information Technology Interchangeable?

Most would find the terms *information* and *information technology* interchangeable from the perspective of running a corporate data center. William R. King[1], a professor at the University of Pittsburgh Graduate School of Business, Varun Grover, also from the University of Pittsburgh, and Ellen Hufnagel, a faculty member at the University of South Florida researched this issue and found that those firms that understood, and reacted to, these differences enabled them to identify and develop strategic applications.

---

[1] William R. King, Varun Grover and Ellen Hufnagel. "Using Information and Information Technology for Sustainable Competitive Advantage: Some Empirical Evidence," *Information and Management* Vol. 17: 2 (September 1989), p. 87–93.

King's team had two major research objectives:

1. To determine the factors that were the distinguishing characteristics, and differences, between information and information technology. King's team felt that the distinction between these two varieties of information resources would enable a firm

> to focus attention on opportunities involving both kinds of resources...to provide the different kinds of support that are appropriate to the development and implementation of the two varieties...to understand factors that may differentially facilitate or inhibit their development.

2. To develop empirical data on a sampling of actual strategic business applications along with the organizational factors that either assisted or impeded the development of each application.

Information technology is commonly defined as the set of nonhuman resources whose tasks encompass storage, processing, and communication of information. It also includes the manner in which these resources are organized into a system capable of carrying out a task or set of tasks. Using technologists parlance, this translates to a combination of hardware and software.

Information refers to that which enables us to make a decision or to narrow the range of possibilities about which we are ignorant. King's team interprets this as "data that has been evaluated in such a way that it alters our expectations of our view of the alternatives that are available." In an interesting twist, King's team also includes the analytic software that facilitates the use of data in their definition of information.

King's team defines information technology much more narrowly than corporate technology staff. Here, information technology is compared to production technology, that is, "the equipment and ancillary resources which convert or combine basic raw material inputs to produce a new product, adding new value in the process." Therefore, information technology would include such devices as computers, terminals, microprocessors, communication lines, telephones, typewriters, and the like. It also includes the software aspect of built-in logic, operating systems, and utilities that maintain data without regard to its specific content or use.

Although most technologists reading this definition would most likely disagree and include analytical software in this definition, thinking about information technology along these lines enables the technology manager to isolate these software/hardware resources into an asset that invariably depreciates in worth over time. Few technology shops, and even fewer corporate accounting departments, carry this sort of technology asset on their books quite in this way. If they did, it might be much easier to justify new acquisitions and replacements of obsolete system hardware and software. A rough estimate would put the percentage of obsolete technology suffered by most firms at a depressing 25. This means that 25 percent of the competitive systems being run today are being run on hardware that is out of date and slow running, on a database past its prime, on a PC the brand of which was discontinued five years ago. Try winning the Indy 500 with one tire manufactured in the year 1960—and used continuously since that time.

On the other hand, King views information as separate and discrete from the value added by the physical equipment and systems software. Looking at information in this pure form, King asserts, "forces us to consider the informational assets that are at the firm's disposal. How can stores of data collected by existing systems be put to new uses to create value in important ways."

Several pages back, we discussed a method for determining the VOI, or value of information. The schedules developed for the VOI exercise can be used for a second brainstorming session along the lines of King's assertions.

The distinction between information and information technology can be clarified by using two examples from real life. Lee Iacocca dramatically rescued Chrysler by using information in a new way. Although computer technology was most certainly used to analyze this information, it was the information that was pivotal here and not the technology.

American Hospital Supply (AHS), on a tightwire due to increasing competition, determined that it could provide more support to its customers by placing terminals in each customer location. Thus the customer could easily order supplies when desired as well as check out price and availability. The information provided the customer was exactly the same as provided in the old manner when the customer called a salesman. The strategic key here was to provide the information more rapidly—and information technology was the way to do it.

King agrees with the conclusion arrived at in the last section that information and information technology are most often used interdependently to achieve competitive advantage. A good example of a system that follows this pattern is an airline, which has already pursued the use of information technology by placing its computer terminals on the desks of travel agents, that begins to use the information entered by these travel agents to manage the availability of discount seating—and thereby competes more effectively with other airlines.

The King report concludes that when we fail to distinguish the nuances between information and information technology, we are unable to develop strategic systems. This is due to the fact that we have not developed the planning and decision-making processes that enable us to identify and develop the appropriate strategic applications.

To put their theories to the test, King's team surveyed some 84 information managers who were members of the Society for Information Management. Of these 84, 95 percent indicated that their firms were using information technology while 86 percent indicated that they developed strategic information-based systems. The overlap indicates firms that are using the interdependency between information and information technology to gain a strategic foothold.

More important than these statistics was the lists compiled by the King team, enumerating "organizational inhibitors"and "organization facilitators" to the strategic systems development process.

The 84 respondents indicated that the following greatly inhibited the strategic process:

Lack of appropriate planning

Low perceived importance of concept

Lack of appropriate technical support

Budget constraints

Difficulty in assessing tangible contribution

Complexity of idea

High potential start-up difficulties

Lack of organizational/top-management support

Power and politics in the firm

Nature of external environment

Ill-defined management objectives

Other more important priorities

Conversely, the following list of behaviors can greatly assist the strategic process:

Strong market position of the firm

Existing information technology leadership position

Strong planning capability of the firm

Extensive computer facilities within the firm

Strong organization/top management

Pressure from competition

Strong technical support/expertise within firm

Strong financial position of the firm

Need for uniqueness or innovation

The ultimate result of the strategic use of a combination of information and information technology is a competitive edge. But information technology itself cannot achieve this goal. Nor can information. It is the use of these tools by the worker, whether the tactical or strategic manager, that will ultimately perform this feat.

The Age of the Intelligent Worker

Ray Kurzweil may have been one of the first people to understand the potential of machines as assistants in man's quest for superior intelligence. In his book, *The Age of the Intelligent Machine,* Kurzweil vividly documents the advances made in the final frontier of information technology.

The advances Kurzweil describes are generated by a subfield of computer science known as artificial intelligence. AI, the acronym by which artificial intelligence is known, is the field of study that works at narrowing the differences between computers and people. There are several branches of AI that pique our interest. Expert systems is the one we seem to be interested in the most with neural nets running a close second.

An Expert System Boom

Over the last several years, over 80 percent of the Fortune 500 companies have explored expert system techniques. The usual selling point is that expert systems encode the knowledge and reasoning skills of resident staff experts. It permits users to conduct dialogues with automated systems, providing an enormous boost to productivity, and dramatically extending the power of the computer.

In 1985, E.I. du Pont Nemours & Company, realizing the strategic value of this type of technology, made a wholesale effort to train anyone on the staff who was interested in expert systems to build their own. Today, there are reportedly more than 600 expert systems installed in Du Pont's business units. What's even more interesting is that this effort has saved Du Pont some $100 million. Along with making a great impact on the P&L statement, the goal of more than one of those 600 expert systems is to get Du Pont a greater percentage of market share— or even to break into a market that they were never in before. An example of this last strategy is a system that Du Pont has named the Packaging Advisor. This expert system is used for designing rigid plastic food containers. This expert system helped Du Pont break into the very competitive barrier resin market.

Digital Equipment Corporation, another pioneer in using artificial intelligence, has some 50 expert systems in place, which has lead to a $200 million savings to their bottom line. The expert system they are best known for is named, appropriately, XCON which is short for expert configurator. XCON automatically writes the technical specification for a minicomputer configuration. Since a DEC minicomputer can have from 200 to 8,000 parts, the human technical writer, whom XCON replaced, made more than a few errors. One of the largest expert systems on record, XCON, with a rulebase of over 10,000 rules, was one of the key elements responsible for making DEC such a strong competitor to IBM during the 1980s.

But what are expert systems? In a human resources knowledge base, for example, there are no facts and figures—only stored knowledge about how the human resource department works. It's this expertise that makes the company competitive.

Expert systems are found in a myriad of other areas as well such as geology, information management, law, manufacturing, medicine, meteorology, the military, and space. In the world of agriculture, an expert system predicts damage to corn due to cutworm. Another expert system manages apple orchards. In the world of chemistry, the expert system "Dendral" can determine the molecular structure of unknown compounds from mass spectral and nuclear magnetic response data. In the area of engineering, the "Reactor" expert system can help operators in the diagnosis and treatment of nuclear reactor accidents.

If we analyze the attributes of this short list of expert systems we can draw two conclusions:

1. Some of these systems are used for packaging expertise for use by non-experts

2. The use of these systems serve the purpose of improving the performance of technicians

As a result, the company that can make its decisions faster, more accurately, and with greater consistency will most definitely increase its market share. For example, a large midwestern insurance underwriter experienced a troubling bottleneck when it took over another insurer. Since one of their strategic mandates was to be able to turn around an application in a short period of time, the company knew, before they even made the acquisition, that something would have to be done to process this huge flow of data efficiently and quickly.

The potential bottleneck stemmed from the fact that the insurer would need to hire new data-entry workers to keypunch the underwritings into the system. Since the underwriting applications were so complex, it took an average of six months to train and get a new employee up to speed. Using an expert system front-end, the insurer was not only able to take students from the local university and turn them quickly into experienced workers, but it was also able to put some "underwriter expertise" into the data-entry front-end, eliminating the need of their professional staff to handle rote, trivial detail.

Knowledge Is What Drives an Expert System

The secret behind an expert system is its knowledge. The first hurdle to overcome is recognizing expertise, which is not always necessarily connected to the "smartest person around." In a study entitled, "A Day at the Races" authors, Ceci and Liker[2], found even racetrack handicappers with relatively low IQs could beat the experts and professionals at their own game. What this seems to be saying is that expertise may be less a function of intelligence, and more the product of skillful coding of experience. This coding of experience is not done consciously by the expert, but is more the result of unconscious organization and structuring of new experiences.

Most people believe that the major difference between experts and nonexperts is in the quantity of knowledge the expert has managed to accumulate. Certainly quantity is one aspect, but there are qualitative differences as well.

The most obvious difference is that experts have experienced, according to Niels Bohr who was a Nobel prize winner in physics, "...all the mistakes which can be made in a very narrow field." Experts have such depth of experience that when a new problem comes their way they can see the whole picture. Novices, on the other hand, possess little experience and thus "don't see the forest for the trees".

Perhaps the most interesting difference is that the expert's knowledge is organized more efficiently than the novice's. Even with the same stimuli, the expert is able to recall more readily the pieces of the stimuli than can the novice. This was proven in a memory experiment done in the early 1970s, where novice and expert chess players were shown boards of games in progress. The experts were able to recall more pieces than the novices, since they were able to recall more patterns up from their experience. A corollary experiment was done by showing the expert and novice a gameboard with pieces strewn randomly about. Neither the expert nor the novice did better at this experiment, certainly proving the pattern-recall hypothesis.

What this seems to indicate is that the expert, by virtue of a good deal of experience, learns certain patterns that seem to be almost "burned" into memory. A new problem exhibits certain traits that are similar in some ways and dissimilar in other ways to the experience-set in memory. In fact this is so burned in that sometimes it leads to rote decision making. This "robotizing" effect was demonstrated in a study by Frensch[3], using bridge playing guinea pigs. In this study, the rules of the game were changed dramatically. Here each subsequent hand was to be led by the player who had played the *lowest* card on the last hand. This confused the dickens out of the expert bridge players, and adversely affected their playing skills. It didn't much bother the novices. Since their experience was not as yet ingrained, they had a much easier time adjusting to the new rules. What we have here is

[2] S. Ceci and L. Liker, "A Day At The Races: A Study of IQ, Expertise and Cognitive Complexity," *Journal of Experimental Psychology* 115, 1986 pp. 255–266.

[3] P. Frensch, "Expertise and Knowledge Modification: When Bridge Isn't Bridge Anymore," Unpublished paper, 1988.

deep-down knowledge at an almost ingrained level. The ramifications are significant for the knowledge engineering team.

For the most part, the first generation of expert systems relied on surface knowledge. This is knowledge obtained through a process of direct articulation, typically acquired through a series of loosely structured interviews. This laborious process is labeled a bottleneck by Ed Feigenbaum, one of the pioneers of the expert-system trend. Here, the knowledge engineer asks rather spontaneous questions as the expert describes a particular case or actually goes through the paces of solving the problem. The loose structure of this method of knowledge acquisition serves only to capture procedural knowledge at the most superficial level. It does not capture the expert's more abstract ability to apply this procedural knowledge at a more tactical level. Schon[4] in his work, *The Reflective Practitioner,* has labeled this deeper knowledge "knowing-in-action."

A second generation of methodology for knowledge acquisition comes from the research of psychology and computer science departments at various universities. Research has shown a better way at grabbing the knowledge residing deep inside the expert. These methodologies have been slowly making their way out of the laboratory and into some innovative corporate AI think tanks.

The Next Step—Neural Nets

Neural nets simulate a network of hundreds of parallel processing interconnected units, shooting messages to each other at a rapid-fire pace. The job of a neural net is to receive the input and respond. This may first look like a task that can be handled as adequately by conventional means, but neural nets are computer programs with a difference. First, neural nets have the capability of recognizing downgraded inputs. This gives us the capability, for the first time, of processing data that is either incomplete or missing. An example of this is handwriting recognition.

Handwriting recognition is being attempted today at financial institutions such as Banc-Tec. Deluged by thousands upon thousands of checks each day, the veracity of the check's signature is a big business. No one signs their signature in exactly the same way each and every time. Neural nets can be trained to recognize signatures of even those people who sign sloppily in a hurry.

Neural nets can do much more than recognize variations on penmanship. John Loofbourrow, chief of John W. Loofbourrow Associates based in New York, used a $995 package that runs on an IBM PC to develop a system that

---

[4] D.A. Schon, The Reflective Practioner: *How Professionals Think In Action* New York:(Basic Books, 1983).

forecasts the Standard and Poor's 500 index. It took Loofbourrow just 12 hours of entering the eight variables chosen as components of an arbitrary model. Data for 10-week intervals for the years 1974 through 1987 were entered for the high, the low, closing price, and volume. This was done for IBM stock, the price of gold, dollar/yen, dollar/Eurodollar. He also entered the result into the net and for this he selected the Standard and Poor 500 index.

When the net is turned on, it searches laboriously for patterns on the input side that result in a particular output—in this case, a particular rise or fall of the S&P 500 index. Neural nets are data hungry. The more input it has, the more accurate it becomes. This, of course, makes perfect sense, as a neural net mimics the way the brain learns. When confronted with many examples leading to a particular output, our brains learn that this is the normative response to these inputs. Soon, the brain can anticipate the answer even though the inputs might be slightly irregular. Just as we still fail to fully understand the working of the brain, we humans have no idea how the net performs its task. On its own, the net develops an algorithm to accomplish its task.

How Campbell Soup Adds a Pinch of Knowledge to the Broth

When you think of Campbell, you most likely think of soup, since Campbell has seemingly cornered the market in this product for over 40 years. Campbell also holds the number one or two brands in its frozen, baked goods, beverage, and grocery business units. Annual revenues worldwide are around $6 billion. Over the last decade or so, however, Campbell has seen their market share eroding as more and more aggressive rivals added their soup cans to the supermarket shelves. Given the problem of narrow margins and severe price competition, Campbell needed to reassess their strategy and move in new directions.

To become more competitive, Campbell did the expected and developed new lines including a low-salt line and a line of more gourmet soups. But equally important to the Campbell company was maintaining its image as a company with a quality product.

To do this, Campbell embarked on a course of using advanced technologies within their company that predates all other companies within their industry as well as most other companies outside it. Perhaps the premier example of this aggressive use of technology is a system fondly named Cooker.

Capturing an Expert's Knowledge

In 1984, Rubin Tyson, Campbell's Director of Manufacturing Technology, was presented with the problem of a valued and experienced worker on the verge of retirement.

Aldo Cimino's job as a Campbell production engineer was to diagnose problems with what is known as a hydrostatic sterilizer. In 1984, Campbell made soup at six locations in the United States, one in Toronto, and one in England. Each of these plants had at least one hydrostatic sterilizer, or cooker. A cooker is a unit about 30 feet square, over 70 feet high and able to process tens of thousands of cans per hour.

The problem with these 70-foot cookers was that it was not unusual to incur significant lost production time on each cooker malfunction. It would take at least a day for Cimino to arrive at the plant—one day before diagnosis and repair could even begin. Losses could be substantial if you multiply the number of hour eight work shifts lost due to malfunction by the tens of thousands of cans it could produce, but did not, per hour.

Cimino had been performing his job at Campbell for over 44 years. Knowing that the loss of Campbell's most expert troubleshooter could possibly hurt their competitive position, the company decided to try to capture Cimino's knowledge in what was in 1984 a brand new and untried commercial technology—an expert system.

The system had two primary goals. The first was to be able to replace as much of Cimino's diagnostic judgment as possible. The second goal strived for a final product that would be useful as a training tool for production and maintenance engineers.

The final product was an expert system that contained Cimino's experience distilled into 151 rules. The system has the capabilities of giving advice about the operation as well as the start-up and shutdown of the hydrostatic system.

Since Campbell soup was embarking on a path with which they had little familiarity, the company enlisted the services of an outside firm that had extensive experience in the field of artificial intelligence. Texas Instruments had developed one of the first commercially available expert system products; it was this product that was used to build Cooker and its siblings.

Success Begets Success

Once Cooker demonstrated its worth to Campbell in the manufacturing technology, there was no stopping Rubin Tyson from using the same technology to solve other, similar problems.

Closer was the first Cooker spin-off. Like Aldo Cimino, Francis Andriella was an engineer with 51 years of experience with an in-depth knowledge on the canning machines used in the soup-process lines. And like Cimino,

Andriella was getting close to retirement. Andriella's expertise was in troubleshooting the canning machines used to seal the three-piece cans in use at Campbell at the time. Since the canner was a very critical piece of machinery, a major problem with it could shut down the entire production line.

Within five months, using the same techniques used when building the Cooker system, Campbell had successfully acquired and represented Andriella's knowledge in a new expert system called Closer. Within a short period of time after the system was completed, Closer was up and running at the eight Campbell production plants.

Cooker and Closer spawned a whole new generation of expert system development at Campbell. COIL LINE was an expert system based on the knowledge of an engineer, Jerry Crawford, who was expert in diagnosing problems with Littell Coil Lines. These coil lines are the first step in the manufacture of cans, cans' bodies and ends. In all eight manufacturing lines, expert systems were built that offered a diagnostic capability based on the expertise of one or more long-term Campbell employees.

AI in the Age of CIM

Eventually, the age of CIM (Computer Integrated Manufacturing) descended upon Campbell, as well as every other company involved in manufacturing.

For Campbell, the changeover to CIM meant a change in the plant computing environment as well. The platform that the Cooker-type expert systems formerly ran on, independent PCs, were no longer a viable option on the newer plant floors. In addition, the type of problem solving that these charter expert systems solved were no longer necessary due to the new equipment, which obviously experienced far fewer malfunctions.

However, even in the CIM environment, there was still a profound need for intelligent systems. Campbell soup, now greatly experienced in the art of building expert systems, was up to the challenge of integrated AI into the CIM environment.

One of the first systems built, after the move to CIM, was SIMON. Federal regulations required special handling of any processed food product in the event of a cooker malfunction. Before the advent of SIMON, this was done by telephone. The problem plant would contact the appropriate department at the home office in Camden, New Jersey, who then interviewed the plant staff.

SIMON, developed by the Process Safety department of the Campbell Institute for Research and Technology, automates this process. Based on information about the malfunction, mathematical analysis, and rules based on Federal regulations and Campbell standards, SIMON produces a product disposition report. According to Michael Mignongna, Director of

Process Safety, this particular expert system saves Campbell millions of dollars each year.

Since Campbell was so successful in their AI endeavors, company personnel strongly leaned towards using advanced technologies wherever possible. For example, at the Maxton North Carolina plant, the existing soup line is being replaced with a flexible line able to process multiple soup products, with processing speed controlled by the demands of the equipment further up the processing line. One of the requirements, demanded by engineering personnel, is to employ some form of AI to assist in maintaining the flexible line.

Campbell is one company that has understood the very tangible benefits of using advanced technologies such as AI. It is interesting to note that their very early adoption of the AI technology has, to some degree, given them a competitive edge.

American Express Is a Smart Creditor

Another early adopter of the AI technology—that also saw its image gain a new luster as a result of an early adoption of an advanced technology—is American Express.

American Express is one of the largest, and most profitable, of American companies. With approximately 130,000 employees, it runs a host of diverse business enterprises—all of which heavily depend on technology.

Roy Lowrance formerly headed up the Corporate Technology Strategy department, which is a staff function reporting to corporate strategic planning. Since its formation, about five or six years ago, the group has been working on technology strategy issues. The interesting thing about the creation of this department is that the idea came from the very top ranks of the company in the form of the chairman, Jim Robinson. Robinson had long been pushing to get technology concepts more embedded in the business.

One of their main strategies is an major investment program in advanced technology. Amex has invested consistently, year after year, in these new technologies, trying to get them to work in their environment. The main thrust behind this program was the feeling that they could be successful in building a system that couldn't be built by anyone else, if it took the chance and proved successful, the net result would be a major improvement in Amex's competitive position.

In following this strategy, Amex looks for projects where there is a reasonable chance of failure but which, if successful, has a possibility of very high returns. According to Lowrance, this is the inverse of the capital asset pricing model. In other words, if you take more risk you have a higher rate of return.

Most technology companies are very conservative, risk-averse. There are a lot of projects that are out there that nobody will undertake, because they can't absorb the failures, and those projects are available to anyone who wants to invest in them. So, all we're doing is simply making those investments. Every year we invest in a new set of projects that have a high risk of failure.

The first project that was tackled in this dramatic, and risky, way was a system that is known as the Authorizer's Assistant. The goal was a difficult one. Amex wanted to use advanced technology to solve the problem of increasing bad debt and fraud in the use of credit cards. Since conventional computer systems didn't make much of a dent in reducing this problem, the idea of an expert system became more and more appealing.

American Express began development of their expert system in the early days of commercial expert system acceptance. Since few companies tread where American Express dared to go, it developed new techniques which, years later, many other financial companies have endorsed in their own forays into expert systems.

One of these strategies was to create a corporate group that would coordinate this new technology among its several subsidiaries. These subsidiaries were already tackling other expert system projects in such diverse areas as trading, customer service, back-office support, and insurance underwriting. This reflects the wide variety of American Express business interests.

The Authorizer's Assistant was destined to become the "pièce de résistance" of the American Express company, and perhaps the single most visible expert system anywhere in the annals of financial services.

In a nutshell, the system assists operators in granting credit to card holders, based on a review of the customer's records. Since there is no preset credit limit, this process can be a bit tricky. The authorizer usually is called into the picture if the customer is making a purchase outside of the limits of the normal computerized system. This means that small purchases can be approved by using the ubiquitous telephone automatic approval device. Here the store clerk slides your card through a slot which picks up your card number, enters the amount and waits for an approval code. It's when the amount is over a certain amount, which is different for each store, that Authorizer's Assistant goes into play.

Developing the Prototype

In developing the system, American Express chose the path of utilizing an outside consulting firm. In this case, the firm was the vendor of the product that it chose to use during prototype mode. Inference Corporation sells a heavy-duty expert system tool called ART or Automated Reasoning Tool; it also sells its services that offer knowledge engineers. American Express took the package deal.

The goal was to build a system that would assist, but not replace, the human credit authorizer. Using the five best senior Amex credit authorizers, Inference Corp's knowledge engineers went to work at eliciting their knowledge. Their knowledge allowed them to determine whether a current transaction should be approved.

In making this determination, the senior credit authorizers reviewed many items such as customer's outstanding charges, payment history, and buying habits. You see, the American Express philosophy is that you can charge anything as long as you pay your bills on time. Gradually, over the years that you have your credit card, you can build up the amount that you spend on your card.

The system required about four and a half months to prototype, and consisted of about 520 decision rules. It ran on a stand-alone Symbolic work station. The system permitted the authorizers to speed up their review of the customer's files to grant that request faster. This assistant has the capability of guiding the authorizer through phone dialogues with merchants and card holders. If the situation warrants, it prompts the authorizer for an appropriate inquiry to make of the customer. In addition, as is the forté of expert systems, the system can display its line of reasoning which is a marvelous in the training of new authorizers.

While the prototype contained 520 rules, the pilot contained over 800 rules. When it came time for American Express management to review this pilot, and provide a yea or a nay for wholesale deployment, they reviewed astonishing statistics. They found a 76 percent reduction in bad credit authorizations. They also found the system to be accurate 96.5 percent of the time as compared to the human rate of 85 percent. Management gave the nod, and the team started to plan for deployment of this system to the 300-odd authorizers.

In order to make this system work, the expert system had to be connected to the mainframe as a coprocessor. The system also had the constraint that the hardware currently used could not be changed. The authorizer workbench consisted of an IBM terminal connected to an IBM mainframe. Since American Express already made a huge investment in this hardware, it was decided to keep it and "embed" the expert system. In embeddable expert systems, the expert system component is called by the conventional mainline processor. It's not obvious to the user that this is an expert system; they just noticed that extra ingredient of intelligence.

Authorizer Assistant Competitive Impact

At the time, the Authorizer Assistant was developed it was a very risky proposition. AI was a young technology and American Express couldn't guarantee that their idea would work at all. And if it did work, they knew that there would be tremendous difficulties in getting it to run in a functional environment.

The raison d'être behind the system was an improvement in the customer service department. A secondary, but little publicized goal for the Amex expert system was to improve the expert. Most expert systems are built to provide an expert's advice to less senior, or experienced, personnel. Few, if any, expert systems are built with the goal of improving the expert. In fact, Lowrance, shares some valuable insight with us, "What you sometimes find out when you build an expert system is that the expert wasn't really an expert. The expert was really a journeyman-practioner." This is important point since it will require another round of investment by management to make this a true expert system.

An Important Capital Investment

Many companies make the grievous mistake of scaling down advanced technology projects during hard times. Lowrance, and most of the other senior officials interviewed for this book, think that this is a perspective that is in error. By and large, American companies have access to the capital markets. Using this resource, they should make all the investments necessary that yield more than their average cost of capital. In terms of the Authorizer's Assistant, if American Express found itself in the situation of needing more capital to build a more robust system, if the predicted returns on the system are sufficient, the company should go out and borrow the money. In other words, building systems that increase competitiveness should not be capital constrained.

Security Pacific
Makes Smart Loans

Loan underwriting is as tricky a business as credit-card authorization. Make enough mistakes, and a bank could suffer severe losses. But fortunately, enough statistics have been collected on the credit patterns of borrowers that it is possible to accurately predict the credit-worthiness of most individuals.

Actually, most banks actually rely on the services of outside companies to perform this process which is known as credit scoring. These external companies are referred to as scorecard vendors which present delay and expense problems to banks that wish to lower their rates, and their turn-around times, to compete in the burgeoning consumer and auto-loan markets. It was these scorecard vendors that Richard Clements, the manager in charge of AI Technology for Security Pacific in California, wished to replace with some form of automation. Given the patterned nature of the input and the predictive nature of the technology he decided that neural nets were the way to go.

The loan underwriting system examines 27 factors to arrive at one of two conclusions: strongly applicable to an acceptance or strongly indicative of a decline. If the loan is declined, then as one might expect, it is kicked upstairs to an human underwriter who ultimately decides the financial fate of the borrower.

To train the neural net, Clements provided more than 6,000 prior loan underwritings out of the 10,000 loans they had on file. Clements found what others before him have found. That is, a large percentage of your intended input is not appropriate to use as training data for a neural net due to corrupt or inconsistent data. Still, a training base of 6,000 loans was considerable, and provided the groundwork for what turned out to be a very successful loan underwriting system.

Loans make great fodder for neural networks. Clements realized this, and proceeded to move neural nets into other areas. Commercial loans was next on his list. These types of loans are far more complex than your average consumer or auto loan. The vagaries of business are such that such factors as type of management control need to be factored in to achieve the mix of inputs that will ultimately yield correct output. The commercial loan system outputs a number from 0 to 9, reflecting the level of confidence that the bank has in the company being able to repay their loan.

Before Neural Nets, There Were Expert Systems

Security Pacific is no stranger to artificial intelligence. Bank management understood the competitive significance of this type of technology long before neural nets became popular. One of its first forays into using AI was as an assistant in the very complex task of consumer real-estate appraisal in its mortgage-lending department. For this, it used an expert system the goal of which would be to review the results of the appraisal task.

The form the appraisers fill out, the Uniform Residential Appraisal Report, is logically broken down into sections. The appraiser walks through and makes judgments on such things as neighborhood, site, room, improvements to the property, interior, cost, market, and finally, value. Each section of the report has its own set of policies and procedures that an appraiser would know or look up when forming the final evaluation. These policies and procedures have been turned into expert system rules.

Security Pacific decided to use this smart new tool for appraisal review and for training. Since mortgages are the bread and butter of any bank, it was important not to let the system take over and be the final word. The human appraiser could choose not to use the system at all. If the system was used and it made a mistake, the human appraiser takes the responsibility, giving them the impetus to observe carefully the prowess of the system. The human appraisers found this system so beneficial, they gladly took responsibility for it; after all, it reduced the review process considerably. In some cases, the review time was cut down from an hour to less than a half-hour.

The appraisal process is more complicated than it looks. Appraisers look at such things as too many houses in the neighborhood to nearby garbage dump locations to quality of schools to you name it and it's included. So it's no wonder that the appraisers took to RESRA like a fish to water. With its 650 rules and "smart" data entry component, RESRA made the process of real-estate appraisal easier and, more importantly, much more accurate.

Some Caveats on Building an AI System

The goal of this chapter is to introduce the reader to the strategic benefits of investing in such advanced technologies as artificial intelligence. There is no doubt that companies such as American Express reaped larger-than-average rewards by being early adopters of this technology. But even if a company is not an early adopter, it is still very possible to gain strategic advantage by using this now mature technology to gain a foothold in a market by being better, more complete, or lower priced than your competition. This is the true benefit that these systems, which emulate the intelligence of human beings, can offer companies smart enough to take advantage of it.

What follows is a short list on how to build an AI system that a manager can use to ensure that the company ends up with a quality system.

- Management support (all levels) is necessary before any further work should begin.

- Training is of paramount importance. Building an AI system is not like building a conventional system; AI training is needed.

- Potential system problems should be screened by a combination of the user community and the technical staff that is developing the system. In other words, not all business problems have an AI solution.

- Do not use more than three experts to build any system unless the group building the system has much experience. Differences in opinion lead to delays and errors.

- Once a problem is selected it should be formally defined. The completed system shouldn't come as a surprise.

- There is more than one branch of AI, therefore the team must decide on the AI approach that should be taken.

- Always insist on a prototype.
- It's not true that expert systems and/or neural nets can't be tested
- The three most important things about an AI system (or any system) is test, test, test

9

Infotrend #8: The Distinctive Edge

Most firms use information technology—but some firms *make use* of it. If this sound like just semantics to you, read on. There probably isn't a firm out there that is not using one or more automated systems. These same firms go about their daily business worrying about market share, about competitors, and about how to make themselves outshine the competition. They do this last one in a variety of different ways: from adopting particular color schemes to composing new jingles. All firms use technology in one way or another. At first, it's just to balance the books or produce a payroll. Interestingly, a large percentage of firms fall into this category. Later, comes the realization that information technology can be used for a distinct advantage when competing with another firm. Perhaps the majority of firms fall into this category. Seldom, however, do you hear of a company that uses information technology to gain that distinctive edge. These are those firms that apply planing and innovation to the principles of strategy to produce competitively active technology.

Finding Out If an Organization Is Competitively Active

It is reasonable to assume that all firms at least understand the relationship between technology and competitive advantage. Given this assumption, it is possible to break the population of firms down into four quadrants which will assist in ranking a particular's firm's chances at success in employing technology for distinction. At minimum use of a matrix, as shown in Figure 9-1, should illuminate the deficiencies a particular firm exhibits and provide a clear path for correction.

Across the top of the matrix are two labels. On the left hand side is a box called *competitively aware*. These are the firms which understand that information technology can and is being used by companies to gain an advantage. Some, not all, of the firms in this category may have dabbled or are dabbling with technology in this vein. On the right hand side is a box labeled *competitively active*. These are the firms which are actively pursuing the use of information technology as a competitive edge in one or more projects.

Along the side of the matrix are the two categorizations of technology literacy necessary to become even a player in the "technology as competitive edge" game. For the most part, the majority of firms fall into the second of these two categories. Even though a company many spend millions on technology, this does not necessarily mean that any true competitive advantage

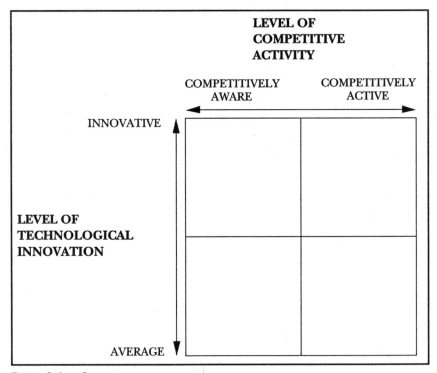

Figure 9-1.   Competitive awareness matrix.

is derived from this spending. Also, the appointment of a CIO (Chief Information Officer) doesn't necessarily mean movement toward a competitive strategy. As mentioned, the majority of firms, although cognizant of other firms' competitive advantage through information technology, are woefully unprepared to move in this direction.

Some firms, such as those discussed in this chapter, can be considered innovative in their use of technology and in its application to business strategies. These firms are the risk takers, continually reviewing new technologies to determine applicability to their business goals. American Express has an entire department dedicated to researching new advances in AI and other new emerging technologies. They are willing to take many risks in applying these newer technologies to their business. These are the innovators.

In correlating the competitive and technological axes, we can reach some conclusions. On the low end, firms that are of average technological skills and incentive but merely competitively aware run the risk of failing in their competitive bid if other business strategies, such as advertising and pricing, are not aggressively pursued. In fact, in tight competitive arenas where pricing is controlled and advertising serves little to distinguish one competitor from another, technology just might be the tie breaker. Look to the discussion on the airline wars that follows in this chapter.

The New York Stock Exchange is a good example of a firm both competitively aware and of average technological prowess. Since the next section of this chapter deals in depth on this issue, it is sufficient to note that the Exchange's tradition of limiting expenditures on automation coupled with its historical preeminence in the securities industry and a plethora of highly political constituencies has kept it from pursuing an aggressive technology program. Hence, usurpers tried, and succeeded, in winning extraordinarily large percentages of market share. Although very aware of its faltering market position, the Exchange's position on the matrix precludes it from using technology to even act defensively.

The matrix also indicates the steps necessary for a firm to move from one quadrant to another. In the Exchange's case, it is not possible to move directly from its position to one of Innovative/Competitively active without first passing through either Average/Competitively active or Innovative/Competitvely aware. To do this requires resources and time, the delay further eroding the Exchange's historical position as market leader.

The NASD Makes a Move on the Big Board

You may have seen the commercials. In one, the camera pans in on a eerily deserted room. Chairs overturned. Cobwebs. Dust. As the camera sweeps around the room, the voice-over describes the major overhaul that the London Stock Exchange went through in the late 1980s. The world called it the Big Bang—for good reason. Its ramifications were surely felt around the globe. This major event was the elimination of the trading floor of the London Stock Exchange in favor of all-electronic trading. As the camera focuses on two massive doors slamming shut (obviously on the old vanguard), the voice-over informs viewers that the London Stock Exchange got this novel automated system from the NASD; and the NASD has had it for some 20 years.

Just a mere 10 years ago, the National Association of Securities Dealers (NASD) had a reputation as a slightly disreputable marketplace of equally disreputable over-the-counter securities. In 1979, the NASD cornered only a 28.3 percent market share. Today, it's more like a 45 percent share. The reason? The NASD's unflagging dedication to technology.

The Nasdaq National Market System is the premier electronic marketplace, the model for the London Exchange and a leg up on the New York Stock Exchange. So how did the NASD manage to pull itself up by its bootstraps to its current exalted position?

Dick Justice is one of the men who built those sturdy bootstraps. At the NASD for 23 years, Justice has watched the seeds of the NASD electronic market grow into a market system that comprises over 4,000 listed companies and to ranking as the fifth largest equities market in the world. As chief technology officer for the NASD, Justice was instrumental in developing the totally automated, and off-floor, trading system (NASDAQ), that is being emulated today by stock exchanges all around the world.

In spite of the revolutionary effect of NASDAQ on the securities industry, the heavy orientation toward technology was more of an evolution. As Justice says, "It just happened." The basis for the NASD's technological growth was the great emphasis management place on the NASDAQ system. In fact, NASDAQ is often synonymous with the NASD. There would be no NASD without the system—and no system without the NASD.

The Technological Future of the Marketplace

According to Dick Justice, all exchanges everywhere will be totally dependent on technology. Each regional exchange has built its own trading support system, in which they have made a major investment. In order to survive, they'll have to continue to invest in technology.

In other words, they'll be forced into it. Just as the NASD was 20 years ago. If you try to tie a market together that is essentially a geographically decentralized collection of offices, technology is the only effective way to do that.

Technology has always been a major component of the marketplace. But it wasn't always digital. There was a different form of technology before—

voice-communications. Each exchange would invest in its own voice communication system which they would then go out and hawk. For example, an exchange's salesman would visit a broker out in Iowa and say, "I'll put in telephone lines for you if you give me your order flow—and you don't have to worry if you get an order then you just call me up and I'll execute it for you."

NASDAQ is an evolution of that kind of technology. It permits people who are geographically remote to communicate with each other. The thing that NASDAQ introduced was the sudden availability of low prices for everybody.

The Future of the NASD

In spite of its increasingly respectable market share, the NASD still sees a need to overcome the perception that the NYSE is the major market player. The premier way that it's accomplishing this feat, aside from its riveting commercials, is through the timely creation of innovative technological products. Its most recently announced innovation is the Portal system. Portal is perhaps the first electronic market for issuing and trading private market securities. Subscribers to the system can perform a multiple of functions, such as check prices in real time, launch issues, buy and sell orders, and even clear and settle trades in any of the world's major currencies. Another of its timely systems, especially in the era of Ivan Boesky, is the Market Surveillance system.

As have most on the street, the NASD has ported some of its complex systems to the high power of the workstation. Market Surveillance is one such system. The goal of this department is to monitor the marketplace, especially noting inconsistencies or aberrations. Of course, when a stock seems to be acting erratically, it really could mean a number of things, the company made an announcement, the President of the United States made a speech, new economic indicators were announced, or there really is hanky-panky going on. Given the complexity of this job, analysts performing it need a very smart tool to help them keep track of the thousands of securities being traded every day. Justice's department, in a little over a year and a half, solved this problem.

The first task that Justice's team tackled was in developing a set of statistical algorithms that could help pinpoint trading problems. For this, they turned to several professors from George Washington University and Penn State. Once this basic work was done, the NASD had it reviewed by a couple of Noble prize winners from M.I.T.

Once assured that the new algorithms could pinpoint, with a fairly high degree of accuracy, strange happenings in a particular security, the algorithms were programmed into the workstation. But that wasn't all. The NASD used the advanced windowing power of the workstation to display, for the market surveillance analyst, such niceties as Dow Jones and Reuters information and so on.

The NASD's market surveillance system demonstrates how good planning and intelligent use of resources can get a rather complex system to market before the competition. The NASD's prime competitor, the New York Stock Exchange, was also in the running with a similar system, but technical problems, confusion among the diverse and numerous working teams, a bureaucratic management as well as a massive turnover turned their very worthy effort into a lengthy four-year (and, finally, successful) project.

The NASD has always planned an evolutionary path for its systems. But now, facing the most competitive of all marketplaces as well as rapid, dramatic change in technology, Justice has decreed that it is necessary for the NASD to take another, further step along. He still calls it evolution, because the NASD isn't shutting everything down and starting from scratch, but it is planning to step off into the unknown.

The NASD has evolved into viewing itself as an *information enterprise.* In this model, data processing doesn't sit over to one side as mere support staff. Since their organization as a whole deals in information the role of technology is folded into the role of the firm. As Justice puts it, "It's all part of the same process."

To accomplish this goal, Justice is turning to a technique that is just coming of age in the 1990s, called enterprise modeling. Although actually quite complex, since a model of the entire working organization is necessary, Justice's explanation of the process makes it seem simple:

> The first task is to recognize that there are multiple, separate systems operating each on its own, individual database. In most cases, these databases sport some common pieces of data, but are each treating the data in a different way. The NASD's goal is to create a central database that is going to support everything that the organization is going to have to do, so all systems will rely on this central database. If you want to make a decision, the data is there. It's correct. And it's consistent.

An Organizational Way of Looking at IT Staff

Perhaps it's not fair to use the NASD as an example of a firm that uses technology competitively. After all, even Dick Justice admits that it evolved this way from the very start. But isn't this exactly what we are after? To find out how the seeds of technological innovation were sowed so that we can transplant them into our own organizations?

If Justice had to describe one system that exemplified the approach the NASD takes to technology, it would be the original NASDAQ system. This was its strategic entree into the market. From this, the NASD learned alot about developing strategic and distinctive systems.

The key factor in effectively using technology is to define requirements accurately at the start. Don't try to make the problem fit what the company has in the way of a solution. In other words, don't force-fit the problem to the first solution at hand. Look at the problem, and determine what has to be done. One of the things that made NASDAQ successful is that the work performed to define the initial NASDAQ system was done in this vein.

NASDAQ was created by a combination of Arthur D. Little staff and a team of people Justice had hired and staff. Interestingly, not one of these people were technologists. They were people, however, who understood trading—and were able to define the requirements in such a way that the system was a very good fit. So good a fit that it just naturally evolved in the marketplace.

Today, the organizational approach to developing technological solutions is similar to the one that the NASD used to develop its successful NASDAQ system some 20 years ago.

Many NASD systems analysts don't have a technical background. They pick up enough knowledge as they go along. Of course they can't write programs. Justice's solution is to create a group of people who writes programs, and a separate group of people who act like business analysts and define the requirements.

The NASD has harkened back to a structure that has become less and less popular over the years. In the 70s, the role of business analyst was a productive and meaningful role. During the 80s, the business analyst went the way of the dodo bird in most organizations—if the classified pages can serve as a barometer. The programmer/analyst seemed to take over. The programmer/analyst became omnipotent. He, or she, not only has the skills to write the most complex of programs, but this person also has an in-depth understanding of the business process.

Sounds too good to be true? It is. Think about it. Where else in the organization is one person assigned the role of expert in two different jobs? Are your marketing mavens also expert in finance? Are your economists also expert in sales? So why should your programmers be experts too in marketing? Or sales? Or any other area they support? It's just too much to expect.

Dick Justice knew that he was advocating something that had become less popular over the years. But he knew that the technology-driven approach just didn't cut the mustard. He simply didn't believe that it would work. He thinks that the NASD has been successful largely because they've been able to integrate technology into business, and not vice versa. And one of the ways to do this was to organize according to their business lines.

The NASD's technology group is well-distributed. There's a group of people located in New York City who functions as business analysts. These are the folks who know the business cold. They're located in New York City since this is where—in spite of the recession and encroaching globalization—the action is. Attached to this group of business analysts is a small team of technically oriented designers with whom the analysts have a close working relationship.

The primary NASD computer is located in Connecticut where the majority of technologists live and work. Along with a large group of designers and programmers, this is also where the systems operations and quality assurance group make their home.

The NASD headquarters happens to be in Washington, D.C. And it is here where Dick Justice has installed his technical planning group. Up to a few short years ago, the administrative technology group was located here as well. A relocation to Rockville, Maryland gave the NASD not only newer quarters, but more space to run the ever-increasing number of systems into which Justice dug his teeth.

Will America Harbor the Electronic Trading Exchange of the Future?

In spite of the NASD's role as originator of the concept of floorless electronic trader, some pondits wonder whether the electronic trading floor of the future will be located in the United States at all. For along with the rise of their economies, matching a parallel decline in the economy of our own country, has been a solid foreign investment in some pretty high-tech trading technology.

Of these, perhaps the London and Japan Stock Exchanges are the most publicized. However, the Paris Exchange, known as the Bourse, has quietly wedged itself into the number one position—and, some say, become a role model for exchanges everywhere.

The Parisian road to success began in 1983 with the elimination of paper-stock certificates. This was the first of a three-phase plan then will ultimately see every exchange function automated in a paperless manner.

Back in 1986, the Bourse installed software originally developed for the Toronto Stock Exchange. Known as CAC, its purchase was the culmination of a worldwide search for sophisticated software that would fit the Bourse's requirements.

The Bourse's decision to purchase rather than to develop poses some interesting insight into its strategic thinking. Most companies that seek a competitive edge through the use of technology are keen on developing their software internally. Creative in-house solutions offer more of a panacea from a public-relations perspective than a mere purchase-and-install solution. If this automated floor trading system was the Paris Bourse's ultimate goal, then, undoubtedly, they, too, would have developed their own solution. But, as previously mentioned, the Paris Bourse had a three-phase plan, and installation of the CAC was only the second phase. Planners who participated in the search for the ultimate trading system were no doubt confronted early on with the question of whether or not to automate or purchase. In searching out competing products, they realized that there was no value added to developing a competing system in this area when there was already a strong product available. I believe that the planners innately understood that there could be no competitive advantage to in-house development when the final product would be little better than already existing ones. As a result, planners at the Bourse pinned their marketing hopes on the final stage of their three-phase plan. In doing so, the Bourse knew that it was of paramount importance that the third phase begin as soon as possible.

The third phase, the one that would mark the Bourse as an innovative leader, was to be a back-office settlement system. Relit would ultimately be the marketing sword that would give the Paris Bourse the reputation as one of the most technologically advanced exchanges in the world. The name Relit is a shortened form of two french words, *reglement* and *livraison,* which can be translated to settlement and delivery. These functions are perhaps the least visible, but most important part of the trading function. In the early days of the stock market, a trade would be accompanied by a two people exchanging cash for the paper security. In the markets of today, obviously a two-person settlement is infeasible. American exchanges have long automated this function. But Paris' completely electronic Relit system goes a step beyond what is available today on other competing exchanges.

When combined with CAC, Relit completes the long-term plan begun in 1983 enabling the Paris Bourse to sit in a pretty position to handle, and profit from, the trading surge created by the long awaited creation of the borderless European Economic Community.

Technology Flies High

The discussion of globalization of the securities industry, in the last section, makes one pause to think about an industry that has been necessarily global from its very outset.

The airline industry must track a myriad of details on many continents. For the traveling public, the problems of this burdensome set of tasks is all too evident. For the ailing airline industry, maintaining customer satisfaction levels is **the** competitive issue—and one increasingly being handled by technology.

We've all had, or will have, this particular problem at one time or another. We check our luggage in, and when we get to our destination, our luggage just doesn't come out. The problem is that we flew to Chicago but our luggage, obviously with a mind set of its own, flew to New York. Except the airline won't know this until 24 hours after our important meeting which we had to attend in tennis shorts.

We're all experts when it comes to the airlines. We keep track of their delays, their promotions and, most importantly, their fares. Basically, what this all boils down to is competency in a very complex environment. In the days of government regulation, the airlines could comfortably control their environments ever assured of their equalized market share and their guaranteed profits. With the advent of deregulation came the necessity of each airline finding an edge that could be used to distinguish itself from the competition.

In a sturdy economy, the tool most often used was advertising. Who hasn't seen the print ads of faraway places beckoning the reader with the punch line always being the name of the airline? For a long while, this ploy worked well—but things change. Turbulent economic times had a number of effects. People traveled less, or maybe not at all. The buy-out boom of the 1980s hit the airline industry particularly hard. For the first time, airlines, once stocks that were the most inviting for widows and orphans, began to travel the rocky road to bankruptcy. The tragedy of Pan Am and near tragedies of Eastern Airlines and Continental loomed large. Frank Lorenzo's name would hereafter become part of airline legend. If this wasn't enough, political unsavories began to use airline flights as targets. The age of terrorism had begun—and there was no end in sight.

Already staggering under the weight of ever-increasing fuel bills and increasing competition from a plethora of domestic and foreign carriers, airlines began to rethink their strategies. How can we attract more customers while streamlining costs? This became the war cry heard in more than one airline board room.

Back in New York, our luggage sits unattended, while we're in a meeting in Chicago dressed rather inappropriately. We want to know where our luggage is, but the airline hasn't yet tracked it down. If there was some sort of system in place where an airline could immediately locate lost luggage, then we'd opt to fly that airline all the time. Wouldn't we?

United Airlines Airport of the Future

This is one of the United Airlines goals as they pursue their "airport of the future" project at Philadephia International Airport. United's mission is to automate every facet of the airport for both employees and customers. Working with Covia, a partnership of several airlines of which United owns half, the team hopes to change the way customers think about airline flying—and about United, in particular.

When we check in at a United counter, all flight and passenger information is encoded on the ticket and matched with the flight data system-wide.

It is envisioned that the luggage tags will be electronically encoded, allowing the airline to track a bag at any point during transit. This will have secondary benefits, since by using laser scanners in the baggage areas and magnetic readers at boarding gates, security is greatly enhanced.

Technology improvements on board the aircraft are also part of the grand scheme. Robert Enrst, who is United's director of on-board services, predicts that United customers might soon see data terminals which would provide customers with electronic libraries of information helpful to travelers interested in customs or other information about their destination.

Airport 2000

United is the airline industry's market leader, on the forefront of applying information technology to its business. But there are many other airlines which recognize the need to invest in this brand of high technology to remain competitive. Unfortunately, many of these firms do not have the financial resources nor the technical skills to develop their own "airport of the future."

For these firms, the entry of IBM, Unisys, and others into this marketplace comes as a mixed blessing. From one perspective, being able to purchase a ready-made hardware and software solution enables these airlines to buy a less expensive, but equally competitive product. Not having to cope with programming delays or cost overruns gets the airline into a competitive position that much faster and less expensively.

A purchased solution, on the other hand, might just backfire. When a new service is unveiled to the public, it is usually accompanied by a flurry of excitement and increased sales to the industry innovator. Over time, as industry competitors unveil their competing service, the novelty of the innovator's offering begins to fade. A service or product developed in house has the capability of being altered as the aura fades to constantly introduce new services, bringing back those customers attracted by the bells and whistles offered by a competitor. Often, a purchased solution is proprietary. That is, it cannot be tailored or altered specifically for the company that purchases it. In essence, if 10 airlines purchase an airport of the future product, then all 10 airlines will be have the same service. There is no competitive advantage in similarity.

The resolution to this dilemma is to ensure that a purchased solution is modifiable to the unique specifications of the purchasing company. This will enable the company to put a unique stamp on the product such that enables customers to differentiate one from another.

Perhaps the best example of a vended airport of the future product is the one being developed by Unisys. Airport 2000 is a far-reaching concept based on the understanding that if an airline is to survive its turbulent competitive wars, then it would have to strategically automate every facet of its business: from passengers to aircraft parking to operations to decision support. Unisys has developed a blueprint that is using some of the most advanced technology techniques and tools.

Dave Roberts, Unisys' Airport 2000 program manager, admits that this is a nascent field and the Unisys offering is in its incubatory period. They do have one module available that is currently being tested by AeroMexico. Although a foreign airline, AeroMexico can be thought of as a global representative of the entire industry.

Until recently, Mexico's airline industry was federalized. Over the last few years, however, Mexico has privatized this industry. For the first time, Mexican airlines has found itself in the position of having to compete—not only with other Mexican carriers, but with foreign carriers flying in and out of Mexico. Since AeroMexico had neither the funds nor the technical resources to fund its own state of the art solution to this problem, it turned to Unisys.

The component of Unisys' Airport 2000 that AeroMexico is currently using is called the Airport Passenger Processing System or APPS[1]. Since most of us are experts when it comes to how we are treated by the airlines, it will be worthwhile to spend a few minutes describing APPS to see how different it is from what we experience.

According to Roberts, a passenger never remembers the good things that happen with an airline, only the bad. With this in mind, there are many potential areas of service improvement.

APPS uses Unisys workstations connected by local-area networks. Each workstation area is equipped with printers and readers for automated tickets and boarding passes as well as bag tags. Additionally, the workstation, at the preflight stage, can call up flight information, reconcile passenger and baggage for an extra safety feature, or collect statistics as well as produce management reports.

The APPS information displays may be used elsewhere other at the agent's desk. Rather than installing costly information boards at central locations only, the system can be distributed throughout the airport. This can be done with a variety of cost-effective, programmable information displays that would show flight and other urgent information. It is then possible to list flight numbers, scheduled and estimated arrival and departure times, gate assignments, and special messages. These messages can be used to redirect passengers and agents to a new gate assignment, or they can advise passengers to proceed to the gate area as a flight approaches closeout status. These displays are a combination of the well-known flight informa-

---

[1]Airport Passenger Processing System. White paper. Unisys, 1991.

tion display or a newer, and more visible, display which will serve to rapidly notify the passenger of important messages.

Central to APPS is the use of automatic ticketing printers and readers. Using magnetically encoded tickets, the system can verify passenger information and prints boarding passes immediately. It also automatically produces a bar-coded bag tag, improving passenger-to-baggage reconciliation as well helping to track lost luggage that much more quickly.

The key principle behind APPS is to keep the system operable even when the host system is off line. This is accomplished by APPS maintaining a local copy of selected host data on the local area network connected workstation. It is believed, by Unisys, that local processing protects against flight delays and inconveniences that can have a negative impact on an airline's image and profitability.

As a stand-alone system, APPS can function equally well as a one-stop passenger check-in for either individual passengers or groups. Seat selection is performed easily be accessing a seat map which, when seats are selected, will automatically trigger a printing of the boarding pass and bag tag.

Unisys believes that positive boarding control functions can provide the basis for improved passenger, baggage, and standby processing. For example, to ensure that passengers are boarding the correct flight, the system can verify seat assignments during boarding.

Unisys is, of course, just one of the contenders in the race to total airline automation. But its system provides some good insight into what it means to look to technology as savior in the competitive wars. American and United known this only too well. From United's Airport of the Future in Philadelphia to Unisys' Airport 2000, the key is indeed technology. As the race for a distinctive edge wears on, soon everyone will serve a five-course meal on china and have similar types of seats, so it will all boil down to who can serve the customer better in areas that are important. And in this quest, information technology is the key.

The Competitive Edge in Customer Service

Most of us travel on airlines relatively infrequently. But we do use one form of travel rather continuously. Perhaps even more frequently than the ubiquitous automobile. What is this form of transportation? The elevator.

Believe it or not, even in this industry, competition is raging, and companies, such as Otis Elevator, are beginning to look at information technology in a new light.

For Otis, the idea of applying information technology to customer service came in the late 1980s. At that time, most elevator companies were providing good, reliable elevators. In searching for a way to differentiate itself, it decided that providing extraordinary service just might be the lift that it needed.

The company had already installed an 800 telephone line so that customers could call to request a repairman. It was the application of information technology to this phone line, hereafter called the "Otisline," that made headlines.

The first step Otis took was to load all information about repair calls into a customer database. This database was made easily accessible to a repairman who could check a customer's file and receive a complete repair history. But this alone was not what helped Otis increase its sales in 1990 by 21 percent from the previous year. The technological innovation that performed this miracle was the introduction of a tiny computer chip into each Otis elevator.

This chip monitors the elevator continuously. If it detects a problem, it can alert Otis headquarters so that a repairman can be immediately dispatched. Sometimes, Otis calls a customer about a problem in the elevator before the customer is even aware of a problem.

What Otis, and others, has discovered is that the new battleground for the 1990s is being able to provide the most satisfying ownership experience for customers; in two words: customer service. According to Daniel P. Finkelman, a principal with the New York-based consulting firm McKinsey and Company, not only can a company not be competitive without a high-quality product, neither can it gain much market share with product improvements alone.

According to the American Marketing Association, it costs five to six times as much to cultivate a new customer as to regain an old one. According to industry studies:

- The majority of customers who switch banks do so because of poor service.

- 60 percent say past satisfaction, 32 percent say low prices when asked why they purchase from a particular company.

- 70 percent of the time a supplier is dropped because of its "indifference" to the customer.

- Companies that implement a customer-service program increase their market share by 2 points, even when they increase their prices.

Unfortunately, customer service is a hard thing to provide. Markets change continually and rapidly—too rapidly to keep up. This is why computers have become a staple technology. In fact, many industry consultants agree that the computer will become the key to building market share in the next decade. Some companies, such as Otis, are using information technology in new and unexpected ways. Companies like these are finding the distinctive edge.

How to Use Information Technology as a Customer Weapon

Even though the decade of the 1990s has been termed the "decade of customer service," the idea of applying information technology to customer service and using the combination as a competitive weapon is not new.

In the 1980s, Metpath, a well-known clinical laboratory, provided terminal hook-ups to physicians who, for a small fee, who could retrieve medical test results. At the time, Metpath was competing in an extremely tough business where services to customers were similar, leading to a lack of customer loyalty and frequent price discounting.

According to Wiseman[2] Metpath was strategically using information technology as a competitive weapon in two ways:

> (1) to build barriers against new and existing competitors by raising the information system ante; (2) to gain competitive advantage over other labs by differentiating an otherwise commodity service by keeping records of patient data on file and by offering financial processing services through billing and accounts payable applications.

Probably the best example of using information technology in this manner is the American Airlines and United Airlines creation and deployment of their reservations systems, Sabre and Apollo, respectively, into thousands of travel agencies. Even though these systems list all flights at all airports, these systems harbor a bias toward the developer of the system. For example, a travel agent who uses American's Sabre system to request a listing of flights between New York and Chicago will invariably see the American flight schedule first, even though it may not be the most direct way—or the least expensive. This prioritization procedure can lead to as much as 20 percent additional business.

Wiseman and MacMillan have devised what they call an *option generator* which may be useful to the reader in the search for strategic opportunities. Using a series of questions, a business unit should be able to generate at least 100 possibilities for using information technology to create a competitive edge. In Wiseman and MacMillan's experience, not one company that has seriously attempted to find an edge, using this methodology, has failed to do so.

What Is the Strategic Target?   Figure 9-2 shows a matrix from which the procedure can take shape. Across the top of the matrix are three choices for

---

[2] Charles Wiseman and Ian C. MacMillan, "Creating Competitive Weapons From Information Systems," *Journal of Business Strategy* (Fall 1984).

the major question, *"What is the strategic target?"* There are three possible choices. Suppliers are those that can provide either raw materials, services, capital, or labor. An example of supplier as target is the Equitable Life Assurance Company which developed an inventory control and purchasing system. This system gives them leverage with the suppliers since the Equitable has access to an on line database that permits them to check the terms of all recent deals struck for the items they want.

The second target choice is customers. Customers, in a broader sense, includes consumers as well as retailers, wholesalers, distributors and potentially anyone to whom a company sells. Otis, American, and United provide good sources of examples in this area.

The third target choice is competitors. This includes those currently in the industry, possible new entrants, other industry firms offering substitute products, and other organizations competing for scarce resources. The brokerage community's use of information technology as a manufacturer of tailored products is a good example of this third strategy. Merrill Lynch's Cash Management Account depends on its database and laser technology, while Shearson's managed commodity account is directed by a computerized portfolio management system.

	Suppliers	**Customers**	**Competitors**
Differentiation			
Cost			
Innovation			

Figure 9-2.   Major options in securing a competitive advantage.

What Strategic Thrust Can Be Used Against the Target? On the left side of the matrix in Figure 9-2 can be seen the different choices used in answering the question, *"What strategic thrust can be used against the target?"* There are three: differentiation, cost and innovation. Correlating the option choices leads to nine possible major options to gain a competitive edge.

The goal of a differentiation thrust is to either increase a company's differentiation advantages with regard to suppliers, customers and/or competitors or reduce the differentiation advantages that suppliers, customers, or competitors enjoy. A good example here is the use of information technology to control labor in the displacement of controllers as a result of the air traffic controller strike.

Prior to the strike, air traffic controllers were seen as highly trained, and indispensable, specialists. At that time, however, a new information system had just been built that had the effect of reducing the differentiation, and clout, of labor. According to M.I.T.'s Harley Shaiken, a labor relations expert, the government's use of information technology doomed the strike. It kept air traffic moving, gutting the striker's leverage. Soon after the walkout, 75 percent of the commercial flights were operating, even though 75 percent of the controllers were on the picket line.

The goal of the cost thrust is to either reduce or avoid a company's costs with regard to suppliers, customers, or competitors; help suppliers or customers reduce their costs with regard to the company so the company gains preferred treatment; or, increase the competition's costs. Hartford Insurance Company provides customers with a computer-generated loss control analysis. For those customers who have complex exposures and multiple claims, this leads to substantially lower premiums—and more business for the Hartford.

Finally, the goal of the innovation thrust is to find new ways of doing business through the use of information technology. Examples Wiseman and MacMillan supply are using technology to transform steps on an existing industry chain, diversify into new markets, create new businesses, or redefine businesses. When Toys "Я" Us decided to enter the children's clothing market, they knew that competition would be fierce. Since they had already become masters at automating a tracking system which provided them with the information they needed to keep the shelves stocked with selling merchandise, they applied this same technology to their new venture.

What Strategic Mode Can Be Used? After strategic target and thrust have been selected another set of options is generated by *determining the strategic mode to be used*. Information technology can be used either offensively, to increase an edge, or defensively, to reduce an edge now held by one or more targets.

American and United provide good examples of the use of an offensive strategy. Airlines that are carried on the Sabre and Apollo systems are at a distinct disadvantage to American and United. In fact, several have complained that their cash-flow problems were a direct result of this self-favoritism.

From the defensive perspective, a law firm's use of its telephone information system to ensure billing accuracy, or use of a telephone system to impede employee overuse, are good examples of this strategy.

What Direction of Thrust Can Be Used?   Now it is necessary to determine whether the system is to be used by the organization internally or to be provided for outside use. Asking the question, *"What direction of thrust can be used?"* uncovers a dual answer. Therefore the answer is not mutually exclusive.

A system that contains marketing information used by sales reps would be an example of *usage as the direction.* Systems of this sort capture and display information about sales penetration, district profiles, and much more. On the other hand, Merrill Lynch's Cash Management Account is an example of *provision as the direction.* Merrill provides an automated system to customers with high minimum balances. Through the system customers can obtain a variety of services that are extremely palatable. With this system, Merrill dominated the market for up to four years, the time it took for a competitor to strike a defensive countermeasure.

What Information System Skills Can We Use?   Finally, we must look at the last option by asking the question, *"What information system skills can we use?"* Wiseman and MacMillan categorize three separate areas of information technology: information processing, information storage, and information transmission. Strategic systems can be built based on any or a combination of the three.

Programs that process statistical data are examples of *processing as the skill* used. National Decisions Systems, in 1980, was the first to see the value of providing an analytical tool for use in generating analytical displays from raw census data. Ford Motor Company's auto parts inventory system, permitting dealers who need auto parts to search each others inventories, is an example of a system using *storage as the skill used.* Ford's bonus was an increase in customer service and dealer loyalty.

The third possibility, *transmission as the skill used,* is exemplified by the now proliferating use of on-line database services such as Dun and Bradstreet.

Synergy with Competitive Business Strategy.   The Wiseman/MacMillan option generator should not be filled out in a vacuum. Systems developers should work hand-in-hand with the business units to perform this exercise. In fact, performing this exercise in conjunction with a business unit's development of their competitive business strategy provides, perhaps, the optimum solution.

10

Infotrend #9: Ushering in the Age of Techno-Business or IT as a Profit-Center

Carmine Vona, of Banker's Trust, said it best when he insisted that in order for a company to be successful it was necessary "to make technology an integral part of the fabric" of that company. The companies discussed in this book seem to understand well the need for information technology to stand side by side, arms linked, with the business units.

A simple way of thinking about this merger of technology and business strategy is to visualize a planet—the planet earth. At the center of planet earth is its core, or heart. Surrounding the earth's core is the mantle which is topped off by the earth's surface where all manner of things live, breathe, and work.

Viewed from this perspective, an organization, in this analogy, has at its core its business strategy. Organizations who take great stock in information technology, like Bankers Trust and the NASD, surround their core with a **mantle of technology** (Figure 10-1). Organizational staff use the power of the technology mantle to perform their tasks and activities more competitively than those without this mantle.

But what if the position of core and mantle were reversed. Instead of an organization using technology to fulfill its business strategy, *what if an organization's business strategy was technology*—in essence—a techno-business? To coin a phrase, a techno-business is one whose rise to prominence is

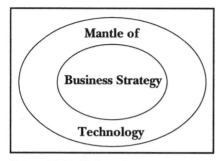

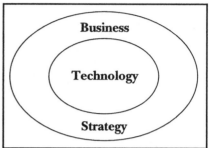

Figure 10-1. Traditional organization's technology strategy

Figure 10-2. A Techno-business

predominantly technology driven. In Figure 10-2, we clearly see that the heart of a techno-business is surrounded by corporate business strategy, in a reversal of the more normative position discussed above.

The very essence of a techno-business is the Memphis-based Federal Express Corporation. Their rise to an almost unbeatable competitive position is due, almost entirely, to their insistent dedication to the use of technology in all facets of their business. Since Fedex has achieved an exalted, almost folkloric, position in the annals of American business, this chapter will explore that company in some depth.

However, before we undertake this tour, it is important to understand that the very nature of a techno-business is neither black nor white. Not every company aspires to emulate Federal Express, nor needs to go as far; there are gradations.

Many companies have honed their IT skills to an exacting science, and are representative of the firms discussed in this book which have managed to interweave IT and strategy successfully. Once done, some of the more ambitious and aggressive of this ilk begin to eye the outside world as a possible source of new profits. Thus, a microcosm of the business at large is formed within the IT department as it goes out in search of new ventures.

This is what Kimberly-Clark Corporation did in 1989 when it started up its Kimberly-Clark Computer Services subsidiary. Of course, Kimberly-Clark Corp—the sales of which in 1989 exceeded $5 billion—is no stranger to corporate spin-offs.

The baseline of this new venture is a reengineering tool named K-C Enable/DB2 which converts programs written in a Computer Associate's brand database to the IBM market leader, DB2.

Another brand-name company using IT for profit—this time in the financial services arena—is Morgan Stanley. Morgan has spent millions in upgrading its systems over the years. It recognized early on, according to Robert Gartland, Chief Operating Officer of Morgan Stanley Services, "that technology was going to be a very important factor in our business."

Morgan's goal today is to be a major intermediary in cross-border capital flows and offer services both to the providers of capital and the users of capital. This is the reason for the very existence of Gartland's unit, a subsidiary of Morgan Stanley. The function of Morgan Stanley Services is to market Morgan's operational services to broker/dealers and institutional clients.

Perhaps the organization that has achieved the most publicity with this technique is Mrs. Fields Cookies. What has made Mrs. Fields Cookies intriguing is not the profitability of her firm, but the fact that the entire company is run—from dough to chocolate chips—by computer.

A series of expert systems does everything from keep track of employees to telling the manager when a person should go out into the street, cookies in hand, giving away samples. This feat alone is extraordinary.

What makes Mrs. Fields a good candidate for a techno-business is that the company soon realized that the precision expertise it had in running its stores was a natural as a product in its own right. Today, Mrs. Fields Cookies technology unit has spun off in its own right specializing in expert system technology at the retail level.

Kimberly-Clarke, Morgan Stanley, and Mrs. Fields all have one thing in common. They have leveraged their information technology skills to such a degree that it was reasonable, and advisable, to expand their services externally. The three firms represent the different gradations of those firms that can said to be techno-businesses. Information technology alone wasn't sufficient; these firms needed an astute understanding of the businesses they were in to be able to successfully bring their products to market.

These three companies have climbed to the very top of the techno-business mountain. But atop the summit sits a firm that made the trip a number of years ago. This is Federal Express. And it's now time to unfold its story.

Without Technology, FEDEX Would Just Be Another Delivery Service

Mention Federal Express to anybody and the first image conjured up is overnight delivery. Most lay people are quite astounded by Fedex's ability to pick up a package today and delivery it by 10:30 a.m.—thousands of miles away. They are even more impressed when they find out that all Fedex planes converge on an airport in Tennessee in the middle of the night to redistribute their loads and fly out to all points, north, south, east, and west, for delivery by the next morning. Few realize how large a role technology plays in this somewhat superlogistical feat.

It all started with Fred Smith, founder and still head of the $8 billion Fedex. Legend has it that Smith conceived of the idea for express delivery as a project in business school. No matter how, or why, he came up with the idea, Smith was most certainly a visionary by understanding, as far back as the '70s, the importance of technology to the success of his scheme.

Smith's reliance on technology to build the foundation of his business is more uncommon than first meets the eye. Smith was not, and is not, a technologist. His role is that of CEO. It is an unfortunate truth that most CEOs in the United States are woefully uninformed about the possibilities inherent in using information technology as part and parcel of their businesses. In many cases, this lack of information translates to downright fear and then, perhaps, mistrust. These CEOs, unlike Smith, don't seem to have the vision that would make the best use of the technology tools so readily available. Of course, these CEOs certainly use technology. They probably even have monthly meetings about various and sundry corporate projects but, unlike Smith, they don't seem to be a guiding force in making sure the company infuses information technology dead center into their businesses.

In looking at, and talking to, the myriad companies that have been profiled in this book, the one thing most pronounced is the good luck to have a CEO who truly understands the relationship between information technology and business strategy, and who actively embarks on policies and projects that reflects this commitment. Understanding and commitment are quite different.

Smith represents this most perfect combination. He's a businessman with a keen interest in what technology can do for Fedex. In fact, his interest is so pronounced that it is said that he personally reads voluminous computer trades to keep abreast of any new development that can be leveraged successfully by his company.

Most companies that successfully use information technology have a counterpart to the CEO directly in its midst. This person, sometimes called the CIO for chief information officer, acts as the top-gun liaison between high levels of the organization and the technology department itself. At Fedex, this person was, up until the end of 1991, Ron J. Ponder who then went on to an esteemed career as CIO of Sprint/United Telecommunications. While still at Fedex, Ponder's description of the internal workings of the company, and the systems for which it is famous, makes good reading for those interested in following such a course.

Fedex Technology Unveiled

The Fedex technology unit is made up equally of systems development, computer operations, and telecommunications. As befitting a global express service, the biggest emphasis is on its telecommunications. At Fedex, telecommunications is part and parcel of the technology unit at large, unlike the more common model where telecommunications is administratively and physically discrete from the rest of the technology unit.

With over 2,000 people working on some very complex and important systems, Ponder fully understands the meaning of people-orientation. One can tell that Fedex emphasizes the humanness of working (unlike many companies in the less-than-humane 1990s) in its descriptions of the way certain things are done at the company, for instance, its no-layoff policy, which is heresy today when corporate marching orders appear to be "here today, gone tomorrow." Perhaps Fedex's rather old-fashioned sense of loyalty to its staff is the reason why their people are so committed to the organization. Perhaps this commitment is the reason why Fedex has been so innovative over the years. Certainly, this speculation should give pause to those in corporations who apparently lack the understanding of the relationship between layoffs and resulting job insecurity and its effect on productivity, innovation, and combativeness.

Fedex technology centers, which process more than 14 million transactions daily, are scattered across the globe. The main unit is located at Fedex's headquarters in Memphis, with another center in Los Angeles—as a result of Fedex's acquisition of the Flying Tigers express service—and one in London—created because Fedex wanted to have a unit close to their European customer base. Perhaps their most interesting unit is based in Colorado Springs—not because of the prestigious talent of these people, but because of its location. When Fedex began their quest for the perfect systems, they had trouble hiring the technical people that they needed. Many balked at making a move to Memphis, mostly famous as the birthplace of Elvis Presley.

In the seventies Fedex did a study of what the most ideal place to relocate would be in order to attract the best talent. This turned out to be Colorado Springs. To this day, Ponder believes that this concession to staff morale was instrumental in their ultimate success.

Ponder's first job with Fedex was in operations research. This was in the days before any of the systems Fedex is renown for were conceived. In fact, this is probably where Smith got his first taste of the possibilities that automation power could provide his growing company. In those days, Smith was very hot on operations research tools. From the very beginning, according to Ponder, Smith made extensive use of these tools in running the company: from there, it was an easy jump to the use of wholesale automation.

Even in the early 70s, Smith clearly understood the growing closeness of the world, now called globalization but referred to by Smith then as worldwide logistics. At the same time, Fedex's strategic planning sessions were questioning where the business was going? Where are the competitors going? What did Fedex have to do to stay competitive over the next decade or two? You'll note some interesting things about Fedex that sets it apart from most of their contemporaries in the early 1970s (and even today).

First, it understood the coming push toward globalization—even though this trend is one that most didn't begin to pursue until at least 10 years later. Secondly, Fedex's planning horizon stretched out over two decades, which was more Japanese-oriented than its American counterparts, which usually worked in a window of two to five years. Finally, technology was considered the key part of their strategy.

Ponder describes Smith as, "very learned in terms of the use of systems and computers." Ponder ticks off Smith's technology attributes:

Understands ability and power of technology

Understands use of it

Appreciates use of it

Very much pushes for the use of it

This combination of Smith's ability to visualize a technological advantage led to the creation of the first, and most famous, of Fedex's systems. Fedex, in situating themselves as a company with which it would be very easy to do business, leapt to the realization "that information about the package is just as important as the package itself." This was the guiding principle behind Cosmos.

Fedex reasoned, in building Cosmos, that if a person is going to ship a critical item, then the person is going to be very interested in placing it in a custodial environment where it is secure, tracked, traced, and watched over. This is, in effect, what Cosmos offers.

Cosmos stretches its tentacles across the United States and the world. In fact, the network (Cosmos and its siblings which we'll read about later) is so extensive that there is no one in this country, no matter how remotely located, that a Fedex van can't reach in 15 minutes.

This feat of superlogistics has its base at company headquarters where an IBM mainframe telecommunicates continuously with 17 Fedex "call centers." These call centers can be compared with airline reservations centers. For example, the Fedex call center in Phoenix, Arizona is staffed by 125 people. Ponder emphasizes that these centers are all user-friendly, "We purposely keep the environments small and pleasant in these centers," to maintain a high caliber of staff and a higher level of customer service.

If a customer in the Southwest calls the Fedex 800 telephone number, the call is rerouted to the Phoenix call center. At this point, the customer will be asked for a customer number, if one is available. In this way, the Fedex customer service agent can recall from the computer all the information that Fedex has on that particular customer. Once Fedex is told that a pickup is requested, the customer service agent presses a button on the keyboard which instantly relays a "request for pickup" message to Memphis.

The computer in Memphis then immediately relays a message to the federal express station closest to the customer's location.

Inside each of these stations is a dispatch center that acts as the distributive part of Cosmos. Each dispatch center is equipped with a DEC minicomputer. The dispatcher uses this mini to manage the 65 to 100 vans under his or her jurisdiction.

While the Memphis mainframe sends the pickup request to the local station, the minicomputer is responsible for performing what Fedex calls "dynamic load balancing." Since at any point in time there may be 65 drivers, called *couriers* by Fedex, on the road and with pickup requests coming fast and furious, the computer needs to be able to handle the load efficiently and completely.

Load balancing is handled programmatically by the dispatch minicomputers on an on-line real-time basis. All addresses are apportioned to particular routes by a process known as sectoring. Fedex divides all zip codes in the United States into sectors. These divisions of the zip code are not random. Sectors understand natural boundaries such as bridges and one-way streets. A courier's route is built up of these sectors.

Most mornings, Fedex couriers are working on deliveries, with the afternoon devoted to pickups. If a customer is on the Fedex database (the database is now some 5 million strong), a sector number has already been assigned. So when this same customer calls for a pickup, the sector number can be instantly sent out along with the request for the pickup. This information is transmitted over the network, and ultimately relayed to a particular courier.

Perhaps the courier that received the message for pickup suffers an overload. For example, a firm earlier on the route ships out hundreds of copies of the annual report. The courier in this situation notifies the dispatcher who adjusts the system at the dispatch center. Ultimately, the pickup in question would be rerouted to a courier on a route adjacent to the original courier.

This backbone, which Ponder refers to as an *order entry system,* forms the basis for the original Fedex Cosmos system. The system is online seven days a week, 24 hours a day. Its backup facilities are prestigious. Besides hardware backup, it has a doubly redundant fiber optic cable around the nation. Its run cable under the ocean and uses satellites as backup. The Fedex systems simply cannot, and do not, fail.

Perhaps as important as Cosmos is Fedex's DADS system. DADS, Digital Assisted Dispatch System, was born out of frustration with using radios for communication between dispatcher and courier. Because of its "obsession with running a system that absolutely doesn't fail you" and the problems with crowded radio-airways, Fedex decided to reach its technology tentacles out into the field.

Inside of each Fedex van is a small on-board computer which communicates to the DEC minicomputer located at the dispatch center. The small computer has the capacity to store somewhere near 60 dispatches. The van's on-board computer is communicating, over a 800-megahertz digital link, constantly with the dispatch center. In fact, if the courier is out of the van, the computer receives the request automatically.

The last of the superlogistical links is Fedex's Supertracker system, sometimes known as Cosmos II. Its goal was no less than providing a tracking system that would provide unparalleled customer service. As Ponder puts it, "these systems are the absolute bedrock of quality. You will know immediately whether you have an unhappy customer." Ponders exclamations over quality are not an idle boost. Because of Fedex's use of technology in this manner, it was awarded the prestigious Malcolm Baldrige National Quality Award in 1990. Equally as impressive is the Computerworld Smithsonian Award it also won in 1990.

The goal behind Supertracker, the ultimate vision of Fred Smith, was to have the ability to enable every person in the company that touched a package to record pertinent information creating, in essence, a supertracking system. In order to do this they needed to develop a small hand-held computer that had the ability to scan the bar codes that are on every federal express package. The problem with this idea, at least in the early eighties, was that the technology for it did not as yet exist. Despite scorn from major vendors that it couldn't be done one small Charlotte, North Carolina-based engineering company finally built the ultimate tracking tool. What Hand Held Products came up with was a small, but sturdy, computer that sports 392K of memory that can accept data from key entry, barcode scanning or electronic coupling (i.e., plugging the hand-held device into a port on a computer for the purpose of downloading its data to the main computer).

Today, Federal Express has some 46,000 Supertrackers in use. When a courier picks up a package, the bar code on the packing slip is scanned and the destination zip of the receiver, along with some other required information, is keyed into this hand-held device. Once inside the van, the courier plugs the Supertracker into the small port on top of the on-board computer for an automatic download of the information into the van's on-board computer which then automatically uploads this data to the dispatcher's minicomputer. The final destination of this data is the mainframe computer in Memphis. Total information delivery time is under four minutes. From the time the package is picked up by the courier until it is delivered the next day, the package is scanned some 10 to 15 times. At any point in time, a customer need merely call to find the exact location of an important package.

Cosmos, DADS, and Supertracker (Cosmos II) make up a trio of systems that form the foundation of Federal Express's business. According to Ponder, these three systems, "are their mainstay in their competitive fight."

There are competitors. UPS and even the U.S. mails have followed Fedex's story and are aggressively planning to follow a similar strategy. But Fedex has an almost insurmountable lead—a lead that includes more than just innovative use of technology. The Fedex lead consists of, as Ponder puts it, "not so much the tools, it's the techniques, the environment, the culture, and corporate management."

11
Conclusion: The Technological Advantage

This book has examined nine very different trends. No one organization will fully embrace all nine. Rather, a combination of the ideas that these trends represent should be selected that is most suitable for the long-term strategic business goals of the organization. Before this selection is made, however, the organization must be, as discussed in Chapter 9, "competitively aware." The organization's structure must be receptive, not resistant, to strategic information technology. There must be an "active" correlation between information technology and business.

It is useful to think about the correlation between information technology and business on five levels. While it is understood that all businesses use information technology in one way or another, what we're grading here is how effectively the organization recognizes strategic opportunity and then takes advantage of it with information technology investment.

On the very lowest level are those companies which have not as yet understood the value of the use of information technology as partner to business strategy. These firms most certainly invest heavily in information technology—but have not yet understood the principles of strategic placement of information technology. These firms, according to Federal Express's Fred Smith, will most certainly be, "combatively annihilated." These firms, unfortunately, are not small in numbers.

On the very highest level are those firms, referred to as techno-businesses, the very existence of which depends on the wholesale use of technology. These businesses simply could not exist without a careful infusion of information technology—as for example, with Federal Express. While not every organization need strive to become a techno-business, its structure is a worthy aspiration.

Between these two extremes are two additional levels. Level three organizations approve information technology investments only when it directly supports strategy as stated in corporate mission and goal statements, while level four organizations have begun to structure their organization such that strategic opportunities become more readily apparent and, hence, more open to technological innovation.

These five levels form a technology continuum. It is possible, by comparing an organization with those profiled or discussed in this book, to place it on the continuum. In this way, it is possible to predict the likelihood of a organization's continued and future success. This success will not come easily, though, for strategic use of information technology implies a structural change within the organization.

Market Trends and Strategic Technology

Those organizations that have moved into the competitively active level of strategic information technology utilization are primed to take advantage of the ideas that the trends in this book illustrate.

This will be important as market forces are continually changing. With this change comes erosion of market lead as organizations that are competitively active are only too well aware.

Fred Smith's 100 percent uptime and on-time delivery measures for Fedex will likely become the norm in most industries. Information technology will assist in enhancing product quality standards through the use of technologies such as computer-aided design in the engineering arena to computer-assisted software engineering in the application development arena.

Others will emulate the success of such companies as American Express in the wholesale deployment of expert systems which for the first time, allows human judgment to be encoded and disseminated throughout the company. American Express was able to cut down on its credit-card losses through error on the part of the credit authorizer and fraud on the part of the consumer through the use of meticulously coded expert systems.

The marketing arena will move from a position of information overload to info-marketing. Using a vast array of internal and external databases, marketers will be able to develop micromarketing strategies that will be based on detailed insights into individual consumer tastes and buying preferences. This will lead to greater customization which will put low-technology performers at a distinct disadvantage.

Channels of distribution will be become increasingly automated. McKesson, the drug wholesaler, is a good case study of this particular strategy. But perhaps the best examples are the airlines, notably American Airlines and Delta, which have developed extensive customer reservations systems already in use by their competitors. Proprietary systems, however, may not be in the cards for long. Exorbitant fee structures and unfair advantages on the part of the carrying company will see a push in the direction of development of industry associations pioneering neutral networks.

The trend towards partnerships, mergers, and acquisitions and strategic alliances will be quickened. These IT-enabled alliances may take the form of joint marketing alliances. One example is the coalition of American Airlines, MCI, and Citibank, whereby travel on American Airlines, phone calls on MCI, and charges on Citibank's credit card will also earn the user free trips on American Airlines.

Organization structure will be profoundly impacted. In this vein, technology might be used to permit more formal control over the work of decentralized units while in other areas it may permit a collapsing of a fattened corporate hierarchy, ultimately permitting more decision-making authority to be delegated to front-line managers.

Information technology will be everybody's business. The evidence is seen in the trends discussed in this book—thrust upon us by an economy that continues its dramatic swings between recession and prosperity. These swings will become more dramatic, more sudden, and more frequent. Firms will, as did Bankers Trust, begin to explore ways of expansion into foreign markets, while at the same time, minimizing risk. The only way that this can be done effectively, and perhaps even remotely, is through information technology.

The age of the computer dinosaur, by all accounts, appears to be ending, in spite of a frenzied resistance by mainframe computer manufacturers. Savvy firms have already begun to downsize themselves away from these expensive and less-functional beasts of burden. Firms that have done so have found that moving to a smaller PC or work station offers new opportunities for innovation that weren't present before. More and more firms will take advantage of this lower-cost, but more functional, hardware to create distinctive systems. Firms that remain coupled solely to corporate mainframes will find themselves at a distinct disadvantage.

The move to downsized information technology coupled with an increasing need for more precise information has led many firms to fund massive integration projects. Firms that are able to tie corporate information into one cohesive and easy viewable database will be able to make better decisions, faster. The organizational structure that is becoming popular in the 1990s, a leaner, less hierarchical structure, will require this fast access to corporate information. Integration, though, will be no small accomplishment for firms with large numbers of old systems. Older firms, those that have invested heavily in IT over the years, will find themselves at a distinct disadvantage to newer firms that have the ability to "integrate from scratch."

Outsourcing will continue to be the hot ticket of the 1990s, as more and more companies decide that this may be the only way to get the most for their technology investments. However, there will be some notable failures first in companies which pursue this strategy simply to save money. Outsourcing will become less an external outplacement of the technology department and more of a strategic alliance between a technology vendor and the internal technology department and business unit(s).

Savvy companies will look to IT to as the ultimate marketing ploy. This will be especially true for companies where the products are essentially the same with little price differential. The NASD is a perfect example of this strategy. The NASD began its long ascent from relative obscurity to a market leader through the use of technology. Few outside the security industry fully understand how much of a success the NASD is. Born of a less than esteemed reputation, the NASD was butting heads with none other than the New York Stock Exchange, whose hallowed halls spoke of a 200-year tradition of blue blood and capitalism. Through the use of technology, the NASD has been able to distinguish itself—read that "give itself a distinctive edge," that has its onetime foe fairly running for cover.

Finally, we will see the rise of more and more companies—such as Federal Express which epitomizes that newest and rarest breed of company—that can fully synergize technology and business to create a company that is the essence of "the competitive use of information technology."

This forecast underlies the principle that "technology begets technology." Changing market conditions will preclude companies such as Federal Express from resting on its technological laurels. It will need to continually innovate to stay in the game. But it is by virtue of its technology that it is in the game at all. In the 1990s and beyond, nonplayers will be shut right out of the stadium.

Appendix A
Planning Tools

CASE/MATE (integrated CASE
tool)
D.P.A.C., Inc.
3952 Spalding Hollow
Norcross, GA 30092
(404) 448-0404

The Developer
Sterling Software
200 West Adams
Suite 2221
Chicago, IL 60606
312-263-5250

Excelerator (CASE tool which
assists in creating enterprise
model)
Intersolv
One Main Street
Cambridge, MA 02142
617-494-8200

IE: Expert (enterprise modeling)
Information Engineering
 Systems Corp.
201 North Union Street
5th Floor
Alexandria, VA 22314
703-739-2242

Information Engineering
Workbend (IEW) (CASE tool
which assists in creating
enterprise model)
KnowlegeWare
3340 Peachtree Rd NE
Atlanta, GA 30026
404-231-8575

Irma (enterprise documentation
tool)
Arthur D. Little
25 Acorn Park
Cambridge, MA 02140
617-864-5770

Prism (planning tool)
Intersolv
One Main Street
Cambridge, MA 02142
617-494-8200

Appendix **B**
The Big Ten in Systems Integration

The following list comes from International Data Corporation. It tracks the companies that dominate the top spots in the commercial systems integration industry. These 10 vendors accounted for more than half of all worldwide integration revenue in 1990:

1. Electronic Data Systems
2. IBM
3. Andersen Consulting
4. Digital Equipment Corp
5. Unisys
6. Computer Sciences Corp
7. Boeing Computer Servicers Division
8. Science Applications Int'l Corp.
9. Lockheed Corp.
10. Martin Marietta Corp.

Appendix C
Info-Marketing Resources/Contacts

Automated Idea Generator

IdeaFisher
Fisher Idea Systems Inc.
2222 Martin Street
Suite 110
Irvine, CA 92715
(714) 474-8111

Brainstorm
Mustang Software Inc.
P.O. 2264
Bakersfield, CA 93303
(800) 999-9619
(805) 395-0223

Business Intelligence Tools

SmartForecasts II — forecasting
  software
SmartSoftware
392 Concord Avenue
Belmont, MA 02178
(617) 489-2743

*Customer Information System —
segmentation system for banking
and financial services*

Harte Hanks Data Technologies
25 Linnell Circle
Billerica, MA 01821-3961
(508) 663-9955

Arbitron Ratings Co.
142 W. 57 Street
New York, NY 10019
(212) 887-1300

Claritas Corp.
Prizm — market segmentation
  database
Compass — PC software to analyze
  Prizm data
201 N. Union Street
Alexandria, VA 22314
(800) 368-2063

Information Resources Inc.
150 N. Clinton Street
Chicago, IL 60606
(312) 726-1221
pcExpress
Express MDB
Datserver— decision support system
Coverstory — pattern analysis
Infoscan — scanning data

A.C. Nielsen Co's.
Scantrack — scanning data
Nielsen Plaza
Northbrook, IL 60062
(718) 498-6300

Metamorph — text retrieval
Thunderstone Software
2401 Superior Viaduct N.W.
Third Floor

Cleveland, OH 44113
(216) 771-7880

Commander EIS — Executive
  information system ·
Comshare
3001 South State Street
P.O. Box 1588
Ann Arbor, MI 48106
(313) 994-4800

Marketing Databases
National Decision Systems
539 Encinitas Blvd.
Encinitas, CA 92024
(619) 942-7000

Executive Information Systems
Redimaster
American Information Systems, Inc.
Charleston Road
P.O. Box 367
Wellsboro, PA 16901
(717) 724-1588

Harry
Adviseurs, Inc.
1500 Broadway
Suite 1709
New York, NY 10036
(212) 391-5500

Framework IV
Ashton-Tate Corp.
20101 Hamilton Avenue
Torrance, CA 90502
(213) 329-9989

Forest & Trees
Channel Computing Inc.
53 Main Street
Newmarket, NH 03857
(603) 659-2832

EIS
Cogent Information Systems
830 Morris Turnpike
Short Hills, NJ 07078
(201) 379-7979

Compuserve
5000 Arlington Centre Blvd.
P.O. Box 20212
Columbus, OH 43220
(800) 848-8199

CIO-Vision
One Computer Associates Plaza
Islandia, NY 11788
(516) DIAL-CAI

Access Executive
Dialogue, Inc.
19 Rector Street
New York, NY 10006
(212) 425-2665

Smartview
Dun & Bradstreet
299 Park Ave.
New York, NY 10171
(212) 593-6800
(404) 239-4636 (info-line)

Manager's Portfolio
Easel Corp.
25 Corporate Drive
Burlington, MA 01803
(617) 221-3000

EIS Toolkit
Ferox Microsystems Inc.
901 North Washington Street
Suite 204
Alexandria, VA 22314
(703) 684-1660

Global Information Manager
Global Software, Inc.
1009 Spring Forest Rd.
Raleigh, NC 27615
(800) 326-3444

Holos
Holistic Systems, Inc.
6766 South Revere Parkway
Englewood, CO 80112
(303) 790-7939

Executive Decisions
IBM
Armonk, NY 10504
(800) 426-3333

IMRS Ontrack
IMRS
777 Long Ridge Road
Stamford, CT 06902
(203) 323-6500

Market Research Companies
Donnelley Marketing Information
  Services
70 Seaview Avenue
P.O. Box 10259
Stamford, CT 06904
(203) 353-7474

Urban Decision Systems
2040 Armacost Avenue
Los Angeles, CA 90025
(800) 633-9568 (West)
(800) 633-7184 (East)

*Competitor Intelligence
Consultants*
Herbert Meyer
Real-World Intelligence
P.O. Box 3566
Washington, DC 20007
(202) 338-1237

Society of Competitor Intelligence
  Professionals
818 Eighteenth Street
Suite 225
Washington, DC 20006
(202) 223-5885

The Business Intelligence
  Conference and Exhibit
  Tokyo in June
  New York in September
  Paris in October
Richard Bennett
National Expositions Company
15 W. 39th Street
New York, NY 10018
(212) 391-9111

Society of Competitor Intelligence
  Professionals
818 Eighteenth Street
Suite 225
Washington, DC 20006
(202) 223-5885

Clipping Services
Executive Briefing Service
Western Union Corp.
One Lake Street
4-11
Upper Saddle River, NJ 07458
(800) 422-4664
(215) 526-2860

GEnie
401 N. Washington Street
Rockville, MD 20850
(800) 638-9636

BRS
BRS Information Technologies
8000 Westpark Drive
McLean, VA 22102
(703) 442-0900

CompuServe
CompuServe Inc.
5000 Arlington Center Blvd.
Columbus, OH 94303
(800) 848-8199

Dialog
Dialog Information Services Inc.
3460 Hillsview Avenue
Palo Alto, CA 94304
(800) 334-2564

Dow Jones News/Retrieval
Dow Jones & Co.
P.O. Box 300
Princeton, NJ 08543
(800) 225-3170

NewsNet
NewsNet Inc.
945 Haverford Road
Bryn Mawr, PA. 19010
(800) 345-1300

Nexis News Plus
Mead Data Central
P.O. Box 933
Dayton, OH 45401
(800) 229-9597

Investext
Thomson Financial Network
11 Farnsworth Street
Boston, MA
(800) 662-7878

This number will permit you to request Investext to perform the searching for you. Costs are much lower this way.

Front End Software for Database Searching

These are software packages that make it easier to search databases. These packages permit you to enter a english language command which it will then send to the appropriate database.

Pro-Search
front-end for Dialog and BRS
Personal Bibliographic Software
P.O. Box 425
Ann Arbor, MI 48105
(313) 996-1580

Nexis News Plus
front-end for Nexis
Mead Data Central
P.O. Box 933
Dayton, OH 45401
(800) 229-9597

NewsReal
front-end for Dow Jones
  allows you to create a clipping
  folder and specify searches

FNN Data Broadcasting
1900 S. Norfolk St.
San Mateo, CA 94403
(800) 433-7068

DIALOGLINK
front-end for Dialog
Dialog
Dialog Information Services Inc.
3460 Hillsview Avenue
Palo Alto, CA 94304
(800) 334-2564

Access to Books and Articles

Directory of Online Databases
$175 per year brings you a source which describes more than 4,000 databases, 1,900 database vendors and 600 on-line services.
  Cuadra/Elsevier
  655 Avenue of the Americas
  New York, NY 10010
  (212) 633-3980

Directory of Fee-based Information Services
$49.50 brings you an annual directory which includes listings of more than 800 information professionals.
  Burwell Enterprises Inc.
  3724 F.M. 1960 West, Suite 214
  Houston, TX 77068
  (713) 537-9051

The Federal Database Finder
For $125 you get a directory of free and fee-based databases and files from the federal government.
  Information USA Inc.
  P.O. Box E
  Kensington, MD 20895
  (301) 369-1519

Association of Public Data Users
This service can assist you in finding an information broker as well as checking his or her references.
  87 Prospect Avenue
  Princeton, NJ 08544
  (609) 258-6025

Appendix D
AI: Intelligence Resources

Mercury
Artificial Intelligence Technologies
40 Saw Mill River Road
Hawthorne, NY 10532
(914) 347-6860

ICAT
Automated Technology Systems
90-A Adams Ave.
Hauppauge, NY 11788
(516) 231-7777

IMKA
Carnegie Group Inc.
Five PPG Place
Pittsburgh, PA 15222
(412) 642-6900

EXSYS
Exsys Inc
1720 Louisiana Blvd.
Albuquerque, NM 87110
(505) 256-8356

TIRS
IBM
1133 Westchester Ave.
White Plains, NY 10604
(609) 734-8761

KES
Software A&E
13100 Worldgate Drive

Herndon, VA 22070
(703) 318-1000

AIM
AbTech Corp.
700 Harris Street
Charlottesville, VA 22901
(804) 977-0686

1st Class
KBMS
AICorp, Inc.
138 Technology Drive
Waltham, MA 02154
(617) 661-7900

ADS
Aion Corp.
101 University Ave.
Palo Alto, CA 94301
(415) 328-9595

Framework
Blackboard Technology Group
401 Main Street
Amherst, MA 01002
(413) 256-8990

LogicTree
CAM Software
Westpark Bldg. Ste 208, 750 N
200 W Prov, UT 84601
(801) 373-4080

M.1
Cimflex Teknowledge Corp.
1810 Embarcadero Rd.
P.O. Box 10119
Palo Alto, CA 94303
(415) 424-0500

Mahogony Emerald Intelligence
3915 AI Research Park Drive
Ann Arbor, MI 48108
(313) 663-8757

Gold Works III
Gold Hill Inc.
26 Landsowne St.
Cambridge, MA 02139
(617) 621-3300

CBR
ART
XiPlus Inference Corp.
550 N. Continental Blvd.
El Segundo, CA 90245
(213) 322-0200

LEVEL5
Information Builders Inc.
1250 Broadway
New York, NY 10001
(212) 736-4433

KAPPA
KEE
IntelliCorp
1975 El Camino Real West
Mountain View, CA 94040
(415) 965-5500

Crystal
Intelligent Environments
2 Highwood Drive
Tewksbury, MA 01876
(508) 640-1080

GURU
mdbs Inc.
P.O. Box 6089
Lafayette, IN 47903
(800) 344-5832

NEXPERT OBJECT
Neuron Data
444 High Street
Palo Alto, CA 94301
(800) 876-4900 X 115

VP-Expert
Paperback Software
2830 Ninth Avenue
Berkeley, CA 94710
(415) 644-2116

AI Magazines/Printed Resources

AI Magazine (Official journal of
   AAAI.)
AAAI
445 Burgess Drive
Menlo Park, CA 94025

IEEE Expert (Publication of IEEE.)
IEEE Computer Society
10662 Los Vaqueros Circle
Los Alamitos, CA 90720

AI Expert (Commercial publication,
   available at newstands.)
Miller Freeman Publications
500 Howard Street
San Francisco, CA 94105

PC AI (Commercial AI magazine.)
PC AI
3310 West Bell Rd.
Suite 119
Phoenix, AZ 85023

Newsletters

AI Week
AIWEEK Inc.
P.O. Box 2513
Birmingham, AL 35201

Techinsider
200 West 79 Street
Suite 8H
New York, NY 10024

Glossary

AD/Cycle: This is IBM's application development life-cycle strategy. It consists of a series of methodologies and tools that will greatly expedite the process of software development.

AI (Artificial Intelligence): A subfield of computer science aimed at pursuing the possibility that a computer can be made to behave in ways that humans recognize as intelligent behavior.

Big Iron: A colloquial expression that many in the information technology field use to refer to mainframe computers.

BU: Abbreviation for Business Unit.

CAEL: Banking acronym for capital, assets, earnings, and liquidity.

CASE (Computer-Assisted Software Engineering).

CIM (Computer-Integrated Manufacturing): Manufacturing technique where all processes are automated and all automation is integrated.

COCOMO: Well-known quality measurement, the Constructive Cost Model, which calculates the cost of developing software.

CIO (Chief Information Officer): This is the chief of the technology department, sometimes going by the title Chief Technical Officer.

CSFs (Critical Success Factors): A technique increasingly being used by business to identify the critical tasks that must be completed, and the order of those tasks, to achieve success in a particular endeavor.

Data dictionary: An on-line document that keeps track of all the data elements within a particular vendor's database.

Data-flow diagrams: These diagrams graphically depict the different items in a computer system and their movement from process to process.

Database engine: This is the program, written by the vendor, that controls the adds, changes, and deletes to the physical database.

Distributed Processing: In the early 1980s, the concept of putting the power of the computer in the hands of the business unit was formulated. This came to be known as decentralization—meaning moving away from a large mainframe computer. This has come to be known as distributed processing: where one or more computers are distributed throughout the corporation.

DOS: The first, and most popular, of operating systems for IBM PCs and compatibles. It is an acronym for disk operating system.

Downsizing: Moving from a larger computer to a series of networked computers.

EDI (Electronic Data Interchange): This is a standard telecommunications methodology used to facilitate the passing of data between firms.

Embeddable expert systems: In these systems, the expert component is "buried" within the traditional data-processing system. In other words, the traditional program calls the expert system module when it needs to provide some judgment to the process. The end-user usually does not know that an expert system is even being used.

Enterprise model: A model of the business organization which includes all data, functionality, and relationships.

Entity-relationship diagram: A diagram which shows the relationship between two objects.

First Mover: A type of competitive strategy, defined by Michael Porter, in which a firm gains an advantage by being first with a new product/technology/service.

Function Points: Perhaps the most popular measurement in use in today's technology groups. Function points assess the functionality of software as it relates to some 14 criteria.

Info-marketing: Using creative and robust techniques to foster business intelligence and thus gain a competitive lead.

Insourcing: Consolidating internal IT development and operations and making it a stronger group. This technique concentrates heavily on a people perspective.

IT: The technology department has many names. Currently it is usually referred to as information technology—IT for short. In the past, and in some firms today, this department is referred to as IS, short for Information Systems, or MIS which is an abbreviation of Management Information Systems.

JIT (Just In Time): A manufacturing technique where supplies are available basically just in the nick of time. This technique cuts down on the inventory, and the expense, that a company must bear in the manufacturing process.

Object: An entity capable of exhibiting a defined set of behaviors and interacting with other objects.

Object-oriented technology: A collection of languages, tools, environments, and methodologies aimed at supporting development of software applications centered around interrelated, interacting objects.

Open systems: The philosophy by which vendors adhere to a common standard such that organizations can easily integrate and/or switch software tools.

Outsourcing: Disbanding one or more IT operations and turning it over to be run by an external vendor.

OS/2: The IBM PC, and compatibles, has two premier operating systems. The original DOS and now OS/2. OS/2 is IBM's entry into the market, while DOS is Microsoft's.

Prototype: Building an initial shell of the system so that the user can see how it looks and feels. Using the user's input it is possible to develop systems more accurately using successive waves of prototypes.

RAD (Rapid Application Development): RAD is a set of processes that are used to quickly develop computer systems. Popularized by James Martin, this technique relies heavily on prototyping.

Reengineering: The process of taking old systems and programs and through a combination of software engineering tools and techniques reworking them into more efficient and more modern systems.

Repository: A central data dictionary for all the data items a company owns—whether it's in a computer system or not.

Techno-business: A firm whose main strategy is technology.

Total Quality Control: Hewlett-Packard's quality approach to developing software.

TQC: Abbreviation for Total Quality Control.

UNIX: This is the operating system that is most popular for workstation devices.

User interfaces: The manner in which the application is displayed to the user on the computer screen. Originally user interfaces consisted of nothing more than black-and-white lettering with one command at a time being entered. Today, there is a wide array of choices including windows and full color.

Warnier-Orr Chart: Diagram of the hierarchy of data within a system.

Bibliography

Chapter 1: Techno-Strategy

The Conference Board. *Information Management: The New Strategic Weapon*, RB 220, 22 pages Conference presentations. New York, 1988.

The Conference Board. *Information Technology: Initiatives for Today—Decisions That Cannot Wait*, Report 577. 50 pages. New York, 1972.

The Conference Board. *Taming the Information Monster*. New York: ATB, Nov., 1986, p. 33–38.

The Conference Board. *Information: The Great Equalizer*. New York: ATB, July/Aug., 1986, p. 5–6.

Morton, Michael S. Scott. *The Corporation of the 1990s: Information Technology and Organizational Transformation*. New York: Oxford University Press, 1991.

Porter, Michael E. "How Information Technology Gives You Competitive Advantage." *Harvard Business Review*, Jul/Aug 1985, p.149.

Chapter 5: Integration

Fisher, Alan S. *CASE: Using Software Development Tools*. New York: Wiley, 1988.

Chapter 7: Info-Marketing

Jerome, Marty. "What's The Competition Up To?" *PC/Computing*, September 1990.

Lesko, Matthew. *Information U.S.A. 1986*. New York: Penguin.

Chapter 8: Turning Data into Knowledge

Barr, Avron, Feigenbaum, Edward A. and Cohen, Paul. *The Handbook of Artificial Intgelligence, Vols. I, II and III*. Los Altos, Calif: William Kaufmann, 1981.

Buchanan, Bruce G. and Shortliffe, Edward H. *Rule-Based Expert Systems*. Reading, MA: Addison-Wesley, 1984.

Feigenbaum, Edward A. and McCorduck, Pamela. *The Fifth Generation*. New York: Signet, 1984.

Frenzel, Louis E. *Understanding Expert Systems*. Indianapolis, Indiana: Howard W. Sams, 1987.

Harmon, Paul and King, David. *Expert Systems*. New York: Wiley, 1984.

Hayes-Roth, Frederick, Waterman, Donald A. and Lenat, Douglas B. *Building Expert Systems.* Reading, MA: Addison-Wesley, 1983.

Keyes, Jessica. "The New Intelligence." *HarperBusiness,* New York, 1990.

Maus, Rex and Keyes, Jessica. *The Handbook Of Expert Systems In Manfacturing.* New York: McGraw-Hill, 1991.

Mishkoff, Henry C. *Understanding Artificial Intelligence.* Dallas, Texas: Texas Instruments, 1985.

Nagy, Tom, Gault, Dick, and Nagy, Monica. *Building Your First Expert System.* New York: Halstead Press, 1983.

Peat, F. David. *Artificial Intelligence: How Machines Think.* New York: Bean Publishing, 1988.

Rich, Elaine. *Artificial Intelligence.* New York: McGraw-Hill, 1983.

Schoen Sy and Sykes, Wendell. *Putting Artificial Intelligence To Work.* New York: Wiley, 1987.

Tanimoto, Steven L. *The Elements of Artificial Intelligence.* Rockville, Maryland: Computer Science Press, 1987.

Waterman, Donald A. *A Guide To Expert Systems.* Reading, MA: Addison-Wesley, 1985.

Chapter 9: Distinctive Edge

Sheeline, William E. "Who Needs the Stock Exchange?" *Fortune,* November 19, 1990.

Stern, Richard L. "A Dwindling Monopoly." *Forbes,* May 13, 1991.

Eichenwald, Kurt. "Wall Street's Cutbacks Sidestep Fat Budget's For High-Tech Trading." *The New York Times,* April 7, 1991.

"The Shrinking of the Big Board." *The Economist,* February 16, 1991.

Cone, Edward. "Trading In A New System." *InformationWeek,* March 4, 1991.

Brennan, Peter J. "OTC Trading Systems Lead in Race to Automate." *Wall Street Computer Review,* November 1990.

Van Slyke, Richard. "Rust on Wall Street." *Information Strategy: The Executive's Journal,* Winter 1990.

Forsythe, Jason. "The Big Board: Boxed In By Automation." *InformationWeek,* May 20, 1991.

Index

About the Author

Jessica Keyes is president of New Art, Inc., a high-tech consulting firm based in New York City. Previously, she was managing director of technology for the New York Stock Exchange, and an officer at both Banker's Trust Company and Swiss Bank Corporation. With more than 15 years' experience in the field, she is also publisher and editor of the highly respected *Techinsider* newsletter, author of *The New Intelligence,* and coauthor of *The Handbook of Expert Systems Applications in Manufacturing.* She has over 100 articles in print in numerous prestigious journals from *Software Magazine* to *Computerworld.* Ms. Keyes is in great demand as a seminar leader on advanced technologies. She has a Master's degree in Business Administration from New York University.